SAGA B
IRELAND

C000103534

by
J.I.C. Boyd

THE OAKWOOD PRESS

© Oakwood Press & J.I.C. Boyd 2006

British Library Cataloguing in Publication Data
A Record for this book is available from the British Library
ISBN 0 85361 651 5
ISBN 978 085361 651 1

Typeset by Oakwood Graphics.
Repro by PKmediaworks, Cranborne, Dorset.
Printed by Cambrian Printers, Aberystwyth, Ceredigion.

'There is properly no history; only biography'

Ralph Waldo Emerson

Title page: A Strabane-bound goods train backs into the siding at Castlefinn to allow the railcar to pass. May 1959. *Author*

Published by The Oakwood Press (Usk), P.O. Box 13, Usk, Mon., NP15 1YS.
E-mail: sales@oakwoodpress.co.uk
Website: www.oakwoodpress.co.uk

Contents

GNR class 'S' No. 171 at the west end of Portadown station. Note wagons of Scottish coal in background. March 1964.   *Author*

Foreword

It may seem strange to the modern reader that when I met with James Boyd in 1948 to discuss the publishing of his first book (*Narrow Gauge Rails to Portmadoc*), there were doubts about its financial viability. It was a large book, and the number of modern enthusiasts for the narrow gauge was then not known. In fact, his book was widely welcomed and he soon became renowned, not only for his histories, but also for putting restoration into practice. We enjoyed many excursions together while his books multiplied in numbers and popularity. In Ireland the narrow gauge remained available for many years on both sides of the border and James took full advantage of this. Now after 11 books and many reprints, he can be proud of the fact that people say 'if it's in Boyd, it must be right'.

R.W. Kidner

J.I.C. Boyd in his den. November 2005.   *Douglas Robinson*

Author's Note

Memory can be fickle. These reminiscences cannot therefore be taken as 'gospel'. Rather, they are the recollections of a lifetime, some incidents having taken place 70 years ago. Events have moved so swiftly in that time that scarcely any of the subject matter can be experienced today; accordingly, these accounts have taken on a historical significance.

As time has gone by, my sketchy knowledge of those early subjects has been enhanced by later fact-finding in locations then surviving but now obliterated; I have incorporated this extra material into the text to give it more substance.

Finally, readers who expect to find some gems of research herein will be disappointed but to counter this there will be others who will read me with a certain amount of envy!

For this is how it was.

J.I.C. Boyd
Colwall

Preface

I am often asked to set down something about my lifetime's interest in railways; it is a reminder of my age and of opportunities which some people wish they could have experienced themselves.

Herein I bow to their wishes. It must be understood that I had no conception that in later life notes begun when I was a teenager would be interesting to many today. Similarly, that photographs taken with a simple camera might become a rarity. Some things I saw I did not fully appreciate on the first occasion. With the optimism of youth, 'there would always be another opportunity'. But when it came, they had gone …

My field notes and drawings began in 1933 and were made in a rather expensive Sketch Book from Reeves which I obtained through the school Art Room so that it might appear under 'Extras' on my father's termly bill rather than deplete my pocket money. I soon learnt that a Woolworth's penny note pad was sufficient for the rough and tumble of rucksack, bicycle bag and railway environment!

My parents inherited a love for the Isle of Man from their own parents and I was seduced by its narrow gauge railways from the age of five. This may explain why Ireland also became a happy hunting ground for similar (and other) railways, and why I begin by a book set in that lovely country. Professor Geoffrey Platt encouraged me to draw a plan of every railway junction and station I encountered with signalling. It was good advice.

And so to Portadown!

Chapter One

Portadown - A First Visit:
August 1933

'Portadown? Why Portadown? Has it a narrow gauge railway?' Such was the comment of a colleague in Manchester who had heard of my intentions. 'Are you going to write a book?' I explained that I had a school friend, Brian Greaves, who lived there and by staying with him it would be a staging post *en route* to Burtonport by train, and that beyond Strabane the journey would be on 3 ft gauge railways. 'You lucky bloke', he retorted enviously.

To be honest, this conversation took place in early 1939 but I had to go back to August 1933 to explain how the seeds were sown for my visit six years later. At that earlier date I had not even set foot in Portadown, let alone an Irish train!

Brian's father owned The Portadown Weaving Co. Ltd, a business at the 'fine end' of the linen trade which finally succombed in 1959/60. His mother hailed from Birmingham and was born Marian Janet Cadbury; she had married Geoffrey Hoyland, Headmaster of the Herefordshire school where I met Brian. His parents were both Quakers and the school was a Quaker establishment. That is how Ulster came into my life.

Brian and I shared the same hobbies and we both worked on the school's miniature railway. So it was I came to spend a number of school holidays in Portadown, a town then closely wedded to the linen trade. In the period of this account the town 'enjoyed a certain Puritan atmosphere' [*sic*] which may explain why Brian's father was courted by the local Plymouth Brethren - but to no avail! My railway interests were further sharpened when told that no love was lost between Lurgan and Portadown (the station prior to Portadown for westbound trains) to the extent that Portadown home-based engine-drivers, if stopped at Lurgan, were quickly off again on seeing the guard's green flag. On the other side of the coin, the Portadown enginemen were said to be a surly lot …

I digress. In those days the only way to reach Belfast was to use the excellent 'miniature liners' which plied from Liverpool nightly. They were superbly fitted out compared to the utilitarian floating garages which do duty today. My mother would drive me to Liverpool, and settle me into a Saloon Cabin after a suitable word with the Stewardess (which dented my ego somewhat) who was quite used to seeing unaccompanied children travelling on their way to and from boarding school. The Stewardess had a formidable presence, dressed like a School Matron in starched white.

Brian's mother had written to mine some weeks before this and recommended that I bring some 'sensible clothes' as life at 'Ardeevin' was informal, save for that one feature of family life in those days - Family Prayers in the Dining Room after breakfast, with the domestic staff present. Thus early one morning the ULSTER MONARCH nosed against Donegall Quay in the Lagan River without noise or fuss; the early morning sunshine heralded a new experience and revealed a fascinating web of dockside railway tracks which held my gaze as I looked down from the ship's rail.

0-4-0ST class 'N' No. 16 on Belfast Donegall Quay, August 1939. This was the sole example of its type: note the useful stool to assist tank-filling!   *Author*

Portadown roundhouse. August 1939.   *Author*

Two steam locomotives could be seen busying themselves among rows of countless covered vans on the quay. Years later I learned that the smaller was ex-Northern Counties Committee Railway class 'N' 0-4-0 Saddle Tank No. 16, built 1914 for shunting at Belfast Harbour, and the only one in the class. The larger was Great Northern Railway of Ireland class 'RT' 0-6-4 Side Tank built 1908-11 for shunting at Belfast Harbour and Maysfields Goods Yard. It had very large buffer heads to avoid interlocking on sharp surves, and was one of four built. I also came to know that all Irish railways favoured the covered van and that all other types of goods wagon were in the minority.

Brian's parents met me off the ship and we set off for Portadown by car. *En route* Brian whetted my appetite by telling me of the various railway outings we might take on succeeding days; each was enticing. What surprised me was Brian had never done any of them himself and I assumed that his mother had waited until my visit when we could more safely be left in the custody of each other!

This theory was put to the test on the following day when Brian suggested we go to Portadown station on our bicycles; in those days it was sited close to that of the second station of 1863 and stood on marshy, low lying ground some distance from the town centre. It was subject to flooding by the Upper Bann River. To conect it with the town a Great Northern Railway (Ireland) (GNRI) bus plied 28 times daily.

We thought our school Rugby shirts were suitable attire for the trip: we could choose between red or green and selected the latter. Passing through some back streets we became target of a cluster of rough little boys who threw stones at us. Emboldened by their indifferent aim, we turned around and ran the gauntlet again. This time they had added broken bricks to the ammunition. We had inadvertently been wearing the wrong coloured shirts when passing through a Loyalist Area! So much for the 'Puritan atmosphere'!

Something of the unusual background to Portadown station as it was in 1933 is worth attempting. It stood as it were, at the top of a tree trunk, from which several sturdy branches forked. The trunk was the oldest portion. It had its base in Belfast and ran west to Armagh; opened in 1842 as the Ulster Railway, it was built to a gauge of 6 ft 2 in. which caused all manner of problems in days to come. The second 'branch' and the second to be built led southwards eventually to reach Dublin. The last led northwards to Omagh and later, to Londonderry. Each had been built by a separate company and to a different gauge - a truly Irish situation. Of course, all this detail was unknown to me at the time.

Portadown was the most westerly destination on the suburban train services from Belfast. Fast trains with no intermediate stops could cover the intervening 26 miles in a little over half an hour; they collected no cobwebs and of their type were unsurpassed in Ireland. Portadown was the focal point of the Ulster railway system and a busy interchange point. The junction of the three routes just described was just west of the station, beyond a fine bridge which carried the railway over the Upper Bann River. The station had four platform faces - the central island platform was the most recent - and four subways, though the fourth was closed about the time of our exploration; it led down to the river and excursion boats.

We dumped our bicycles against a wall and roamed the premises quite undisturbed. They had the dismal appearance of certain stations around

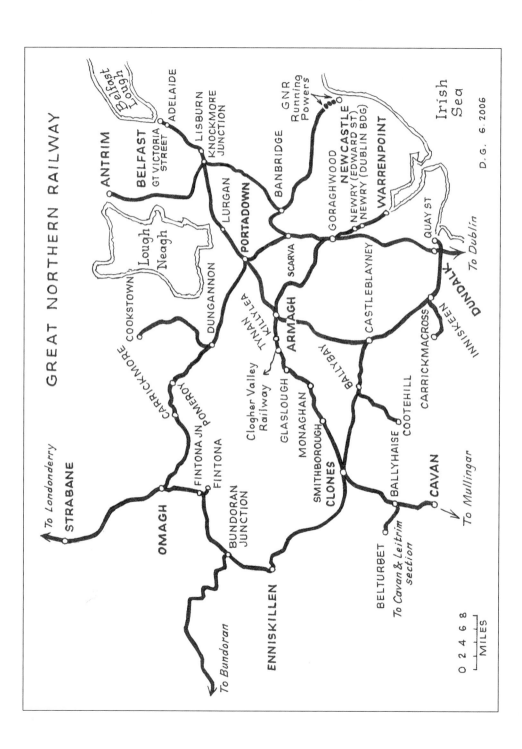

GREAT NORTHERN RAILWAY

D.G. 6. 2006

Irish Sea

Belfast Lough

ANTRIM

BELFAST
GT VICTORIA STREET

ADELAIDE

LISBURN

KNOCKMORE JUNCTION

GNR Running Powers

NEWCASTLE

WARRENPOINT

NEWRY (EDWARD ST)
NEWRY (DUBLIN BDG)

BANBRIDGE

LURGAN

PORTADOWN

GORAGHWOOD

QUAY ST

To Dublin

DUNDALK

Lough Neagh

SCARVA

CASTLEBLAYNEY

DUNGANNON

COOKSTOWN

CARRICKMORE

ARMAGH

TYNAN
KILLYLEA

Clogher Valley Railway

BALLYBAY

CARRICKMACROSS

INNISKEEN

GLASLOUGH

POMEROY

FINTONA JN

FINTONA

MONAGHAN

SMITHBOROUGH

COOTEHILL

To Londonderry

STRABANE

OMAGH

BUNDORAN JUNCTION

CLONES

BALLYHAISE

CAVAN

To Mullingar

BELTURBET

To Cavan & Leitrim section

ENNISKILLEN

To Bundoran

0 2 4 6 8
MILES

Manchester. There had been an overall roof but it was demolished during World War I. We spent the morning soaking up the atmosphere of the GNRI. There was a constant stream of arrivals and departures, most frequently to and from Belfast Victoria Street, trains which were handled by 4-4-2 tank engines of Beyer, Peacock origin. I emphasised to Brian the importance of this Manchester firm to the history of the GNRI. At that time my only knowledge of it was limited to glimpses over its Gorton walls from the upper deck of an Ashton-under-Lyne tram as it made sporadic progress along Hyde Road with its circuit breaker blowing out with a loud bang from time to time!

Concerning the westward-bound trains making for Armagh and beyond, my imagination pictured them ending the journey near some Atlantic shore on the Irish west coast. The trains were headed by elderly 4-4-0s, not unlike those ex-Great Central Railway engines which passed through the fields at home on their way to Chester. Did I but know it, steam trains were soon likely to be confined to destinations beyond Armagh as new railcars replaced them on the Portadown-Armagh service.

But in 1933, steam was almost supreme here. The express trains on the Dublin line were managed by the-then nearly-new three-cylinder compound 4-4-0 tender engines, confined by their weight to this route only. Such trains only stopped at Portadown between the two capital cities and as we admired them from the platform end we saw there was nothing to compare them in size in England with its smaller loading gauge. They were reputed to resemble the last batch of 'Midland Compounds' built by the London Midland & Scottish Railway in 1924, but were considerably bigger - and of the Southern Railway's 'Schools' class too. At first they were painted black but after my visit, blue. Handsome engines indeed.

Finally, there was the line which curved northwards from the junction, known as 'The Derry Road'. It seemed to be the custom for its trains to leave from the north face of the island platform and the congestion when a train from all three routes was timetabled to make connection here was chaotic, especially as luggage, parcels etc. had to be exchanged between vans. Luggage trollies ran over the tracks on levelled sleeper crossings while passengers jostled in the subways. Portadown was the busiest intermediate station in all Ireland; sometimes called the 'Crewe' of Ireland it had the character of a frontier post.

On The Derry Road passenger trains appeared behind haughty high-pitch-boilered 4-4-0s with tall smokebox saddles. We were impressed and could identify and compare their various controls and fittings with the engines at school. Their ample cabs allowed curious small boys to gaze within while their crews seemed struck by our interest! They told us the engines were a rebuild of the 'Q' class 'and had been rebuilt by Mr Glover with a raised boiler to clear the new 8 in. piston valves and cylinders $18\frac{1}{2}$ in. x 26 in.' We nodded dutifully and imagined that Mr Glover was a frightfully ingenious man working almost single-handed to perform these mechanical miracles in some almost-forgotten railway shed. Additionally, we were told that the engines were limited to seven bogie carriages and a four-wheeled van. We did some more nodding.

(Years later I rode on one of these engines. Of them R.M. Arnold relates 'that these delightful engines tore down the hills and round the curves of The Derry

Dublin express and local trains meet at the west end of Portadown station. August 1939.   *Author*

GNRI class 'A' No. 60 at Portadown engine shed. March 1964.   *Author*

Road but still retained their original frames, repeatedly patched after many fractures. No doubt the hard running to Derry was responsible. Some enginemen found them shy for steam but an experienced GNRI fireman, a well burned-through fire and four or five shovelfulls of coal of any quality along the sides of the box, could restore steam pressure'. It was to be 1939 before I came to know The Derry Road.)

There were long intervals between these frenzied train exchanges but we found interest in the long rakes of goods trains coming from Belfast and passing through the station *en route* to sidings beyond the platforms. They were hauled by 0-6-0 tender engines of identity unknown and were often made up of loaded coal wagons. The coal was shipped from Scotland or Whitehaven and destined for the linen mills of the Province. There were also long trains of cattle vans up to 40 vehicles long, making their way to Belfast for shipment. Each van was copiously daubed with white disinfectant. Such trains rumbled over the pointwork with considerable clatter, each van nodding and swaying as it nosed those alongside.

Most of the cattle came via the Sligo, Leitrim & Northern Counties Railway and Enniskillen, so a patient member of the station staff informed us. Enniskillen? It had obviously been omitted from our geography syllabus. We learned much at the station!

One thing we had not learnt was that the GNRI was embarking on an experiment of fitting railway wheels to road buses and using them to build up a railcar fleet which could replace expensive steam trains on lightly-worked lines. The GNRI had been alerted to the economies of this exercise as co-owner of the County Donegal 3 ft gauge railway system, in which it was a pioneer. And one of the first fruits of this exercise was resting, unattended, at the up platform further along the station! It was railcar 'B' which had been built at the GNRI Dundalk works some months previously. Was it then on trial? At that date it was fitted with diesel-electric drive and weighed only 21 tons. (Some years later it was converted into a steam-hauled trailer, thus converting it into the type of vehicle it was intended to replace! Before that conversion I rode in it from Belfast to Newry and back; it was noisy, slow and uncomfortable. At the time of this account we gave it scant attention.)

That first Irish visit left many impressions; there was a 'handwriting' in the design of station buildings which gave me the feeling of a uniform hand especially on the Portadown-Clones line. Later I found it all in *Railway Construction* by W.H. Mills. Would there be more books of this calibre! The main lines of chaired rails had the keys inside the rails. The secondary lines used flatbottomed rail. This was also found in yards and sidings and where the two rail sections were joined it was often done on an *ad hoc* basis. Travelling over the flatbottomed sections produced a different sensation and noise, six-wheeled carriages swayed and induced sleep. The railbuses tended to dance about once they had left the better chaired rail.

In the 1930s, the period of these recollections, the GNRI enjoyed a plenteous provision of attractive semaphore signals, as did the Lancashire & Yorkshire Railway in England. This may have been due to their both being loyal customers of The Railway Signal Co. of Fazakerley. No upper quadrant arms

GNRI class 'SG3' No. 49. Portadown. March 1964.   *Author*

GNRI class 'AL' No. 36. Portadown engine shed. March 1964.   *Author*

Westward-bound goods leaving Portadown for Clones. March 1964.   *Author*

Portadown engine shed. Piston trouble! March 1964.   *Author*

here! There was a plethora of signals for every movement, actual or postulated. Different too were the distant semaphores which unlike the English yellow, were painted red; so too were their matching levers in the signal cabins - the GNRI did not use the term 'Signal Box'. Perhaps there was economy also in the company's use of a round telephone post instead of the square section signal post common in England.

Portadown boasted two Cabins, North and South, while a third controlled Portadown Junction and dated from 1924; it been built around its predecessor! Notably, the section of railway covered by the North and South Cabins was linked by cabins which possessed no block instruments, only a telephone!

It is convenient to append some more recent events which took place after my earliest holiday. Until 1940 in the block sections north of Portadown towards Knockmore Junction and Belfast, the cabins contained Preece's Block Instruments but in the early 1940s they were replaced by Harper's Instruments manufactured by W.R. Sykes. South of Portadown Harper's system survived, possibly from the original installation. The up distant signal and the up home signal in the North Cabin were 'slot controlled' by the South Cabin. The down home signals in the South Cabin were 'slot controlled' by the North Cabin; the down distant signal was fixed at Caution.*

In earlier times the engine sheds at Adelaide, Belfast had provided the lion's share of motive power seen around Portadown but in 1925 a large roundhouse in concrete was built there where the bulk of the locomotives was based.

Almost everything in my essay has now disappeared, so I make no apologies for being tedious. I venture to think that small boys in green shirts are still the targets for their counterparts in loyalist streets. That aspect, at least, has not disappeared.

The Greeves family drove us to Belfast for my night sailing back to Liverpool. With time to spare we interrupted the journey at Belle Vue Zoological Gardens where we were promised a ride on the miniature railway; it was dusk but the crowds in the pleasure garden were so great that I saw little of the railway. The carriages were open and the steam locomotive in front was the strangest I had seen. Much later I read that the line was of 15 in. gauge and that the engine had been built in Germany by Krauss of Munich in 1926 at a cost of £350 delivered. It was a 0-4-0WT with outside cylinders and Stephenson valve gear and been employed in the construction of the Romney, Hythe & Dymchurch Railway (RH&DR) in Kent where it was named JEAN. Unsuited for further work it was sold to the Blackpool miniature railway along with some coaches in 1933 and then re-sold to 'Belle Vue Park Railway'. It returned to England again later after discovery under a pile of scrap iron and found its way to the RH&DR once more. It was renamed THE BUG and still survives. It was a fitting end to the holiday.

---

* IRISH RAILWAY RECORD SOCIETY JOURNAL Vol. 21 June 2001 p. 89 for details of Block Instruments. Signalling details supplied by Thomas McGauran of Lisburn.

Chapter Two

Beyond Portadown - A Second Visit, August 1939

It proved to be August 1939 before I could fulfil my ambition to return to Ireland and travel over the 3 ft gauge railway to Burtonport on the north-west coast of Co. Donegal. Much had happened since my school holiday back in 1933. Brian had left Campbell College, Belfast and was reading Engineering at University. Meanwhile, I was 'apprenticed' to the family textile business in Manchester and being sent to various manufacturing concerns 'to learn from the floor'. Under such circumstances there was little opportunity to broaden my knowledge of Ireland which offered no avenues in the commercial direction I sought. I took the opportunity to read about north-west Ireland in particular and luckily the newly-launched Oakwood Press began publishing small booklets on minor railways, and that covering Ireland became my Alma Mater. It sustained my interests in several unencouraging surroundings!

I was preparing otherwise for the journey which was taking on something of an expedition; the territory I sought was, from what I read, an expanse of wall-to-wall saturated bog. I had already bought from a shop in Blandford near school a pair of 'waterproof' boots which I studiously saturated in dubbin each time I came home. The smell reached every corner of the house. I bought a rucksack and a pocket-sized map book but as my weekly wage was 10s. I had to save carefully towards the cost of fares.

In those times the annual holiday meant 14 days away from work, some of which would have be used to reach Portadown *en route*. To me a holiday in North Wales, Southport or the Isle of Man was elisium; the thought of travelling further stirred the blood! The journey would entail leaving Portadown by GNRI to reach Strabane where, by changing to the 3 ft gauge, I might attain Letterkenny. Here I must change again onto another 3 ft gauge system which would take me a further 49¾ miles to Burtonport. It was going to be a long day. Where I might eat or sleep did not trouble me. The railway journey was the thing.

Back in Manchester it would take me seven minutes to walk from our Works or less by tram to the fine new Central Library where after a frugal lunch I could examine the locally published *Bradshaw's Monthly Railway Guide* in whose ultimate pages some of the lesser Irish railway timetables appeared. There were some dispiriting blanks although the GNRI services were shown and I could see that the Portadown-Strabane trains made frequent stops. The narrow gauge lines beyond Strabane and out to Burtonport were not given at all and I was left to assume train times were seldom altered from one year to the next. I soon learned to write to the company concerned for a timetable, footplate pass and permit to travel on non-passenger trains! These were always forthcoming.

Brian met me off the Liverpool boat at Donegall Quay; he was now the proud owner of an Austin Seven and, being a big lad, drove it everywhere though still under age. While passing through Lisburn's wide street *en route* for Portadown, a large black dog dashed out from between some houses and attempted to cross our path at high speed. It collided with the driver's door and buckled it so badly

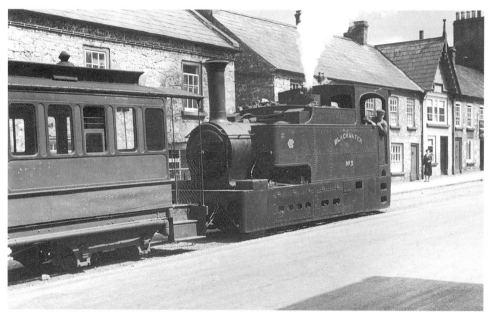

Train passing along Caledon main street.   *Stewart Dewsbury*

No. 5 BLACKWATER at Tynan. August 1939.   *Author*

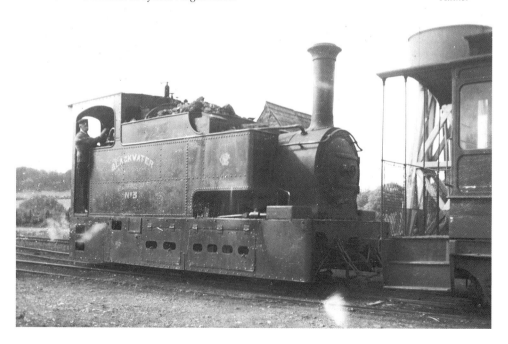

it would not close. The dog just disappeared. On the journey Brian suggested some mouth-watering suggestions as to where we might go before I left for Donegal. We decided on Tynan, an interchange station between the GNRI and the 3 ft gauge Clogher Valley Railway (CVR).

With the driver's door tied up with Brian's sister's skipping rope to secure it, we were soon at Tynan next day. The station was impressive, a cross between a Hunting Lodge and a church. There was a Custom's Post on the platforms. A Clogher Valley train stood in the station yard. The CVR had no station proper of its own but shared the use of the GNRI facilities. The GNRI line here connected Armagh and Monaghan on what had first been the Ulster Railway (UR). The CVR, on the other hand, was little more than a roadside tramway and in fact was an intruder so far as the GNRI was concerned. Forced to find space where it was permitted, the CVR goods yard, engine shed etc. was a quarter of a mile west of Tynan station which was the original UR property and in the Gothic style favoured by the local estate.

The GNRI had relinquished the use of one platform to allow the CVR room for passenger traffic; the result was curious. When we arrived the CVR train (tram engine, BLACKWATER, one bogie coach and passenger/goods van for the guard) was just preparing to leave for Augher and points west. We had no idea of its timetable but assumed from its dilatory shunting that there was no hurry. The driver, like many enginemen of that period, seemed as old as his charge. He had a heavy, drooping moustache and that, together with his accent, prevented us from understanding much of what he said but we gathered we might ride down to Caledon (the first station) free of charge if we did not mind walking back. We did and we didn't. We were the only customers in the spartan balcony-ended coach which, with its long bare seat along each side put me in mind of the lower deck of a Manchester tram.

The ensemble crept out of Tynan yard without ceremony or fuss, the engine leading cab foremost so as to give the crew a clear view ahead, and rounded the long curve of 110 ft radius falling at 1 in 35, almost the steepest on the system. In about half a mile we reached the main Belfast road and took up a position on the left of the highway. The screech of protesting flanges on the long curving section now abated. We made the briefest stop and one passenger jumped on. There was no indication that this was a formal stopping place.

A little further on we ran longside the Ulster Canal where, on turning right, there was a mandatory stop before we made a nasty crossing of the road from left- to right-hand side following which we crossed, at snail's pace, the canal and Blackwater River by stone-arched bridges shared by road and tramway. The guard came along and explained that this was the lowest point on the entire tramway system, more I thought to satisfy himself that we were genuinely interested in all around us!

Caledon, a pleasant, picturesque village, lay just beyond; we trundled down its main street and alighted. The appearance of this neat community was explained by its proximity to Caledon House. We were loathe to leave the tram, delighted by the free ride, enchanted by our luck and the novel experience. The heavy blasts of smoke and steam from the engine as it laboured up the hill beyond the village stayed with us as we walked back to the car. The next day would be an anticlimax, come what may.

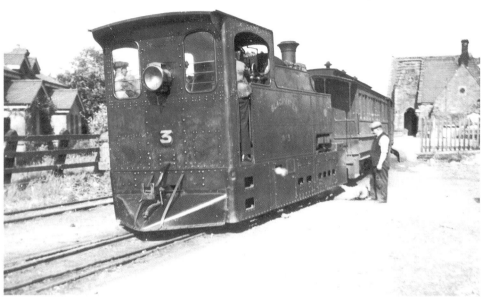

Train ready to depart Tynan station. August 1939.   *Author*

Aughnacloy works yard.   *Author's Collection*

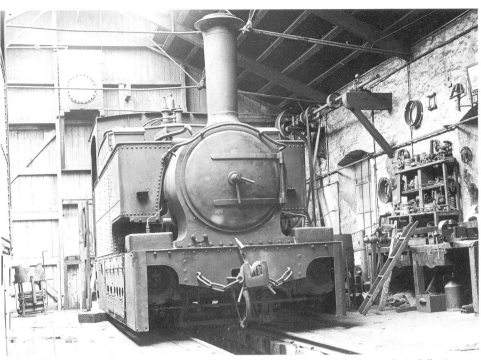

Aughnacloy works interior.

Author's Collection

Coaling gantry Aughnacloy.

Author's Collection

Walker-built railcar No. 1.   *Author's Collection*

Open wagon transferred to Cavan & Leitrim section. May 1958.   *Author*

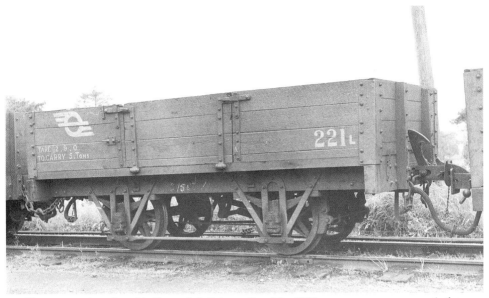

Open wagon transferred to Cavan & Leitrim section. May 1958.   *Author*

Open wagon, built by Bristol Wagon Works Ltd, transferred to Cavan & Leitrim section. January 1961.   *Author*

(Many years later Edward Patterson's book on the CVR rekindled youthful memories of this, my first encounter with the Irish narrow gauge. The CVR closed to all traffic in winter 1962 with a memorable BBC radio broadcast and the next time I arrived in Tynan it was on the footplate of a GNRI 4-4-0; the site of the CVR yard was under an immense sheet of water. Floating majestically thereon was a child's lonely chamber potty.*)

The following day, 29th August, 1939, was that for which I had planned so long. I was embark on the journey with anticipation and slight foreboding for Burtonport seemed as distant as Vladivostok. Like others of my time, life had been insular until now. So I found myself on the 11.30 am from Portadown to Londonderry, a though working from Belfast which I would use as far as Strabane. The carriage was handsome, comfortable and spacious and, being alone I could dash from window to window in reckless observation. There was a 'Q' class 4-4-0 in front to handle the four polished mahogany bogie carriages, and their impression of width was most striking; they must have seemed palatial to the users of their six-wheeled predecessors which had served so long on The Derry Road. With a width of 9 ft 6 in., passengers could sit three per side on either hand of a central gangway. (Even these did not compare with the 10 ft wide ex-Lancashire & Yorkshire Railway electric stock which I occasionally used between Liverpool and Southport.)

The countryside north of Portadown was most pleasant and we passed through many apple orchards for which it was acclaimed. Through the open window I caught the occasional whiff of turf smoke from a passing dwelling. Many farmsteads were neatly thatched. Carts with shafts upright leaned against their walls, as if on regimental parade; they were all of one colour - red oxide. Beyond the cultivated land the terrain was rough and unkempt, and this became more pronounced as I travelled further west and north.

---

* BLACKWATER was one of a class of six 0-4-2 side tank tram engines supplied by Sharp, Stewart Ltd of Manchester in 1885-7 for the opening of the tramway. From ground level it seemed to be an elephantine machine probably due to being completely encased by side skirts which hid wheels, cylinders and motion. Set in the skirts were hinged openings giving access to the mysteries behind. There was a large cab with generous spectacles in its rear sheet. Inside, the driver, George Leahy, stood like a supervising Guardsman on the footplate whilst his young fireman busied himself at ground level attending to all those things expected of young CVR employees - mainly with an oilcan. It was a cameo that lives with me still. What I have described as 'spectacles' were really windows to enable the crew to enjoy a bounteous view of what lay ahead - a most essential feature on the CVR which dashed from field to roadside and verge to verge in a manner common to most Irish tramways. To economise in water the class was fitted with condensors whereby, with suitable controls, the exhaust steam could be directed into the side tanks instead of up the chimney. This practice might make the feed water so hot that the injectors would not work. The CVR was not unique: condensors were frequently fitted to tramway engines as they softened the chimney blast which might frighten horses.

The CVR locomotives sported brass bells which operated from the cab. As built they carried enormous oil lamps to illuminate the way ahead (that on BLACKWATER was missing). In this rural backwater a night-time encounter with such a machine must have made many a child hide under mother's skirts. No. 6 was Leahy's usual engine; it was kept immaculate in red lake livery. The hidden driving wheels were 3 ft diameter and the weight almost 24 tons. I promised the CVR a return visit but World War II denied me the opportunity. The last train ran on 1st January, 1942; I was fortunate to have known it.

By Irish standards I was using the main line between two of its major cities, Dublin and Londonderry, a north-south artery which seemed to my mind, to overlook the requirement of connecting Belfast at all! (Experience would ultimately correct my mind. Belfast was clearly Ulster's starting point by rail.) The drum of the wheels over the rail joints caught my ear and we seemed to be making a good speed. It dawned on me, however, that though the sounds from the engine's chimney were encouraging, things were not as they sounded for this part of The Derry Road was still laid in short 45 ft rails. One could still enjoy the same cacophony of sound whilst travelling over original parts of the old North Stafford Railway south of Macclesfield.

There was something of a 'chocolate box lid' about the scene yet Arnold describes it as 'revealing the monotonous Co. Tyrone bush'. But then, he was an Ulsterman. I found it fascinating.

We reached Dungannon, junction for the Cookstown branch. The empty branch 'train' stood patiently in the adjacent platform; it comprised a converted GNRI road bus. Its original wheels had been replaced with others having flanged steel tyres. These were a little disappointing as I was hoping to see the new Howden-Meredith type wheels which could exchange rubber-tyred wheels for a flanged steel set by a jacking system. Nevertheless, it was an interesting encounter.

GNRI railbus at Dungannon.   *Author*

Beyond Dungannon I looked out for the exchange of the hand-held single-line token between engine crew and station staff but did not know that the GNRI-designed - but clumsy - automatic exchange apparatus had been fitted to some tenders. This ejected the tablet so forcibly that the public was cleared from the platform when certain trains were due. Exchanges could be made at 30 mph as against the 10 mph of the manual system.

It was interesting to note the hush which surrounded trains as they waited at rural stations. There would be the sound of the hissing injector and the ring of the fireman's shovel as more coal entered the firebox. Then a plume of black smoke rose from the chimney as the unburned coal smothered the fire. These little aural cameos were a part of the commonplace.

On again. The labouring of the engine became more pronounced as we climbed through Pomeroy. The speed dropped to walking pace as we threaded its deep cutting. I could discern the nonchalant engine crew as they waited patiently for the gradient to ease and the engine to recover speed. With Portadown far behind I spared a moment to renew my knowledge of the 'saw tooth' profile of the gradients. There were steep undulations out of Portadown and from Donaghmore an eight-mile climb northwards across a spur of the Sperrin Mountains. The watershed just beyond Pomeroy marked the second-highest point on the GNRI system, exceeded only by the 600 ft summit on the Castleblaney, Keady & Armagh line, by then abandoned. Arnold, who spent his schooldays hereabouts, describes the surrounding countryside as 'brown, boggy and deserted'; perhaps he was homesick for the town!

On coming to write these reminiscences 65 years later I am much aware that my mind was focused on the 3 ft gauge railway portions and that the 5 ft 3 in. line on which I now travelled was just an aperatif to what was to come. Would that I had paid more attention to it at the time! I recall the valuable role The Derry Road played in communications north of Portadown as far as Dungannon; the alternative to the railway was a 'narrow rough road' which even a motor cyclist took with great care. Liddle refers to the railway, 'to call it undulating would be mild'. Steam trains were limited to 45 mph and railcars 60 mph. On the section known as The Long Moss the spongey ground and instability of the formation made it difficult to maintain. It became an easy prey to road transport. Northwards the line suffers from speed restrictions due to its many sharp curves; it was said that if one had not noted the engine at the head of the train, the curves enabled one to do so.

And so onwards to Omagh, the county town of Tyrone with its considerable station, and in those pre-World War II days, a bustling railway centre with an engine shed providing locomotives for much of the GNRI. From the south, the former Irish North Western Railway made junction with The Derry Road which came in from the south-east. My train was now on part of the route of the erstwhile Londonderry & Enniskillen Railway, single-tracked then and now. In fact there had been several changes from double to single line since Portadown but I did not note each one. I anticipated Victoria Bridge and hung through the window hoping to glimpse some reminder of the Victoria Bridge & Castlederg Tramway, but there was none.

Chapter Three

Into Donegal, August 1939

A long curving feature on the west side of the train caught me unawares, so much so that my favourite pipe, which lay on the seat close beside me, fell between the cushions and was lost - to eye, much to my chagrin. I followed the curve which in due course came up beside us and assumed this to be the 3 ft gauge County Donegal Railways (CDR) line from Stranorlar to Strabane where it made a mixed gauge junction with the GNRI. My long interest in the Donegal railways was taking tangible form at last. I was absorbed by the complex environs of Strabane station as we entered it; we were in the platform in no time and I made a hasty exit - thus the loss of my pipe!

My preparatory reading about this part of my journey had revealed that the 3 ft gauge line which had run beside us into the station had begun life as the 5 ft 3 in. gauge Finn Valley Railway but had later been converted to 3 ft gauge. Its locomotives had been sold and might still exist on some railway backwater in Co. Cork. Thirteen miles long from Stranorlar to Strabane, it had opened in 1863 and worked in conjunction with the Irish North Western Railway.

It was evident on alighting from the train, that the line from Stranorlar had itself been joined by a second 3 ft gauge line - again by a sweeping curve. I guessed this must be the line from Letterkenny over which I would travel later that day ... I sensed that Strabane would not disappoint!*

Apart from my brief encounter at Tynan earlier that week, this was my first experience of a mixed gauge junction station with the added complication and bustle of a Customs Post. On the GNRI side of the station the mileage posts read from Dundalk (not from Portadown), a reminder of the historic commencement of the line.

There was plenty of opportunity to explore the station before the Letterkenny train departed. The extent of the land which the station occupied was considerable and reflected its cheapness before the railway age; it is a sobering thought that by end of the 20th century it had become a vaste expanse of waste ground! Not so in 1939. Both GNRI and CDR each had enough work to keep a station pilot engine occupied throughout the day, the former coming from Omagh shed whilst the latter was housed in a two-road open-fronted building at the north end of the complex. The GNRI was confined to the east and the CDR to the west of the site. The eastern island platform used both faces for GNRI use and the western similarly for the CDR. There was a narrow strip of no man's land in-between and a long connecting covered footbridge. It was the practice here to exchange consignments by hand between the gauges and for this purpose the GNRI stabled a bogie luggage van on the west side of the eastern platform. GNRI vehicle No. 400 (built in 1893 as Saloon A2) was kept solely for this assignment; it was unique.

A feature that emphasised the near-presence of the Free State border was the Customs occupation of certain station buildings whose boundaries were

---

* Strabane, Raphoe & Convoy Railway. (Opened in 1909.)

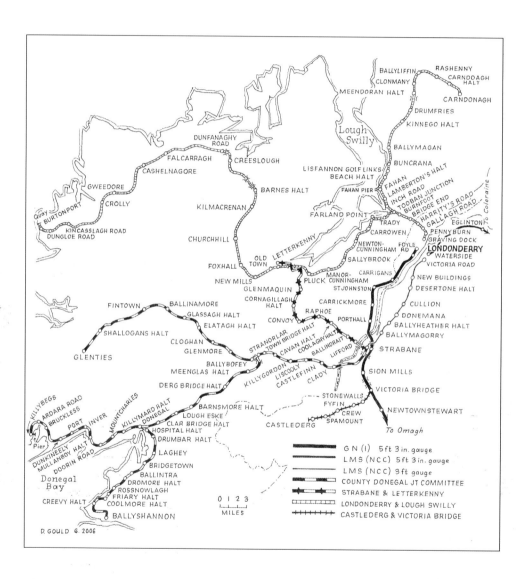

determined by crude wooden fencing which projected onto the platform. This was, at the same time, an eyesore, impediment and a joke!

What stirred my wanderlust was a platform sign - the like of which I had only seen at Ruabon - stating: 'STRABANE change for LETTERKENNY CREESLOUGH GWEEDORE & BURTONPORT. DONEGAL STRANORLAR KILLYBEGS GLENTIES.' The display was arranged to denote that the first-named stations were on the Lough Swilly system and the remainder on the Co. Donegal. What the *cognoscenti* knew but what the sign wisely did not indicate was that it was also possible to reach Londonderry from here either by GNRI or CDR, along opposite banks of the Foyle River.

There was an eye-catching turntable of sorts accessed by both gauges, each on a different level; this enabled narrow gauge wagons to be carried on GNRI transporters. Such were not to be seen but I once saw a similar arrangement on the Leek & Manifold Valley Railway at the age of eight! It was the first narrow gauge system I had seen. Strabane rather luxuriated in turntables - they were located at various places for turning railcars.

Concerning the resident shunting engines: the GNRI's representative was an elderly six-coupled tender engine of class 'PG' while the CDR example was the unique ex-Clogher Valley Tramway one-time steam tractor No. 8, built in 1928 by Atkinson-Walker Waggons Ltd of Frenchwood Works, Preston, Works No. 28. Much of its duty around Strabane was on mail trains and inter-running between the Customs Posts. In the form I saw it, it was diesel-engined, numbered 11 and named PHOENIX.

The CDR office at Stranorlar had sent me a copy of their Working Timetable, a single-folded foolscap sheet which proved to have little relevance to what took place. Such was the intimate nature of the concern that re-printing to keep it up to date was not a priority in an organization where everyone knew everyone else and Job Description was a pointless phrase. To me the Timetable was the embodiment of the independent nature of Ireland's remote north-west; it was a region apart. Its railways took scant heed of Dublin, Belfast or even Londonderry. Hereabouts, Letterkenny was the nerve centre of movements.

From this disarmingly simple yet informative missive I saw that the Strabane-Letterkenny line was worked from the latter place; according to my 1938-dated copy there was only one return steam train each day. All the other workings were made by railcars. The steam operation was a mixed train hauled by a 2-6-4 tank engine shedded at Letterkenny which left there at 9.30 am. The return working had already left Strabane before my arrival, so there was no movement on that line to watch. The Londonderry line, worked as a continuation of the Strabane line, had fallen into a post-prandial slumber. There were various stationary railcars about the place which perhaps at the sound of a bugle, might spring into action? As at scattered junctions I had come to know - for instance Crewe, Hereford, St John's Isle of Man, Portadown-Strabane would become a hive of activity interspersed with long periods of hibernation? The Letterkenny line was fortunate with five return trips per day and, except for the aforementioned steam train, relied on railcars entirely. Better still, for when I made enquiry I learned that an extra railcar now ran and had been doing so for the past six years; my informant explained that the timetable I had been given was 'quite old'.

Strabane with CDJC *left* and GNRI *right*. The GNRI parcels van is No. 400 built 1893 as saloon
A2. December 1954. *Author*

GNRI class 'T2' No. 62 at Strabane. June 1962. *Author*

A mixed train, steam-hauled, ran in from Killybegs and Stranorlar. All its passengers alighted but none went through the strategically-fenced Customs area. Then a railcar, hauling a small covered trailer, appeared and rounding the long curve, drew up at the most westerly platform face and emptied; an intriguing gaggle of country people emerged, mostly women clutching an assortment of bags, baskets *et al* but the men were empty-handed. It was curious to note that most of the women were smoking … quite unlike women at home who seldom smoked in public. It had not occurred to me that I should have broadened my knowledge beyond a map and timetable; a note of Fair and Market Days would have been informative. The Customs was ignored by everyone. I sat down and sampled one of Mrs Greaves' sandwiches. A few people were entering the train for Stranorlar and beyond; 2-6-4 tank No. 6 was in charge. Others were hanging about, awaiting railcar No. 15 with a trailer and open wagon attached, which had been turned and now stood at the west platform with its engine running. It would take me northwards. Behind it, on the same track, two more railcars drew up. Quite impressive! No one stopped to enquire directions. I was the only foreigner.

A strange impression came over me. The countryside, which had had a familiar ring about it at breakfast time was now a changed environment; I seemed to have crossed a Railway Rubicon and was now entering a new and strange one. I can offer no explanation for this but it is not confined to Ireland. Some have explained that it is due to a change in geology. The impression grew as I travelled further into Donegal and became aware of distant mountains which gave the region an identity all its own. I thought the people were different. They reflected a life-style stemming from a proximity to the Atlantic Ocean and the railways hereabouts had the character, pace and timetable which matched it. Their existence was wrapped up in the price of cattle and the size of the herring catch. While most homesteads had battery-operated wireless sets few boasted a telephone. Milk was a universal commodity but mains water was a luxury. Widespread electricity was a novelty though small turf-fired generating stations were springing up. Turf from the bogs was the domestic fuel: sanitation was basic. Alongside the railway, unsprung carts were used on unmade roads and decrepit bicycles spawned everywhere, usually carrying up to three children! These, and similar scenarios filled my head as I munched my sandwiches and digested the changing scene about me.

In the interests of cost-cutting, the three foot gauge railway builders ignored many smaller clusters of population by using cheaper routes. Some remote stations were consequently centres where both vehicles and quadrupeds were stabled whilst their owners made use of its infrequent trains. A small station would have a bar which gave the station an important niche in the social life of an area which would otherwise be denied to it. As a young man from urban Manchester this observation was unexpected, as was the expression, following the recent Irish civil unrest, that the hinterland was 'good Bandit Country'.

Some of Strabane's signals were of the somersault pattern frequently favoured by the Northern Counties Commitee (NCC) which was currently responsible for the CDR signalling. A modern-looking NCC signal box looked out of place; it transpired that some native signal boxes had been destroyed during the Civil War, and had been replaced. I had much to learn.

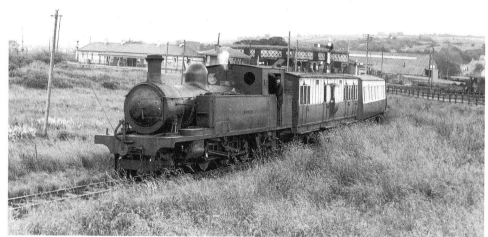

Letterkenny train leaving Strabane.   *Author's Collection*

Strabane-bound, a train leaves Raphoe.   *Author's Collection*

Enough of day-dreaming. It was time to make a move. The August afternoon was hot and sultry and some folk were beginning to board the railcar. I half glanced at its windows and was dismayed to see they were of typical roadbus variety with narrow opening lights the top. All were open but they could not compete - the interior was like an oven and the fug of stale cigarette smoke and shag could be cut with a knife. Additionally there was a strong hint of hot sweaty humans and domestic animals. Taken together they took much of the novelty off the experience - trains in England did not display such qualities!

Clearly, most of my fellow passengers had attended the Cattle Market, as was evident from their footwear and the category of their belongings. The guard entered and began to check tickets. He obviously knew all his customers and ticket collection was more like a social gathering; my paper ticket was to him an unexpected surprise but he offered no comment. Then the engine driver climbed in wearing a life-expired cloth cap on the back of his head. He revved up the engine as does an aircraft prior to a charge down the runway, and filled the bus with diesel fumes. The elderly woman sharing my seat had lost her ticket and without ceremony dumped a small pink piglet wearing a harness on my lap whilst she searched for it. Luckily it was house-trained and rather beguiling! Further along the journey its mistress alighted to the trackside and made her way through a nearby farm gate: the CDR prided itself on these unscheduled rail-side courtesies.

By now my feet had swollen with the heat and my dubbin-treated boots were insufferable. The railcar made numerous lineside stops and there were two substantial stations, Raphoe and Convoy - each had lost its passing loop. When on the move the railcar had a curious motion as the driver's portion was loosely articulated to the passenger unit behind. Its engine was incredibly noisy as were the connecting rods on the driving bogie which clanked incessantly and sounded as if they about to fall off.

At Raphoe and Convoy the yards were choked with covered vans fitted with corrugated iron roofs. It appeared that 95 per cent of traffic was conveyed in such. Some goods vans were lettered DR in white while others had the two letters overlaid as if there was insufficient space to paint them apart.

The falling approach to Letterkenny and the wide expanse of the Swilly estuary beyond, took me by surprise. The town sprawled in the river valley below, dominated by St Eunan's Roman Catholic Cathedral. I knew little about the Celtic saints and their names, only learning in years to come that in any Irish town of consequence the church is prominent but may be surpassed by the police barracks and railway station. The place is a model of its type with the railways crossing the Swilly River where the broad lough narrowed. The railcar rattled downgrade and there was a momentary view of the Lough Swilly Co.'s line from Londonderry coming towards us, also *en route* for Letterkenny. Without warning we crossed over its track by a concrete bridge. I attempted to absorb this sudden intruder and take stock of the nest of railway sidings which it spawned; preceeding them but below our railcar a branch led off the Swilly's line towards warehouses and a small quay on the riverside. Clearly there was much of interest here - more than the time available would permit before I caught the Burtonport train.

The Port, Letterkenny. March 1953.   *Author*

We ran into the Co. Donegal's station, well befitting the status of the county town. It lay to the north of, but side by side with, the Swilly station, and was obviously the newer, incorporating all that was best in model railway trends of that time - island platform with all-over roof and a neat station entrance surmounted with a plaque, '1909'. It was straight out of the Bassett-Lowke catalogue depicting: 'A Terminus Station'. Contrasting with it were the 1903 premises of the Londonderry & Lough Swilly Railway (L&LSR), so much more a typically Irish rural through-station … plain, and without squitter! As if anxious to outdo the other, each system possed an engine shed, turntable, carriage shed and signal box plus an impressive display of semaphore signals. (It was years later when I came to examine the umbilical cord which linked the two stations through their goods yards. Relations between the companies were seldom cordial and seemed to be emphasised by the catch point which prevented the Donegal from trespassing on Swilly tracks; the locking key was kept in the Swilly signal box!)

I hurried along the short distance to the Swilly station at whose platform the Burtonport train was already waiting.

Letterkenny terminus. *c.*1910.   *L&GRP*

Chapter Four

To the Farthest North-West,
Letterkenny to Burtonport, August 1939

Although in close proximity, there were many differences between Letterkenny's two stations. The Swilly's had formerly been the terminus of the Letterkenny Railway but in the form I now saw it, it was a through station. (It was to be 1951 before I had the opportunity to explore them both and by then a one mile stub of the Burtonport line beyond Letterkenny was all that remained of the erstwhile Burtonport Extension.) Compared with the Donegal Railway's terminal which I had just left, the Swilly's was the poorer relation, but no less interesting.

The connection for Burtonport was due to leave about 6.15 pm and had done so since the Extension was opened. It was the second and last daily working over the entire route from Londonderry. I deduced that a Letterkenny-shedded engine had worked the first eastbound train to Londonderry and returned to Letterkenny again. Here it had been changed for the 4-6-0 tank engine which even now was waiting patiently to depart 'for the far northwest'. Behind it were two depressing-looking grey-painted painted bogie coaches bearing a diamond-shaped green logo, 'LSR'. I concluded that the Company did not value their appearance with esteem! They compared badly with the smart red and cream railcars of the CDR. Following in turn was a rake of motley four-wheeled vans terminating in another grey-painted carriage having a guard's compartment. It struck me that the guard was well isolated from his responsibilities in the front portion of the train.

There were about 20 people in the forward carriages. I managed to secure a compartment to myself. It was bare with lath-boarded seats. The electric lights did not survive and the window-opening straps had disappeared - no doubt to serve as razor strops - to the effect that when the window was up it did not fully close, so making the last part of my journey cold and miserable. The luggage rack brackets were intact but the racks had gone. I spread a map over one seat where later it became peppered in soot from the open window. Departure time came and went; various folk still stood around and gossiped while packages from the CDR railcar were brought across from the other station; these were mainly crated hens and ducks which were seemingly regular passengers to judge by the containers and well-used labels in use. I had noticed that the guard's van was awash with feathers.

With an absence of haste prevailing, I took the opportunity to walk the platform and examine the engine which, compared with the drab coaches, was immaculate. I had learned that the Swilly men took great pride in their engines and that they were shedded near to home if possible so that they received careful attention at week-ends; the L&LSR favoured black paint for its locomotives. The Burtonport Extension had a nominal allocation of them, this example being No. 3. It would remain at Burtonport overnight. Messrs. Andrew Barclay & Sons had built the class in 1904 to a design by T.M. Batchen of the Irish Board of Works. (Incidentally, there were six similar Neilson-built engines

Letterkenny L&LSR station, towards Londonderry. March 1951. *Author*

of 1893 on the Donegal Railway and a single Kerr, Stuart product of 1903 on the West Clare Railway.) No. 3 seemed small for such a long run. Like its sister engines it was lettered 'L&BER' and remained in traffic until the system closed. The tanks and bunker were rather undersized but we were to make numerous stops for water and would begin the journey with coal generously heaped over the footplate floor, and a brimming bunker! By the time we had reached Burtonport I was filled with admiration for this plucky little engine. How proudly did its Scottish hooter echo amongst the Donegal hills!

Writing of coal, at that age I gave it scarcely a thought; it was a commodity every railway stocked and whence it came and how, I had little knowledge. The L&LSR supplies came by sea from Scotland and was loaded into L&LSR wagons on Londonderry's River Foyle quayside. The Harbour Commissioners had a steam locomotive with draw and buffing gear to suit both gauges which would quickly shunt such wagons between riverside and L&LSR tracks; that company had no suitable engines for this task as the dock line curves were too severe to employ them.

I returned to the compartment to reconsider my position. The afternoon was already well-spent yet here I had quite 50 wild and winding miles still to travel that day. Was there sufficient food left in my rucksack and where would I sleep that night? I was fortified by the correspondence I had received from Harold Fayle of Boscombe, a contemporary of my father at Owen's College, Manchester, now Manchester University. From him, possibly the foremost authority of Irish railway matters then extant, I had received a sheaf of notes on what the remainder of the day might reveal. After a circuitous route around Letterkenny, the train would travel westwards along the Swilly valley before quitting the river and climbing steeply northwards. At 340 ft above sea level we would reach Kilmacrenan which, like most stations along the line, would be inconsiderately distant from the place of its name. From here the railway fell in surroundings wilder than previously, only to climb again when, after a summit, Fayle recommended me to look out for the bleak and rock-strewn Barnes Gap.

Almost immediately would come the *piece-de-resistance* of the Extension, the infamous Owencarrow viaduct, the site of a spectacular fatal derailment some years before, caused by a ferocious wind. I had seen pictures of the viaduct in its setting - they put me in mind of geography lessons on Afghanistan and the Kyber Pass. This point in the journey would seem to epitomise the whole trip. At the same time I recognised that Burtonport and a night's rest would still be far off.

The late Poet Laureate, W.H. Auden, had been our English master and we were obliged to learn more of any subject chosen for an essay. It was good advice. For my present journey I had searched extensively for articles about north-west Ireland but it did not seem to be a topic which English writers favoured as a subject. In 1939 there were no organizations which promoted Irish tourism!

The railways hereabouts had usually been aided and abetted by a well-meaning Westminster Government which was ready to recognise that parts of the north-west region were impoverished; in official terms, measures 'to alleviate the conditions of life of the inhabitants of certain of the poorest districts of the western coast of Ireland' were taken. A Congested Districts Board was formed in 1891 and in due course the Burtonport Extension Railway would be built entirely within such a District. I found this pertinent especially as the level crossing to the west of the train on which I was about to travel marked the Parliamentary Boundary of the District.

(The great herring fishery off the islands of The Rosses in Donegal dated back to the 1780s when the catch was made from open boats. The fish then migrated only to appear again a short time before my visit. Now the industry had grown sufficiently to attract some Scottish firms with steamers plying to the Clyde with cured fish and fresh herrings. Iced fish in barrels were consigned to Irish, North German and American markets. It was this development which gave the impetus for building the Extension Railway.

Years later, when the Donegal roads were improved and suited to road lorries, the Extension Railway became the victim of change. Less obvious among the reasons for its demise was that much of the permanent way had reached the end of its life-span. The cost of such major renewal was considered to be uneconomic once the highway had been upgraded.)

Back on the waiting train the late July sun, which had shone all day, began to dip over the distant hills to the north. A sudden jerk disturbed my reverie. After standing so passively there now seemed to be some activity afoot. The little knot of men grouped by the engine's cab melted slightly. We were about half an hour behind our published departure time; the Working Timetable gave it as 5.50 pm. The engine sounded a short toot and the coach took a frightful jerk as the couplings on the long mixed train took up the slack; possibly the guard's handbrake had not been fully unscrewed for the character I took to be the guard was still chatting unconcernedly on the platform as the train gathered momentum. As the engine pulled away, from under the floor came the sound of creaking, protesting drawbars. It suddenly ceased - no soubt the guard had boarded safely and released the brake. At last I felt my quest was entering its last phase. The nearby locomotive began to rumble happily along a wooded valley and we passed Old Town, the extent of Letterkenny's southern flank. I realised that it was an opportunity to eat and foolishly spread food, maps *et al* along the opposite seat. It was still a balmy evening and both windows were open; shortly I discovered my food was covered by a thin layer of ash.

The train ran westwards for some miles before the railway turned north. There were undulating gradients but we climbed persistently with a maximum of 1 in 50 throughout. The engine skidaddled along comfortably, running like a well-oiled sewing machine. The sun shone intermittently between the valley's trees. It was cool and pleasant. We climbed about 200 ft from the valley floor and reached 350 ft at Kilmacrenan, the first station proper. I was so busy rescuing my food from smuts that the station caught me unawares. It was an extensive place, well equipped with a stone-built house and goods shed, and a timber signal box. These features proved to be alike throughout the journey.

There was then some protracted shunting. The engine and my carriage were uncoupled from the train to collect a van from a siding and place it along with its fellows i.e. behind my coach, this being done in order to satisfy Board of Trade (BOT) regulations concerning brakes and train make-up, over which the company had been in trouble several times. In the event, and as shunting took place at every station, at succeeding stations where more movements were necessary, it was usual for the engine to draw the whole train clear of the station so as to insert (or remove) wagons as necessary. After finding myself marooned and alone in the carriage, I followed my fellow pasengers as we all left the train while the engine shunted to its heart's content. Meanwhile, the station bar enjoyed a field day; we returned to the train after the engine crew had joined us and I wondered if the BOT was aware how strictly regulations were being observed! Kilmacrenan was like other stations, I could see no sign of a village. It was important as a block-post in the middle of the long 21 mile Letterkenny-Creeslough section.

Our surroundings here were of pleasant upland country. I began to take more notice as we descended into a steep rough valley in the Loughsalt Mountains to thread a narrow pass between Stragaddy and Crocknagrady mountains. The geology had changed; the railway began its penetration into the Donegal Highlands with wild and rocky scenes to either side of the train. I darted from side to side, anxious not to miss this exciting change in our surroundings. But the train speeded on and it was impossible to absorb it all, the summit at 40¼ m., the long fall thence at 1 in 50, the bleak Barnes Gap where railway and road ran together for two miles, the Barnes Gap viaduct 60 ft high with three 60 ft spans and the overall speed limit of 10 mph … a quick change of direction ensued as we emerged onto the edge of the Owencarrow River valley. With dramatic suddeness the whole vista of the Highlands burst into view and the two mountain peaks which I had followed from a distance for much of the day, were almost at hand. They stood prominently above the river, their flanks littered with white boulders, as if with iceing. Furthest away was the dominant white quartzite cone of Errigal, rising to 2,466 ft, 10 miles away. Much nearer was the massive bulk of Muckish, 2,197 ft. Some years later I was to know each more intimately.

The valley was a most peculiar place. It blocked the direction of the railway and obliged it to turn sharply left and right on a falling grade of 1 in 50, in order to cross it at right angles by the unlovely Owencarrow viaduct. To see the site

In 1925 a train was blown off the Owencarrow viaduct by high winds.

of an unusual accident had long been one my ambitions (another was to cross the Forth Bridge by train). And now, here I was in person. The unlucky train was crossing a length which was part viaduct and part embankment, a curiously composite affair. The drama of the occasion was undiminished. I resolved to try to memorise it all again when I returned tomorrow.

All this was now behind us. The train had been brought to a walking pace but the lack of height had taken something off the experience. I watched the driver, whose every movement was under my gaze, open the regulator sharply and we were carried quickly over the lip of the valley on the other side.

The railway now climbed over high ground again to reach Creeslough where there was a village nearby and wonderful views of the north coast. At the station there was a huddle of mixed vehicles as the main road made one of its rare contacts with the railway. Transport by bicycle was the preferred mode and the local children had come to watch the train go by. They rode, three on one machine, without footwear. Their barelegs, feet and clothing were white with quartzite road dust. Here again we spent some time in shunting and there was much to entertain me!

Onwards from Creeslough the arresting views of the Atlantic coastline held my gaze and the Railway descended almost to sea level at Dunfanaghy Road which I deduced to be nearly six miles from that seaside village. The station's title to incorporate 'Road' was a warning to any stranger who assumed he had reached his goal. Once again there was a little straggle of vehicles beside the station as horse and donkey carts loaded people and belongings, and made for home. *En route* between Creeslough and Dunfanaghy, we had crossed the three span viaduct, 50 ft high, at Faymore but I was so attracted to Sheep Haven and the shore of the inlet, that I missed it. In the evening light the coast line took on that beauty which is a feature of sundown in the west.

There followed a long period where the rails traversed the flank of mountain range to the south-west. This section began just after leaving Dunfanaghy and all views of the coast were lost in a long rift valley. To the left the hump of Muckish filled the scene; there was a four mile climb to 474 ft at the 50th milepost (mileages are measured from Londonderry). Here the upland country was wild and bleak and I was glad to put on the cardigan from my rucksack. The sun was now low in the sky and afforded little warmth.

The civil engineering hereabouts was considerable. A long descent brought us to Falcarragh and again there was shunting and a group of folk left, bound for the village four miles away. Three miles beyond here came Cashelnagore which, at 420 ft was the highest station on the Extension. Such was the emptiness of its surroundings that I wondered how it attracted any business. Here and there among the featureless scene would be a small white cottage or cabin. Exceptionally, one could pick out a diminutive turf-fired generating station, with loaded donkey carts plodding their way towards it. So eventually we gained Cashelnagore station for more extended shunting. I was glad to leave the compartment and stretch my legs. Errigal's flanks, near at hand, dominated the background.

We had passed through some of the wildest scenery between Falcarragh and Cashelnagore; it fulfilled my expectations exactly and the overall lure of Errigal captivated. This was the terrain I had imagined, lovely in summer and desolate in winter with a standard of living encapsulated by the solitary dwellings. Their roofs were, by necessity, held in place by wire or rope fastenings, anchored to the ground by enormous rocks which were to hand everywhere. The contrast with industrial Lancashire, its mills and coal tips, was profound and affected me considerably. I realised that one could experience the privations of austerity just as much in this fine mountainscape as in the back streets of Wigan, a town of which I had had recent close experience whilst working with its unemployed coal miners.

Gweedore station came after six miles of intermittent fall from Cashelnagore. It was evidently important by Extension standards as witnessed by the considerable gathering to greet the train and the size of the motley collection of road transport; it had the appearance of a large open-air marketplace. The station was the centre for several large villages on the Bloody Foreland and proved to be the busiest place I would see since Letterkenny. Train apart, the local people used the station as a convenient meeting point for every kind of purpose, be it business, social or domestic and why not combine this with the convenience of travel?! The church would be the only other similar situation, and it had no bar.

I had become wise to the movements of my fellow travellers. Immediately the train stopped there was a rush akin to a rugby scrum making for the try line and aiming for a small ancillary building, the bar. In due course, the men from the train joined us. I made my escape and discovered a small carriage body in use as a store, to learn later it was one of several formerly used as horse trams in Londonderry. I had time to notice the preponderance of elderly people and children. There was a noticeable absence of anyone in the 18-40 age range which bore out the effects of emigration - mainly to the U.S.A. This journey was broadening my mind.

(From 1940 the railway between here and Burtonport would be lifted in an attempt to close the whole Extension, a plan which was thwarted by civil unrest among the local inhabitants to the extent the railway was retained between Gweedore and Letterkenny. Thus Gweedore became the terminus until 1947 when dismantling was resumed. There was much evidence of the litter and rubbish created during this interregnum when some years later my wife and I returned to the derelict station by Lough Swilly bus. By then no nostalgia remained! Worse, I had promised her a meal at the local hotel, important to my mind as being the focal point of Joseph Tatlow's visits to investigate the irregularities which the Government felt were inseparable from operating the Exension. Our bus had an hour to wait amid the clutter of junk and pools of oil between the platforms, before returning; of the hotel there was nothing but a ruin also. We dined on a bar of chocolate and biscuits which the bus crew spared for us.)

I must return to 1939. Frequent stops at small stations which followed Gweedore began to take the edge off the journey. The train began a long descent as it left the Highlands behind and entered a region known as The Rosses, a district of numerous lakes and many rock outcrops. The track wound its way between these outcrops and the lakes, frequently by means of low stone embankments and there were constant changes of gradient. It was a novel situation, well suited to the type of railway. The engine glissaded among the succession of curves and switchbacks. It was going dark and I had no food left. I began to feel cold. My interest in the inevitable shunting had also cooled and when we reached Kincasslagh and I was asked by some young people in the next compartment to join them, I did so. There were no lights in the train but my companions took me to small house in Burtonport where I could obtain a lodging. I noted it was 10.10 pm whereas we were due in at 9.00 pm and wondered if the train ever arrived on time. My experience suggested not. It was now very dark indeed and my journey had ended in something of an anti-climax.

I recall little of that night except that I seemed to be sharing the room with a variety of noisy livestock. My bedroom proved to be an adequate recess in the wall of a larger room over the floor of which various dogs, cats, poultry, etc. seemed to have the right of prior residence. They ignored me. Breakfast was a feast and I was unfamiliar with all the fare 'herself' set down before me; she was very disappointed when I turned down the offer of a third fried egg. Knowing that the train left at 8.30 am I asked how much I owed her. 'Would it be too much if I said 1/6d?' she replied, almost suggesting that she was over-charging me. At this obvious bargain I asked where I could obtain a pipe and tobacco? I was taken through into what was a general store with a rough wooden counter. Her tobacco was not of a type with which I was familiar, but she rolled out a curious blend of shag and measured it alongside a brass ruler on the counter. 'That will be two pence, and the pipe six pence. Will that be all?' I thanked her, said 'Goodbye now' and made my way to the station.

There was little time to explore Burtonport before the train left. There was only one other train that day and if I missed the 8.30 am, I would lose my Londonderry connection and my promise to be back in Portadown. I had only a cursory glimpse of Burtonport. It was a bitter disappointment anyway. I had imagined it was on the Atlantic coast and had visions of a wild vista. As it was there were so many islets with intervening water that the precise coastline was unclear. Houses and sheds were scattered amidst pools of brackish water. There

The 8.30 am train for Londonderry awaits a locomotive at Burtonport. August 1939.   *Author*

No. 14 will take the 8.30 am train through to Londonderry (73 miles). August 1939.   *Author*

was no real centre and the whole community was given over to fishing. Rubbish and smells predominated. I looked westwards in vain for a recollection of ocean rollers to carry home with me, but the many islands intervened.

The station proved to be a simple terminus which stretched along the water's edge for some distance. There was a single platform, station house, engine and carriage sheds, turntable; the Swilly never ran its tank engines bunker first! The whole station area had been reclaimed from the sea with large boulders. The engine shed housed No. 3 behind which I had arrived on the evening previously; it was being prepared for the afternoon working to Londonderry but would only haul it as far as Letterkenny and then return to Burtonport once more. The carriage shed was empty. The 8.30 am train stood in the platform. It comprised a bogie guard's brake at each end of an assortment of covered vans, loaded with fish in barrels which leaked profusely. The engine was one of the Letterkenny & Burtonport Extension Railway's (L&BER) impressive large 4-6-2 tanks which were not, it was said, as popular as the smaller 4-6-0 tanks. It would work the train through to Londonderry.

Departure time came and went and I began to concern myself about my GNRI train connection at Londonderry. There was no one about on the engine or platform. But I had despaired too soon for the guard appeared and we slid out from Burtonport almost noiselessly. We had but a handful of passengers and ran along the sea's edge before quitting the shore and making for the lake-studded Rosses again. We began a long steady climb and I stuffed myself into a corner to see the winding track ahead. The motion of the big tank engine was quite different from that of No. 3 - was much more sedate and ponderous! It was another beautiful day and I decided to sample the Plug tobacco I had just bought but after a few puffs, thought the better of it; it was that or the uneasy ride of the carriage, whichever, I began to feel sick. The shag bore no relation to BALKAN SOBRANIE to which I had been introduced by the Sports Editor of the *Manchester Guardian*, but then it cost 7*d*. per oz. in stout tins which had their after-life in storing small model railway parts.

The train passed a large farm from which a black sheep dog ran out and chased us so closely that I feared for its life. It raced between the rails behind the last carriage for a matter of miles - and probably did so regularly.

On the return journey to Letterkenny I filled my notebook with the many features I had missed the day before. I intended to use the ample waiting time there to eat in the small but useful bar in the County Donegal Railways Joint Committee (CDRJC) station adjacent, there being no such facility in the spartan L&LSR premises. In the bar I was approached by a young man who said his name was Russell. He had noticed me the previous evening boarding the Burtonport train, and had envied me the opportunity - I explained that some of the experience had been a little disappointing.

I failed to note if No. 14 was unchanged for the run to Londonderry but assumed it was. Russell proved to be a considerable talker and well-informed on L&LSR matters. Listening to him I failed to note much of our journey; he left me at Graving Dock terminus. Once there I called in to see James Whyte the L&LSR Manager, who had been so helpful in recommending me to come. Seeking some souvenirs of the visit I asked him if I could have some old tickets.

No. 12 has been left outside the shed for our delight! March 1953. *Author*

'Certainly. Walk down to our Pennyburn station. There is an old wooden building beside the line there. Go in and help yourself.'

I had great difficulty in pushing the door open as the whole structure was collapsing. Inside, and stacked to roof height, bulging sack-fulls of used tickets had been jettisoned. Parts of the floor had subsided under their weight. I made my way carefully - it appeared that every ticket issued since the railway opened might be unearthed here, if only opportunity allowed! An Aladdin's Cave, no less.

But time was not on my side and the GNRI station was some distance away. I sorted out some choice specimens from the breath-taking variety of tickets for which the L&LSR was a byword, and left their equally breath-taking smell behind. As I made my way along the mixed-gauge tracks beside the Foyle River, I felt that the last hour had been a rewarding end to my Donegal venture.

No. 12 had been used in lifting the Burtonport Extension. It will never run again. March 1953.
Author

Chapter Five

North Donegal Anthology, Part One

The monthly meetings of the Manchester Locomotive Society had continued throughout World War II; the annual subscription was 5s. and the venue an upper room of a public house conveniently near to Knott Mill station. Being a pre-war member I attended the gatherings again where I quickly learned that I was but a beginner in my pursuits and that at every meeting, if I kept my ears open, I could learn of railway matters quite beyond the information published in my *Railway Magazine*. More especially this was of railways and locomotives of which I was unaware, mainly in private ownership and in industrial premises, on which several members were well informed. I realised that my interests might be broadened. At the same time, it was curious that no one seemed to be familiar with the narrow gauge systems unless they happened to be in industrial use. The North Wales slate quarry railways were amongst the latter type and, although public transport was still crippled by wartime restrictions, some of my friends were adept at putting their bicycles on the train and visiting remote locations.

Regularly, conversation dwelt on threatened closures and the imperative to make a visit before it was too late. Most of us worked on Saturday mornings so opportunity was limited. I made a list of places I thought were at risk and accessible by rail and cycle. Some extracts from the list make fascinating reading today:

ASHOVER RAILWAY. Steam operated narrow gauge mineral line.
MANCHESTER SHIP CANAL. Steam operated standard gauge canalside system.
WHITTINGHAM ASYLUM. Steam operated standard gauge branch offering passenger service in converted goods brake vans. Lancashire County Council.
WOODHEAD RESERVOIRS. Primitive electric line (narrow gauge) used for maintenance of Manchester Corporation Water Works.
EATON HALL. 15 inch gauge system owned by Duke of Westminster.
KEARSLEY POWER STATION. Standard gauge overhead electric system carrying coal for steam generators.
WALKDEN WORKSHOPS. Central repair for the Lancashire Coalfields' complex of railways.

Even this brief list will serve to show how closely my feet were being directed into avenues of which I had no previous experience. Until now I had thought that the boundaries were set by a conventional interest in railways which might be seen from the lineside, station platform etc. Now the knowledge that, for instance, a railway was being built for the creation of the huge Ladybower Dam of Sheffield Corporation Water Works up in the Pennines, and that it could be accessed on Sundays, was gained through the intimacies of the 'grapevine' which spread such news among the members of that Society. From that time on, I could ponder on fresh strings to my bow.

Oddly, there seemed little awareness/interest among Mancunians towards railways which had drawn me to Ireland (for instance), and to which I wished

Great Victoria Street station with GNRI class 'T2' No. 66 on carriage shunting duty. June 1963.
Author

Great Victoria Street station. NCC class 'W' No. 104 on a Dublin train. June 1963. *Author*

to return at the first opportunity for there was no doubt they were as vulnerable as any on my List! In particular, Co. Donegal offered much 'unfinished business' as the 3 ft gauge lines from Londonderry to Buncrana - and the November 1935 abandoned line beyond to Carndonagh - plus the whole of the Co. Donegal Railways Joint Committee network was waiting to be explored. Rumours that abandonment of the 'Derry based-lines was close were not helpful, nor was the opportunity and the expense.

Our business interests, however, took me to Belfast from time to time and I proposed to use that city as a staging post and means to the end.

The first opportunity came in March 1951. I had had earlier visits to Ireland in 1933 and 1939 before this but not to Belfast. I must explain that we had about 18 business customers in Belfast; though our resident Agent there kept us in touch, no one from the factory had made personal contact with them since before World War II. To offset this, such customers frequently came over to England and would call on us in Manchester; such visits had become essential to them to retain supplies of our products which had become rationed and in short supply during the war and for some time afterwards. For this reason we already had pleasant relationships and I was looking forward to the occasion.

Dorothy could join me as she had approved of Ireland previously. We could time the visit around Easter and the Bank Holidays and if we spent the nights out at Bangor this would give me the opportunity to commute daily to Belfast by the former Belfast & Co. Down Railway (B&CDR) and then walk to the office across the River Lagan bridge and into the city. There was a spur of the electric tramway system into the B&CDR terminus on Queens Quay. It terminated under a fine glazed roof and the tram bay could hold two cars, but such was my business timetable that I never used it and the next time I was in Belfast the tram system had been abandoned!

The Belfast & Co. Down system had become part of the Ulster Transport Authority (UTA) in 1948. It was largely untouched and an experience in itself. It deserves a separate account but served as an hors-d'oeuvre to things to come.

We planned to leave Belfast on Maundy Thursday in the morning and gain Londonderry by the former GNRI lines (now UTA) to Portadown and Strabane changing at the latter to the Co. Donegal Railway system. We could thus arrive in Derry on the 3 ft gauge instead of the more conventional continuation from Strabane on GNRI metals by the same train we had used from Portadown. By this ploy we could walk across Derry to the Lough Swilly's railway yard at Pennyburn by means of the lower deck of the Craigavon Bridge with its mixed gauge tracks, and then follow these same rails up the west side of the Foyle River. Somewhere along here there was a chance we might encounter the Harbour Board's 5 ft 3 in. gauge six-coupled saddle tank with its mixed gauge buffing and coupling gear, shunting stock of the two gauges at the same time. (We were lucky. We did and it was!)

There were still regular movements of wagons along these quays but for reasons to be explained later the L&LSR terminus was now only used for wagon storage and we would therefore conclude our walk by a short visit to the admirable Mr James Whyte in the railway offices - who I had not seen since 1939 - before proceeding to meet the goods train which would take us to Buncrana.

Continuing this itinerary, while the train shunted we could explore Buncrana, return by the same train as far as Tooban Junction and wait there for the Londonderry-Letterkenny afternoon goods. This would take us to Letterkenny where we planned to end the first day of our long weekend. On the following day, our coverage of what remained of the Lough Swilly system being complete, we could transfer to the former Strabane & Letterkenny Railway terminus at Letterkenny and so reach Strabane by the Co. Donegal Railways. We intended to travel to Donegal town, thence to Ballyshannon and back, and take a train to Killybegs where we could overnight. Unlike the L&LSR which had no passenger services, there was a useful timetable (mainly comprising railcars) on the CDR and the day's ambitious programme seemed quite feasible. The Manager of the CDR at Stranorlar must be contacted before we left home!

The history of the L&LSR lines which would thus become familiar to us was slightly complex and at that time there were no useful books on the subject. This Saga is not a history, but a background to where we were going was essential to our fulfilment of the journey. We therefore set about the task of listing promising features under suitable geograpical headings so that they could be noticed *en route*. Large scale maps would be essential if available. Timetables would be needed to plan our movements. Should we leave accommodation to chance? Did we need Passports for Southern Ireland? Would a rucksack each be sufficient? What items were still rationed / unobtainable etc?

To find an answer to such questions about the Irish Free State (which had been independent in the recent war) and particularly on remote parts of Donegal was impossible for us in Manchester. For instance, camera film was then rationed by my friendly local retailer - and proved to be unavailable in Ireland. Accordingly much of our luggage space was used for a stock of films, chocolate, pipe tobacco, soap and the like. We were advised that the Customs Inspectors around Londonderry were especially keen on the smuggling of cigarettes, nylon stockings and such items as listed in the *Post Office Guide*, 'Elm Trees and contraceptives'. Dorothy elected to stuff her precious pairs of nylon stockings in her bra and I supported our photographic equipment with official receipts from well known suppliers to satisfy curious enquirers.

The proposed stop at to call on Mr Whyte was essential to check up on current timings and the operation of the twice-daily Derry-Buncrana and Derry-Letterkenny goods workings, such was the meagre level of trains by this date. He had previously sent me a copy of the Working Timetable which though dated four years earlier had a hand-written note, 'Ignore the date. This is the current Table'.

As we hurried through the streets to the GNRI's Great Victoria Street station for the morning fast train to Dublin (which we would leave at Portadown) I caught the unmistakable sound of short exaust beats from a steam engine working hurriedly. Knowing we were scarcely within earshot of a railway engine I stopped and looked down the street to see smoke billowing up amidst the road vehicles. Coming rapidly towards us and towing an empty four-wheeled trailer was a small road traction engine; it left an enticing smell of hot steam oil as it passed travelling at a fair pace but not too fast to note that it was one of Messrs Harkness' 5-ton Garett steam tractors off in a hurry to fulfil an assignment. The brief episode was a fitting debut to the day.

We were directed to the front of the train at Great Victoria Street: it was composed of a varied collection of teak carriages, some of genuine wood and others in steel with teak finish. There was no opportunity to assess them closely and in any case, I assumed, wrongly, they were little different from similar carriages I saw daily at home on the Cheshire Lines railway. What we could not miss was a gorgeous smell of frying bacon issuing from the kitchen car as we passed; there were flames shooting up from its galley chimney.

I made time to inspect the engine of our train. It proved to be one of five most recently built for the GNRI by Beyer, Peacock Ltd of Manchester in 1948, No. 209 FOYLE of 'VS' class, a 3-cylinder simple expansion version of a similar class but supplied as compound engines. Owing to their weight, the class was confined to the Dublin-Belfast main line. We could anticipate a fast 29 minute run to Portadown, the first stop. In a brief chat with the driver, he commended the new engines but said he preferred the compound version!

Dorothy was completely taken by the spacious carriages which were more sumptuous than those in which we travelled in Eire. I had not been over this section of suburban line since 1939 and was reminded how 'English' it seemed compared with similar routes out of Dublin. In no time at all we were slowing for the Portadown stop where a number of business people left the train with us. Along with a mere handful of folk we made our way under the subway for the Londonderry train standing at the adjoining island platform. There had been plenty of signs of war-time bomb damage around Belfast but Portadown seemed to have led a charmed life; it had obviously been a wise move to transfer all the engines shedded at Belfast Adelaide out to Portadown for the duration of the war!

There was plenty of time to change trains as luggage, parcels etc. had to be brought over as well. It was quite a labour-intensive business; I counted seven luggage trollies involved. The GNRI was the largest employer in Northern Island. There were only three passenger carriages in the train but we had two bogie passenger vans as well so obviously these could accommodate the trolley-loads easily. I suspected the parcels were involved in the mail-order business. The former vehicles were steel-sided but the van of teak. Our engine was one of the rebuilt 'Q' class 4-4-0s by Clifford of 1899, very much used on this line; it would work through to Derry.

I had run over this route on my 1939 journey and was looking forward to a leisurely re-appraisal while Dorothy could absorb the views and monitor our picnic lunch. There was ample seating of 3-per side and a wide central gangway, while our fellow passengers gave us a wide berth suspecting the maps spread out on the seats and frequent rush to the open windows put us in a Nuisance Category.

There were the expected long stops at stations but at Omagh it was especially lengthy while we did a little shunting with much waving of arms and whistle blowing from staff on the platform. Our train drew forward allowing a train behind us from Enniskillen to a detach a single coach bound for Londonderry, to be coupled to our own. This was more complicated than I expected and I failed to grasp the necessary movements: normally I would have alighted on the platform to watch but Irish railway habits had already taught me that English

GNRI Adelaide engine shed, Belfast. March 1964.   *Author*

GNRI class 'VS' No. 207 at Dublin Amiens Street engine shed. June 1965.   *Author*

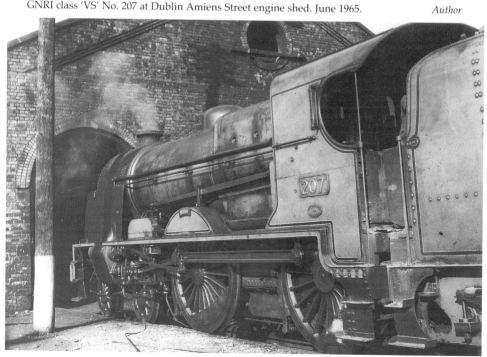

methods could not be taken for granted and I feared that if I left our coach it might depart without me and take my wife with it.

(Omagh was the historic meeting and operating point where the Omagh & Enniskillen section, originally part of the Londonderry & Enniskillen Railway and later part of the Irish North Western Railway (INWR) came together. The importance of it seemed to have lived on in the practice so observed; it seemed that trains from Dundalk to Derry came via the former INWR route and some were married to portions which had come from Portadown. I must check the timetables to see if this was commonplace.)

Remembering how the sudden appearance of Strabane had caught me unexpectedly last time (12 years ago!) we kept our eyes open for the long sweeping curve of the Stranorlar line on the Donegal system as it curled in beside us on the west flank to cross the Mourne River and thus make a two-fold assault on Strabane station. The GNRI lines were entirely to the east of the joint premises, its most westerly being along a face of an ample platform along which we pulled up. Between here and the 3 ft gauge layout lay a useful space across which items from GNRI vans could be loaded into Donegal stock.

As we crossed the footbridge to the narrow gauge side of the station we noticed how its long single island platform was hemmed in at either side by trains. Some were steam-hauled, some by railcars with trailers, others were single railcars. The steam trains faced either way. Dorothy was delighted by the apparent disorder but now knew it was inaccurate to describe the scene as 'typically Irish' but rather exclaimed, 'Presumably some one untangles them all and knows which we must take for Londonderry?' The official we asked seemed very surprised at our question and directed us towards the train we had just left and which, as we had correctly suspected, took every one with it who wanted an expeditious route and arrival near the city centre.

The narrow gauge line which we were taking had its history linked to the very circumstance we had witnessed, competition from the GNR. The GNR passed over to the west side of the River Foyle on leaving Strabane and thus into Eire; the narrow gauge remained on the east side and in Ulster and in consequence had station stops into Derry, so lengthening the journey. Whilst the bulk of the narrow gauge lines became controlled by the Co. Donegal Railways Joint Committee in 1906, for historical reasons the Strabane-Derry line, although operated by the CDRJC, was wholly owned by the (English) Midland Railway and so passed to the London Midland & Scottish Railway in 1923. A truly Irish situation indeed! But of course, our train of Naysmith, Wilson-built 2-6-4 tank engine No. 8, FOYLE and two bogie coaches was a purely CDRJC assembly, and looked like one. We commented on the singular experience of being hauled by different locomotives bearing the same name on the same day.

We climbed steeply out of Strabane in order to cross the Strabane Canal which in its heyday had also been a thorn-in-the-flesh to the railways' business. We were the only passengers. We were ahead of time at Donemana; I noted that the station had been stripped of all inessentials; there had once been a loop with platforms each side but in the interests of economy the site had become a mere Halt. With what high hopes had the promoters intended their system could compete with the GNR line on the opposite side of the river and the adjacent

Strabane station. A Londonderry train awaits departure. Locomotive No. 2 BLANCHE.

Author's Collection

A Londonderry train at Donemana hauled by locomotive No. 8 FOYLE. March 1951   *Author*

road into town! Further, in those days politics played no part and the competitors for business did not have to exist in separate countries. The more I thought about it, the more I felt the CDRJC had been on the losing side right from the start albeit the conception of a through railway link from west Donegal to the city and port of Derry must have seemed sound commonsense to the late Victorians. (How laughable that by the time these reminiscences are being written, railways of any kind in this part of Ireland have ceased to exist.)

Dorothy commented favourably on the carriage in which we rode. I had forewarned her that we would use the very basic vehicles of the Lough Swilly line before the day was out and the smart interior and exterior of the short Donegal Railway train was a bonus. The outside was painted with cream upper panels and red below with black line between. The company crest was applied and the carriage number in gold leaf. Inside the compartment was fully upholstered in brown fabric and above the luggage rack the walls and ceiling were finished in light green. As for our engine, it had been No. 8 RAPHOE until 1937. It was painted in geranium red and had a fruitily - sounding whistle similar to that heard in the Isle of Man.

We liked what we saw of the Donegal train. There were in all six intermediate stations between Strabane and Derry but apart from Donemana we ignored them. They appeared to have fallen into disuse. We came close to the river again before entering the terminus, a broad and lengthy island platform, Victoria Road.

Considering what little traffic it saw, it was adorned with a very adequate overall roof, all on an ambitious scale as if on Bank Holidays the place would be filled with happy excusionists. The guard was busy unloading his van onto the platform but there was no glimpse of any station staff so we wandered off the premises through a neat little building of design so favoured in the catalogue of makers of childrens' toy building bricks, 'This small station building is typical

Londonderry (Victoria Road) station. March 1951.   *Author*

Victoria Road showing 5 ft 3 in. gauge exchange platform. June 1948.   *R.E. Tustin*

Londonderry (Victoria Road) station buildings not in railway occupation. June 1962.   *Author*

of what can be built using our No. 1 Set'. The arched entrance door was embellished with 'O'Neill & McHenry Ltd' but looking through the windows it was clear that the place was no longer occupied by the Railway but had been let to absent tenants. It was all very sad. Steps led to the street while a track on the river side of station continued onto the lower deck of the Craigavon Bridge (built 1933 to replace the Carlisle Bridge) so we found our way onto the lower deck as well while road traffic roared above us on the upper. Here a mixed gauge turntable stood, connecting the narrow gauge station we had just left to the south, with a 5 ft 3 in. gauge connection to the north and the Waterside terminus of the former NCC line to Belfast. The turntable did not exhibit any signs of recent use and it was hard to think that the installation had done more than offer access in emergency. The view west across the gloomy underside of the bridge and over the river was hardly more encouraging. A single mixed gauge line traversed it to another turntable and all railway lines were inset in stout timbers. It was the mixed gauge track which commanded attention; the way the rails were taken from side to side and the unusual dual-gauge pointwork was worthy of note. But we had much to do and see that day, so we let the camera record it all and hurried on. At no location here was any rolling stock seen.

Londonderry (or Derry Columbkille historically) is a city of great interest, being a port, naval base and garrison town. To appreciate these historic links, the visitor is not recommended to take the route along the quays on the west bank of the Foyle, as we were doing. But for us, this course had its own rewards. The first of these was to dispel our notion that wagons over the lower deck of the bridge were moved by the Port's steam locomotive, for along the edges of the bridge was a generous row of bollards which were not positioned to moor boats but to allow wagons to be ropeshunted. Added to the skill of placing each wagon on the turntables at each end of the bridge plus the several shunts necessary both on and off the structure, movement must have been time consuming. No doubt the men involved had become adept as I had witnessed in the below-ground railway warehouses in Manchester. But we were too late to see anything of the sort here in Derry. Along the bridge at least, the practice had become discontinued.

At the westerly end we were alongside the Foyle Road terminus of the GNRI line from Belfast, the last stretch of which we had deserted at Strabane in favour of the narrow gauge. It too had a connection in 5 ft 3 in. gauge only with the bridge, but only by a reversal off the quay system. It all looked abandoned as did the adjoining track and nearby wharf.

Further west the river curved west then north again and, although there was no activity, this section was obviously in use with double or triple tracks and railway wagons hard beside warehouses. There were occasional crossover connections in mixed gauge to link them, all laid in granite setts and using street tramway type rail sections. Round the next bend, beside a large water tank we found the Harbour's tank locomotive, standing unaccompanied. The morning shift had ended. There was a rake of broad gauge covered vans waiting for the next move, a patient horse with dray and some parked road lorries but little else. It must be the sacred lunch hour or perhaps the Angelus Bell we had just heard had called some faithful into church? The standing railway vans posed a question. They could only have been worked on or off the GNRI over that

Londonderry Port & Harbour Commissioners owned two locomotives of 5 ft 3 in. gauge which operated over the mixed gauge tracks on the Foyle River quays. Here is No. 1, an 0-6-0 saddle tank by R. Stephenson & Co. of 1891. Note the dual couplings. June 1948.   *R.E. Tustin*

No. 2, also an 0-6-0 saddle tank, was supplied by the Avonside Engine Co. in 1928. Seen here during the lunch break on the quay in March 1951, be-robed with towing cable, spare hooks *et al.*
                                                                                          Author

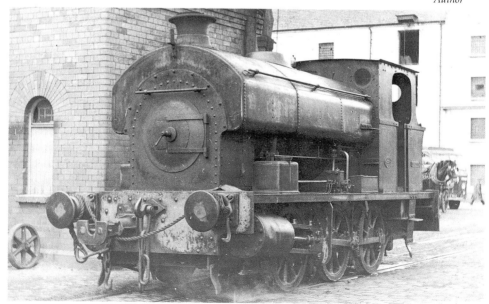

A typical view along the west quay with the Foyle dredger alongside. November 1961.
Author

appalling siding connection we had just noted so, despite our assumptions, the Harbour Commissioners must have had faith in their trackwork! We had also noticed that the train and engine standing in the station at that time was inconsiderately blocking the use of the connection until the train drew out; presumably quay shunting was timed to avoid these little imperfections which might extend the lunch hour a little?

The locomotive was No. 2 of the Londonderry Port & Harbour Commissioners R.H. SMITH, an 0-6-0 saddle tank of 1928 built by The Avonside Engine Co. of Bristol. It was clean and hung about with a collection of gear which allowed it to meet the miscellaneous demands it might incur: spare coupling chains, assorted hooks, a long wire to rope. The buffer-coupling for narrow gauge stock was offset but we were denied a sight of a train of mixed gauge wagons travelling over gauntletted track. Apparently it was not unknown for the engine to drag ships moored alongside the quay by means of an even longer wire rope which was stowed nearby for that purpose. (The same method was used at Neyland in South Wales by the Great Western Railway's shunting engine to drag stranded trawlers off into deep water. It was quite unofficial of course; the trawler's skipper tied a length of heavy aerial wire to the coupling hook and the engine made off along the siding. It could be quite successful and a basketfull of fish would change hands.)

It was a further mile before we approached the Londonderry & Lough Swilly Railway's Graving Dock station, comprising two platforms bounded by rough whitewashed walls and two tracks full of stored wagons. It was part-covered by a 'Belfast roof'.

The lower deck of the bridge with gauntletted tracks, capstans and turntables. November 1961.
Author

Derailments were not unknown. November 1961.
Author

It was not an inspiring goal to end our slog along the quay; I had forgotten what a dismal place it was as, it might have been mistaken for a ship in a port at which cattle were shipped daily. To think that this was the base from which all my railway dreams of 1939 had come made me realise how fortunate my Burtonport journey had begun in Letterkenny!

Opened when the railway was new in 1863, the situation was to remain the same until closure in 1953 (after our visit). True, it had been rebuilt from a wooden erection in 1883 as a goods depot when the Swilly trains ran through to a terminus on the Middle Quay on the Harbour lines, a quarter of a mile distant. There were recurring arguments between the Harbour Commissioners and the railway company which frustrated plans to build a more acceptable station here so this poor relation continued to serve. At the company's office we were shown the several designs which still existed for this idea by Mr McDivott, assistant to Mr Whyte, who seemed overwhelmed by our interest to the extent we were worried about missing the goods train to Buncrana. We were re-assured when told the train crew had had instructions not to leave Pennyburn until we were aboard and were given all-day Paper Tickets as authority.

Just beyond the station we came to Pennyburn engine sheds and had enough time to make quick note of its contents.* The shed itself was timber roofed with corrugated iron sheeting supported by the ubiquitous 'Belfast roofing'. It was well past its 'sell-by' date. If memory was reliable, one or two inhabitants which I had seen there in 1939 had gone, probably in the drive for scrap during the

*	2	4-6-0T	Andrew Barclay	1902	30 Tons
	4	4-6-0T	Andrew Barclay	1902	30 Tons
	5	4-8-4T	Hudswell, Clarke	1912	51 Tons
	6	4-8-4T	Hudswell, Clarke	1912	51 Tons
	15	4-6-2T	Hudswell, Clarke	1899	41 Tons
	16	4-6-2T	Hudswell, Clarke	1899	41 Tons

The above were inside Pennyburn shed, complete but out of steam. No. 16 dismantled for spare parts at rear of shed.

Two engines operative - in traffic:

3	4-6-0T	Andrew Barclay	1902	30 Tons
10	4-6-2T	Kerr, Stuart	1904	35 Tons

One locomotive is outside Letterkenny shed, unused for last two years:

12	4-8-0	Hudswell, Clarke	1905	37 Tons

Used on lifting trains on Burtonport Extension, and laid off when that work was completed. The livery was basically green but this varied according to how much oil had been applied to the cleaning rags! A logo 'LSR' appeared in the side tanks in yellow; lining was also in yellow. In the gloom of the shed it was impossible to be sure all engines bore the same colours - probably not, but the working engines bore a standard finish. The cleanliness of the latter was outstanding and raises several questions. Was their mechanical condition equal to their appearance? Was it in relation to a One Engine to One Crew policy? On reflection it was, but the whole subject is a much broader one since men have nursed and cleaned their machines since earliest times. It is a subject which might be explored more deeply!

West end of Craigavon Bridge. GNRI Foyle Road station upper right. November 1961. *Author*

Craigavon Bridge with the Commissioners' tug. November 1962. *Author*

First encounter with a narrow gauge 4-6-2T. Tooban! August 1939. *Author*

Burtonport train locomotive No. 2. A plucky little machine. Letterkenny, August 1939. *Author*

No. 15, exceptionally clean at Tooban Junction. March 1953. *Author*

No. 3 at Tooban Junction. March 1951. *Author*

Mackenzie & Holland signals. Bridge End. March 1951. *Author*

Trackwork at Tooban Junction. March 1951.

war. Our Buncrana train was waiting just along the yard with its guard coming out to greet and assist us up into a guard's composite coach: the L&LSR no longer possessed any goods brake vans!

Obviously our guard kept this vehicle for his personal use, which was just as well as it had enjoyed some protection from vandals and most of the windows were unbroken. Our compartment put me in mind of the spartan ride I had taken in 1939 in a similar conveyance, bare boarded, without luggage racks and seats of lath strip without any covering, to the *Ultima Thule* of my railway dreams, Burtonport. I recalled the lack of window leather straps and the windows which constantly fell open and when pulled up shut, admitted a fierce draught. I was glad that in the present March weather, we were both wearing coats for with a quick glance under the seats it was clear that heating had never been fitted.

Departure time from Pennyburn was due at 1.22 pm but we took no note of it. Our train comprised No. 10, a single coach, two vans and our composite. There came a short run to Bridge End where we had a prolonged stop for Customs Examination, halted amongst a veritable sea of covered vans. To break the monotony we banged our feet on the floor for warmth and explored our sandwich bag; from time to time we were pushed clear of the station while extra vans were coupled up. After our very early start, the day was already becoming a long one.

Off again, we reached a fork in the railway and took the north-westerly side. This was Tooban Junction, a marshy desolate spot with only a signal cabin and a bare island platform. Stacked all around were rails and sleepers recovered from the Burtonport line. There was nothing to detain us here and, having picked up the single line staff from the signalman without stopping, we continued in the thick of a brief blizzard. More banging of feet.

The train soon entered a narrow strip of flat terrain which took the railway along the eastern foreshore of Lough Swilly. To our surprise it stopped at a small station, Inch Road, and from the building came two men carrying a coffin which they loaded into the van without much ceremony or care; presumably it was empty. The men and the guard had a long conversation which we did not understand but were later told it was in Irish Gaelic; they had come by boat from a remote location along the Lough.

After a short run we came through Fahan, almost on the water's edge, and travelled alongside a grass-covered branch leading to the woebegone remains of Fahan pier where once steamers served Rathmullen and lesser landfalls on Lough Swilly. I wished I could recall the interesting railway and steamer links which dated back to 1866, before the advent of the 3 ft gauge railway. Of more immediate note was the home of our engine No. 10 which was taken to its shed on the pier branch each evening for stabling (and at weekends for cleaning) by the fireman who lived adjacently and could monitor the fire overnight!

It was only a few minutes' journey along the Lough shore until we came to Buncrana, in earlier times the terminus of the original 5 ft 3 in. gauge line. We had had several conversations with local people, all of whom had brought up the same subject when told we were making for Buncrana, mainly recalling the hundreds of day trippers from Derry who descended on the town at week-ends

No. 10 (*left*), No. 3 (*right*) at Tooban Junction. March 1951. *Author*

Goods train from Letterkenny approaching Tooban with No. 8. Burtonport track materials lie on the left. March 1951. *Author*

and Bank Holidays, the Good Old Days, the enormously long, overcrowded trains, the mayhem … etc. Expecting something akin to a Donegal Blackpool, the reality was an anti-climax when we detrained in the middle of another snow shower. The station itself covered a considerable area of ground. Its west edge stood on the shoreline. A long deserted platform bounded each side of the tracks, most of which were occupied by further varieties of the ubiquitous covered vans which the company seemed to possess; perhaps it had no other place to store them? We were reminded that the ample area was a legacy of the time when the station had been the terminus of a 5 ft 3 in. gauge line, further evidence of which was a fine gothic-like stone building at the north end, unsurpassed on the Swilly Railway system. It would have been quite at home as a north-country Town Hall or Public Library.

On this same westerly side of the station was the present station building, an adequate stone affair more suited to railway use and of a style much featured elsewhere on the L&LSR. Also at the north end was a turntable and engine shed. The source of the Carndonagh Extension (abandoned in 1935) could be seen beyond; it must remain unexplored for another day.

Suddenly there came to ear the sound of a steam locomotive travelling fast. It was second time that day and we rushed out of the station to see a large Burrell steam road engine mounted on balloon tyres, rush quickly by! Twice in one day - this must be Ireland.

During this time No. 10 had taken water at the Derry end of the eastern platform and was now shunting vans between that platform and the train we had brought in. The platform itself was well occupied by a number of colourful wooden crates which seemed to contain textiles of unknown origin and made up much of the railway business here. The two platforms themselves, being of ample length and width, were used as a bus terminus for L&LSR roadbuses and goods vehicles. In summer these were driven with extra care as the company still ran extra passenger trains here at weekends even though the regular service had been abandoned; this would account for the existence of those derelict-looking carriages we had noted at Pennyburn!

No. 10 whistled by pre-arrangement announcing that our train was ready to return so we made hurried notes of the signalling. It was always my intent to make a rough track diagram with signalling of every station of interest and the Swilly line was proving to be most rewarding. Here at Buncrana the semaphores were by McKenzie & Holland of Worcester. There had once been signal cabins at both ends of the station, that which survived at the Derry end being of the usual L&LSR pattern, a wooden garden shed with penthouse roof covering the ground frame.

We left Buncrana in fine style with a long rake of vans trailing behind and stopped at Tooban Junction for us to alight. With little ceremony and a little clanging of block bells from the signal cabin, the train was on it way to Derry again, leaving us standing in the open whilst another sleet storm whistled past. Not for long! The signalman shouted for us to come up and inside. He said our Letterkenny train was running late having been delayed by the Bridge End customs.

Tooban Junction was an inhospitable place at this time of year. It was bleak and windswept and situated on a low dyke flanked by drainage ditches.

Buncrana looking north with locomotive No. 10 in the distance. March 1951.   *Author*

Buncrana in a bitterly cold wind. March 1951.   *Author*

Buncrana looking south. Locomotive No. 10. March 1951.   *Author*

Bridge End station. March 1951.   *Author*

4-6-2 No. 10 entering Bridge End with a Buncrana train. March 1951.   *Author*

Luckily the cabin itself was of standard Railway Signalling Co. pattern and would have been equally at home around Liverpool. It was cosy inside from the March wind. I could see the layout was signalled for bi-directional running and the semaphores were of McKenzie & Holland and RSCo. origin. Extra sidings had been added, alongside which Burtonport track had been stacked. This had arrived by the trainload over several years. There was no sign of habitation and only a bridle path link with Inch Island. After what was becoming near the end of a long day, we were not exhilarated by the signalman's reminiscences of long holdups at the Customs. At last the bell rang and was answered. We recogised the block code; our train had eventually left Bridge End at 5.45 pm instead of 3.50 pm. The signalman said this was the worst instance in six months.

Engine No. 3 brought in several petrol tank wagons and a composite coach and the guard remarked that though they were exceptionally late, there was no intermediate shunting to do and we should have a good run home (No. 3 was based at Letterkenny). The guard was pleased to have our company; he was full of stories of Buncrana specials and mishaps, of how the big 4-6-4 tanks on those trains were heavy on coal and suffered broken springs etc. But we were tired, hungry and cold and were poor listeners and took little note of the journey. He told us where to find comfortable lodgings for the night and we were grateful.

We found the house without difficulty and than ran into further trouble. On asking for accommodation we were told they only had one double-bedded room. Saying that was just what we wanted they remarked we looked too young to be married and we seemed to be in danger of being put out in the street. We searched our pockets for evidence of our married state and when we produced photographs of the children they let us in! It was a narrow squeak.

Chapter Six

West Donegal, County Donegal Railways

The problems of reaching north-west Ireland from Manchester were twofold: Geographic and Financial. They always included a time-consuming overnight sea passage in each direction on what was well accepted as probably one of the roughest stretches of water round our coasts; our preferred choice was the old Midland Railway route from Heysham to Belfast. We became stoic as we lay on our steamer bunks to watch our clothes swinging wildly from the coathook in the small hours, consoling ourselves that it was all worth while. On the financial aspect, it was essential to make the most of our travel costs by cramming in as much as possible while we were on Irish soil, for the spectre of impending rail closures breathed hard down our necks. So the opportunity of combining a business trip to soften the cost - as this had done - was welcome.

Now we had reached Letterkenny by means of the GNRI, County Donegal and Lough Swilly, we looked forward to covering the remainder of the CDR and in due course return to Belfast for the night sailing to Heysham. Here there was an early morning through connection to Manchester allowing me to be at my desk only slightly late! The extra day we would need in Ireland to complete our assignment was taken in exchange for a shorter annual holiday from the Works. I would have to disguise my yawns on returning.

As we had completed all we could include of the Lough Swilly system, our next movements involved the CDR. Firstly a return to Strabane, a second train to Stranorlar, a third train (actually the morning goods train to Donegal town), a trip down the Ballyshannon branch and back and finally to Killybegs for the night. On the following day we would return to Stranorlar, see a little of the disused Glenties branch and so to Belfast for the boat.

We had an early walk on 1st April, 1951 to the Strabane & Letterkenny (S&LR) station, a venue I had had no time time to explore thoroughly on my first visit in August 1939. We parted from our overnight hosts as if we had been long awaited relatives in contrast with the difficulties of our arrival!

The S&LR station was alongside that of the older L&LSR one and was almost an exact copy of the County Donegal Railway building at Victoria Road, Derry except that here the date of opening had been been added to the frontage squitter, 1908. The track layout was basically simple with a covered island platform so littered with a plethora of boxes, bags, crates and other impedimenta there was little space for personnel. Beyond the platform was a turntable, engine shed, goods shed, signal box and sidings full of CDR vans. There was a single line connection with the L&LSR which had a trap point inserted worked from the L&LSR signal cabin. There was the now familiar signalling by the RSCo., quite distinct from that on the L&LSR line.

We hurried to obtain window seats in our 8.5 am train which consisted of Railcar No. 15 hauling a red-painted, four-wheeled covered van which was literally stuffed with luggage etc. At this period such Railcars worked all the passenger traffic between Letterkenny and Strabane; there were no steam-

The link line between L&LSR and CDJRC. Letterkenny. March 1951. *Author*

Letterkenny station, Co. Donegal Railways (1908). June 1962. *Author*

Class '5a' BLANCHE, built by Nasmyth, Wilson 1913, prepares to leave Letterkenny. May 1956.
Author

Climbing out of Letterkenny, seen from the footplate of No. 2 BLANCHE. May 1956.   *Author*

The daily goods train for Strabane.

Author's Collection

Seen at Raphoe, the daily goods train with the author on BLANCHE, awaits his pleasure. May 1956.

Author

hauled passenger trains, but the well-loaded goods trains were steam worked. (No. 15 was built in April 1936 by Walker Bros of Wigan.)

We headed out of the station with much clanking of side rods. The sun was rising from the east and it promised a cold clear day. There was a distinct difference about the passengers who were mainly going shopping in Strabane I thought. Occasionally we picked up passengers by the railside without the formality of a recognised stopping place. In this way the murmur of conversation in creased and fug of pipe smoke grew thicker.

There is a long climb out of Letterkenny, combined with curves and the railcar made noisy work of it. First comes the concrete bridge over the older L&LSR line, then a curvacious crawl up to about 350 ft. The engine was worked hard and I wondered whether we were overloaded; the noise was deafening but the driver seemed unconcerned and I came to accept that these units were flogged like this day and night. The sun over the snow-covered fields was harsh on the eyes. Shortly we reached Convoy near the summit of the climb, where the passing loop had been taken out. The surviving sidings held a number of covered vans, no doubt used in connection with the number of woollen mills in this large village, noted for its tweeds, serges and worsteds. The railcar's engine was now reduced to a tick-over and in the resultant quiet we could discern the babble of voices again and the driver leaned back in his seat and lit up a fag.

We resumed the journey and reached Raphoe, but not before making two midfield stops to drop down passengers. We considered how these took place after dark; perhaps the headlight on the front of the railcar was sufficient? Raphoe has lost some of its importance with decline of the flax industry but here is situated St Eunan's Cathedral. Here, too, the passing loop has been taken out but it was possible to use one in the yard. After we had finished station work the railcar set back into it to allow Railcar No. 19 (Walker Bros of 1950 and later sold to the Isle of Man Railway Co.) to use the surviving platform and then run past us *en route* to Letterkenny. There was a goodly number of CDR 6-wheel open wagons, all with flexible wheelbase here. Were they part of the original stock supplied to this railway?

We approached Strabane by means of a long curve - reminiscent of a model railway - which took us into the west side of the station's narrow gauge island platform. The years had not diminished my memory of the place; how much of the premises were devoted to Customs & Excise business, the number of green-painted basket-ware hampered trolleys used by the Irish Post Office, the careful arrangement of wire barriers to oblige passengers to pass through the long trestle tables set out by the Customs, and the way in which those who had just left our train melted from sight mainly towards the bar to leave the platform devoid of anyone save ourselves. Of our connection to Stranorlar there was no obvious clue but we were alerted to an engine whistle down the track and watched No. 14 ERNE (4-6-4T Nasmith Wilson of 1904) draw out of the station along the line we had just travelled on its way to Letterkenny with the 9.20 am goods. In the cold morning air it made a brave spectacle hauling such an impressive rake. This class of engine was justifiably kept for working this section and was shedded at Strabane.

The perpetual sound of a diesel engine came to notice as soon as the Letterkenny goods was out of earshot and we wandered to the other side of the

No. 9 4-6-4T ESKE at Strabane. March 1951.   *Author*

No. 10 4-6-4T ERNE leaving Strabane with a Stranorlar goods train. March 1951.   *Author*

Bridge over Finn River and outer home somersault signal, Strabane. March 1953.   *Author*

Home signals at entry to Strabane. May 1959.   *Author*

The west end of Stranorlar station. June 1948.   *R.E. Tustin*

Former headquarters of the Finn Valley Railway, Stranorlar.   *Author's Collection*

platform to see PHOENIX the rail tractor performing its seemingly endless shunting duties at the north-east end of the station. It had lost much of its lustre and the name had almost gone, suggesting that it hardly remained still for long enough to benefit from a wipe of a cleaner's rag. Certainly it buzzed up and down the yard like an irritated insect.

There were some interesting CDR 6-wheeled wagons standing by, having tubular-built frames and built by Oldbury of Birmingham c.1901. This variety of wagon seemed to be much in favour and when we enquired further about their popularity it seemed they had but one drawback, 'some batches have different dimensions and require care in coupling together'.

There was time to wander down to the south end of the station where I noticed there was a transhipment yard which had previously escaped me. Its heart was a dual gauge turntable, served at one end by the CDR 3 ft gauge and at the opposite side by the GNRI 5 ft 3 in. gauge. By this equipment it was possible to carry vehicles in pick-a-back fashion, though there was a height limit on GNRI stock. From what could be seen, the interchange of specially adapted containers was the principal function of this novel equipment, reinforcing my contention that the CDR was always in the forefront of its day - as it had shown itself to be with its railcar philosophy.

We bestirred ourselves for a knot of people was making for the Stranorlar working, consisting of Railcar No. 10, one of the smallest units with only 28 seats and already crammed with humanity.* The journey to Stranorlar would be along the site of the former 5 ft 3 in. gauge Finn Valley Railway (FVR) which followed the course eastwards of the river and seldom strayed from it. I hoped one day I could visit Cork see where the former FVR engines had gone when they were sold to the Cork Bandon & South Coast Railway!

Along this section the scenery was unremarkable and the ride uncomfortable. The motorised portion of the car seemed to have a mind of its own and Dorothy did not enjoy the motion. Fortunately we had a long wait at Castlefinn and took the opportunity to await the delayed arrival of oncoming railcar No. 12 (GNRI/Walker 1934) with a walk in the fresh air of the platform, and a visit to the little signal cabin.

Soon we were passing rows of stock beside us and there was a general bustle as we approached Stranorlar. We took our time as we knew we were expected and that our connecting train would be held.

Stranorlar marked a point in our travels where we had journeyed over the latest and oldest sections of the CDR by railcar, namely Strabane-Derry/Strabane-Letterkenny and Strabane-Stranorlar and it seems to be a convenient point in my narrative to set down some impressions of railcar travel, for had we not enjoyed certain privileges our whole experience of the CDR would have been solely by this means. Our presence among the passengers had been picked out by each guard as he checked the tickets and noted the unusual format, though never any comment was made. We noticed that the guard often made sign to his colleagues, hence the unspoken welcome to inspect the small signal cabin at Castlefinn; such courtesy was shown everywhere we went. Later

---

* Purchased from the assets of the Clogher Valley in 1942 on which it ran as No. 1. Built by Atkinson & Walker Bros of Wigan in 1932 and fitted with a Gardner diesel engine, it was the first articulated power-bogie railcar introduced in Ireland, becoming CDR No. 10 - the second railcar to carry the number on that system. Ultimately being used on CDR demolition work, it is now housed in the Belfast Transport Museum.

The station, Stranorlar. March 1951.

Author

Old and newer buildings combine at Stranorlar.

Author's Collection

West end of Stranorlar: Donegal line left, Glenties line right. March 1953. *Author*

Finn River bridge, Stranorlar. *Author's Collection*

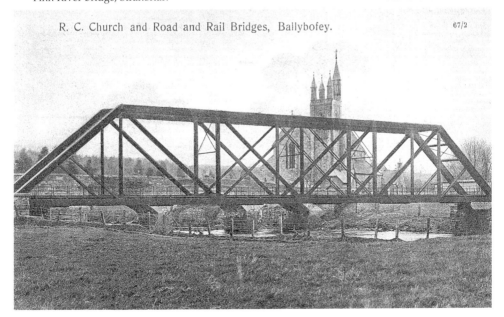

R. C. Church and Road and Rail Bridges, Ballybofey. 67/2

Stranorlar looking east, workshops far right. March 1951.   *Author*

Stranorlar looking west. May 1959.   *Author*

Railcars meet at Castlefinn. The signalling allows two-way running. March 1951.   *Author*

Finn River bridge, Stranorlar. May 1956.   *Author*

Right: Footbridge starting signal for the Donegal line, Stranorlar. May 1956. This signal is now in the Narrow Gauge Railway Museum, Tywyn. *Author*

Below: The daily goods train ready to leave for Donegal. Stranorlar, May 1956. *Author*

we learned that we were travelling as 'friends of Mr Curran' (Bernard L.Curran, the Manager, formerly with the Northern Counties Railways in Belfast). [We were also to learn that over half a century of Irish visits which followed, this natural courtesy and goodwill is not confined to the CDR but is met with all over Ireland.] Even before we had left Strabane for Stranorlar, the driver had come up to me and asked if I would like to travel with him in the cab?

Dorothy was ready to accept such invitations and drivers seemed quite happy to have her bouncing quite unconcerned while trying to keep steady on top of the bonnet! Because of the noise level, conversation was impossible anyway. Even I could not compete with the roar of the Gardner diesel engine and the staccato clank of siderods. The older railcars were the worst, No. 10 especially, where the whole engine was 'naked'. The driver occupied the only seat. He would be confronted by a pillar rising up through the floor in front of him on top of which were only the rudimentary controls. The gearchange lever was adjacent alongside large foot pedals. Gear changing up was done with a screaming engine and the maximum vibration. Dorothy seemed exhilarated by these experiences, which she said were far better than 'standing in front of the sink at home'.

The early railcars were conversions from road buses but these were all taken out of service long before our time. The connection between the driving portion and the bus body behind was extremely flexible as was apparent when looking from one section to another *en route*. The smell of diesel fumes pervaded everywhere. The later railcars were greatly improved in ride and ventilation. As a schoolboy we were encouraged to spend some of our holidays on civic work, and my chosen task was to assist disabled coal miners in Wigan to cultivate vegetables on their allotments near the West Coast main line at Boar's Head - a wonderful location! We were given the opportunity to look round the Pagefield works of Walker Bros who were at that period building railcars for the CDR. It was a happy coincidence and a topic of mutual interest.

So back to Stranorlar as we prepared to meet Mr Curran …

It was clear that there was far too much to absorb here than this fleeting interchange of trains would allow (in fact, this as not achieved until some years later!) and we were assured that he would conduct us round the Railway Works on our return from Killybegs - and before we were to travel by road bus to the Glenties Branch as far as Finntown - the following day. There was just time to notice that the station boasted an imposing building, a legacy of the former Finn Valley owners and that the tracks divided at the west end, the south line heading for Donegal and the north for Glenties, the latter commencing with an impressive steel viaduct over the Finn River.

The courtesies on the platform were brief. Our goods train for Donegal was due out at 11.15 am and it was already 11.40 am and a long train headed by No. 8 FOYLE which was blowing off steam impatiently. Dorothy was to travel in the train and I on the footplate. I had a quick look down the length of the formidable train against the curving platform and was assured to see she would travel in another of the bogie passenger guard's composite vans which would be upholstered and clean though without heat! I climbed onto No. 8 and was given a warm welcome by the driver, an elderly man who was well wrapped

Donegal line in the Barnesmore Gap.

Lawrence

A goods train for Donegal halts at Lough Eske for a railcar to pass. Meanwhile the fireman cleans the smokebox! May 1956.

Author

up against the cold. Mr Curran introduced us and I learned that I should be in the good hands of the undertaking's senior driver whose son was one of Dublin's most respected surgeons. Curran seemed to know the family history of all his men and anxious to demonstrate their loyalty to the company.

No. 8 was a right-hand-drive engine and the guard having waved us off, we made a melodious whistle and set off gently with Dorothy giving me an acknowledgment from the window. I hoped her feet were warm. All CDR stock was fitted with the vacuum brake and we crossed the four girder-span viaduct over the Finn as the driver eased open the regulator and screwed forward the reverser slightly as we began the 5½ mile climb to the shore of Lough Mourne. Described as one of the wildest stretches of any Irish railway, the gradient is 1 in 58-60 throughout and surrounding country bleak in the extreme. Now and again an icy wind blew straight through the cab but the brilliant sunshine made recompense.

The engine plodded up the hill under an impressive black cloud from the chimney as the fireman put on two rounds of coal about every three minutes. Now and again the men looked back to see if the train was following in proper fashion! We were now almost 600 ft above sea level and the summit of the climb could be seen through the cab spectacles. On the left Lough Mourne came up alongside, its surface sparkling in the brilliant sun and the water whipped into white horses by the wind. Ahead the snow-capped peaks of the Blue Stacks fulfilled the memorable moment. We topped the hill. The driver closed the regulator, screwed back the reverser and made a partial brake application to control our descent into Donegal through the Barnesmore Gap.

There was a passing loop and platform for Lough Eske on our way down, but in this remote location it was usually retained for allowing railcars to pass these lengthy goods trains. Once in the confines of the Gap itself the headwind hit us hard; I heard that it had been sufficiently strong enough to stop a train and precautions were taken to divide trains at Lough Eske in these circumstances!

Along this length there was a section of track which had been relaid using ex-Dublin & Blessington Steam Tramway sleepers. During the long descent the driver asked me to keep an eye on the train following as wagons were known to jump the track. I noted there were a number of hot brake blocks and an occasional smoking axle box but these were apparently commonplace! The running of the engine was very steady and smooth, and in quite distinct contrast to our run on the Cavan & Leitrim section in 1949. Here and there the driver dropped sand on the rails to improve adhesion. The gradient eased and we passed an impressive bracket signal and the Ballyshannon branch coming in from the left. I glanced casually at the pressure gauge - it read 175 lb. and did not seem to have moved since we left Stranorlar!

And so we ran into Donegal station, an important junction and point of interchange. Here we would leave the steam-worked goods train to continue its journey to Killybegs while we took another railcar for the ride down the 47 miles to Ballyshannon, southwards and on Donegal Bay. I left the warm footplate of FOYLE with regret to meet Dorothy who said she had enjoyed the scenery but that her feet were numb with cold. Donegal was an interesting station. There were up and down platforms with a bay and no less than three

Above: Bracket signals at the east end of Donegal station. Ballyshannon branch *left*, Stranorlar line *centre*. March 1951.
Author

Right: Goods train from Stranorlar at Donegal Town. May 1956.
Author

Donegal Town station looking towards Stranorlar. March 1951. *Author*

Walker-built railcar No. 20 entering Donegal Town station from Killybegs. (This railcar was later purchased by the Isle of Man Railway.) March 1951. *Author*

Signal cabin interior, Donegal Town. May 1956.   *Author*

turntables (one made from the chassis of a 4-6-0 tank engine), a two-road loco shed and a long siding with turntable for handling transhipment wagons. The signalling was again lavish, McKenzie & Holland, Saxby & Farmer were the suppliers; somersault semaphores were noted. The two large junction bracket signals at the east end were especially imposing and suggested that there were ample funds available for this extravagance! The signal box here was well-endowed with equipment plus rows of potted house plants.

Railcar No. 16 (GNR/Walker 1936) stood in the platform and we managed to find two seats, just. Railcar No. 20 (GNR/Walker 1951; now Isle of Man Railway) stood alongside, also very full and then set off for Strabane. The station had been bustling with activity. The guard said everything was running late due to delays at the Customs. Which Customs? I had forgotten that Ballyshannon was also a border town. We were due out at 1.40 pm and were obviously quite late but there was no anxious scanning of wrist watches by the passengers as there would be back at home. We sensed the unimportance to life's pattern of the prompt running of the train ... and remarked on it ...

The Ballyshannon Extension - as it was formally dubbed - had been a latter-day addition to the CDR and ended up on the steep north side of the town above the River Erne. Notable here are two hydro-electric power stations. If the loading of the railcar was an indication, the line was well patronised. At any other time of year it was popular for the wonderful views of Donegal Bay and the magnificent three mile strand at Rossnowlagh. There was also a Franciscan Abbey in building here which brought considerable pilgrimage traffic. The route of the Extension brought the line within sight of the Atlantic Ocean and huge seas breaking on the shore. In the distance we discerned the fine cliffs which border Sligo Bay; the mirage-effect of the sea caused us to read the map with care! We were astonished to learn that a recent August excursion had comprised 11 coaches and two steam engines. Rossnowlagh station was but a long single platform with a turntable outside. There was no run-round and steam engines were attached to each end of the train. In his book, the *Narrow Gauge Railways of Ireland*, Fayle rather plays down the Ballyshannon run. We enjoyed it.

Within minutes of arriving at Ballyshannon the passengers had surged off the train and disappeared from sight; we found ourselves alone on the station, no staff, no ticket collection ... the railcar trundled off and backed down onto the turntable to be turned by driver and guard. It then returned past the long curved platform and halted outside the signal box inside a deep cutting. Leaving the engine running the crew left it for a siesta in the box where a stove was burning. Outside the box there was another of the three-arm bracket Railway Signal Co. signals identical with the two at Donegal. Additionally there was the foundation of a carriage shed, a small goods yard and shed, a loco water tank, railcar shed and cattle dock but no rolling stock of any nature. It seemed probable that goods traffic had ceased and that passenger-loco hauled trains were a thing of the past. Though far from being derelict, the atmosphere was one of extreme economy.

At the station there was an unoccupied house, its vacant rooms perhaps proof that there was no resident staff? Or was the incumbent snug in the signal box

Rossnowlagh had platforms of exceptional length for excursions.   *Author's Collection*

Ballyshannon terminus from the buffer stops. March 1951.   *Author*

Right: Ballyshannon station. The railcar which has arrived from Donegal Town, sets back to the vicinity of the signal box where the crew can enjoy a cup of tea in the warmth. The bracket signal seems an expensive luxury! March 1951.   *Author*

Stranorlar-Killybegs daily goods train taking water at Inver. March 1951.   *Author*

Mountcharles station looking west. May 1959.   *Author*

along with the train crew? Dorothy decided to explore the 'Ladies' and returned to recommend me to a tour of same as the enamel notices on the cubicles were of curious pattern. They read 'PRESS COIN INTO SLOT & DEPRESS THUMB BIT'. Luckily a door was open and she was spared the risk of operating what seemed to be a lethal contraption which years later was to draw blood from a finger of a male colleague of our party who had mistakenly taken the premises for the 'Gents'. (He received little sympathy except the offer of an appointment to have his sight tested.) The view southwards over the town below and over the river from outside the station was an attractive one. Soon the railcar was back in the platform to form the 4 pm working to Killybegs via Donegal. There was plenty of room to find a window seat each and enjoy the westward views out to sea, but the drone of the engine and warmth of the railcar overtook us and we missed some of them in sleep.

A goodly throng met us at Donegal. Presumably Donegal was the place / town where everyone shopped and gossipped, or we did we interpret all we saw through the eyes of English town-dwellers? Whatever, the buzz of humanity cleared away any inclination for further sleep.

The remainder of our day was to be travelling over the last section of the CDR open to us, the coastal route westwards to Killybegs, a wooded and seaskirt course across the north side of Donegal Bay with some steep gradients of 1 in 40 along its switchback profile. To the north-east the Blue Stack Mountains dominate. The Donegal-Killybegs section was opened in 1893, the latter being a village with great potential as a fishing port, and greatly expanded since that date. The initial steep section occurs just after leaving Donegal and is due to the railway having to cross the first of many drumlins which are a feature of the area and gave problems to the railway builders. Whichever aspect we took across Donegal Bay there were wonderful vistas but the environs of the line itself did not match up to them; the countryside has something of the bleak feel of those parts of western Ireland which bear evidence of The Great Famine years in the late 1840s. Perhaps I do it an injustice. We were tired and hungry. We were learning to live each mid-day on a diet of thermos flask coffee and Irish chocolate. The coffee had passed its best but the chocolate was better than any one could buy in England.

I am afraid we took little note of the journey. At Inver the loop had been taken out and if it was necessary to pass a train, reversal into the goods yard was resorted to. Dunkineel and Bruckless followed, both obviously full stations in earlier days but now merely Halts in our Working Timetable; the railcar stood in the platform at each place and we confirmed how useful were the railcar steps at such locations. We remarked on signal posts with the arms removed. As we passed a small harbour just below the railway I was reminded how much depopulation had impoverished this coast and why Halts serve what were once communities which could support a station.

We reached the head of a landlocked bay which broadened as we neared its head. The railway was carried here along a causeway close to the water's edge. Wrapped in a pall of black smoke we glimpsed the engine shed as we passed. Evidently FOYLE was inside, put away for the night. It was getting dusk as we ran into Killybegs and we saved further exploration until the following day.

THE COUNTY DONEGAL RAILWAYS
JOINT COMMITTEE.

PUBLIC NOTICE.

On the Night of **Wednesday, 17th November, 1920,**

AT INVER STATION,

a Guard of this Railway was dragged from his Van by cowardly masked and armed ruffians: he was handcuffed, was placed against a wall, revolvers were presented at him, and his life was threatened if he continued to carry on the duties for which he is paid.

In consequence of this outrage on an inoffensive Railwayman, the train service on the Killybegs Line will be restricted at an early date, and if further interference with the Railway Staff takes place—in the absence of Military protection — the line between Donegal and Killybegs will be

CLOSED.

HENRY FORBES, Traffic Manager.

STRANORLAR.

Killybegs with sidings to the fish pier and harbour going off right. March 1951. *Author*

Arrival of daily goods train, 'Running if required' with locomotive ERNE, at Killybegs. March 1951. *Author*

Killybegs. Harbour *left*, station *right*. May 1959.   *Author*

Killybegs station interior. Railcars Nos. 18 and 16. May 1959.   *Author*

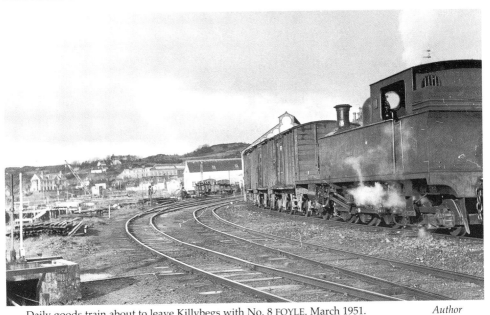

Daily goods train about to leave Killybegs with No. 8 FOYLE. March 1951. *Author*

Railcar leaving Killybegs above the seawall where I had the incident with the fish! May 1959.
Author

Exit from Killybegs with engine shed in the distance perched on the seawall. March 1951.
Author

Early morning in Killybeg, we await the appearance of the engine which is still inside the shed while Geoffrey ponders over the ground frame interlocking. May 1959.   *Author*

Enquiry had told us that there was a small hotel nearby. We could have slept on a bed of nails but were innocent enough to be thankful for a big room overlooking the main street. At that juncture, we were ignorant of the impending Dance and the Petrol Pump!

We decided to have an early night but noticed a poster in the hotel lobby announcing there was to be a dance in the town that same evening starting at 9.30 pm. Ignorant of such functions, we were in the land of nod until woken up by the sound of laughter and commotion in the street below. We checked the time. 4 am. For the next hour we were treated to the sound of cars which refused to start and were being push-started by their inebriated occupants. Worse, directly below our window was a petrol pump which apparently gave free access to anyone. Certain of the cars which refused to start were pushed to the pump and refilled; the pump motor protested with an unceasing scream. In desperation I tried the window but it was stuck, so we hid under the bedclothes; we had to rise early to explore the station and catch the 8.18 am steam-worked goods train to Stranorlar. We resolved never to stay in a town where a Dance was billed … at a later date we added a Circus, but that is another story!

The station had an all-over roof and protecting wall from the sea. There was a single platform. Beyond the platform was a turntable built on the frame of one of the scrapped 4-6-0Ts, only suitable for railcars. One long siding curved off onto a substantial stone jetty and other sidings towards a modern fish factory. There was a small ground frame by Saxby & Farmer on the sea wall. A long train of vans headed by FOYLE (bunker first) was in the platform and our friend the driver assured us that they would not start without us if we wanted to walk up to the engine shed. It had held FOYLE overnight but was now empty. The building was wooden and narrow. Outside a flight of stone steps led to the water. On the bottom step we were fascinated by a very large crab which seemed to be stranded there and waiting for the tide. Whilst we were commenting on its size and colour, we were shocked to see an enormous fish leap from the sea, grab the crab and pull it under. We returned to the station and took our seats in that same composite van in which Dorothy had travelled the day previously. The guard assured her her feet might be warmer as the weather was more mild. I looked favourably on the carpeted floor with its CDR motif. Our visit to Killybegs might have been brief but it had left us with some things to remember which were far from a railway nature!

FOYLE kept up a steady pace on our return to Donegal. The intermission of the drumlins did not appear to affect the speed and the guard confirmed the rake of vans was the maximum number permitted on the branch. When asked about the acetylene gas lighting in the van (and all other passenger stock) he explained that every coach in service had a cylinder fitted at one end which was supplied by plant installed at Stranorlar. 'You should be asking to see it', he added with a touch of pride. I remarked on the smart pace of train and that he never seemed to apply the brake with the vacuum handle in the van. 'Not necessary Sir, and I only use the handbrake when the engine leaves the train.' At Donegal we made an extended stop for water and mugs of tea were brought for the trainmen - including ourselves - a discussion ensued concerning the likelihood of certain winners and, that deliberated, we pulled out to tackle the heavy climb ahead.

Killybegs station and harbour.   *Valentine*

Killybegs station from the fish pier. May 1959.   *Author*

There is something utterly relaxing about retracing a railway journey one has done before and does not feel obliged to make notes and absorb everything which passes the window. Then there are sections of the route which are so interesting that one lowers the window to see more of the lie of the railway before and behind, with the added risk of collecting some persistent smuts in the eye as the locomotive belches out fire and soot along the roofs of the train ... I know to my cost, having spent some in the surgery while the nurse tried to remove some obstinate matter thrown out by a labouring engine on the Somerset & Dorset Railway ... So it was for most of the way back through the Pass and the Donegal Highlands; we could sit back and enjoy a peerless Spring day as the anticyclone persisted. Not only did we have the train to ourselves, but the countryside too was bereft of humanity. It was a moving scene especially for our enjoyment.

Our reverie came an end when we crossed the Finn River viaduct and came immediately into the long curving main platform at Stranorlar. The guard bid us goodbye and screwed down the van handbrake as the engine was detaching a number of vans from the front of the train here, and would then go down the yard to collect others for coupling up; the whole assembly would then leave for Strabane. Mr Curran was on the platform to greet us. He had a rolled object under his arm which he presented to Dorothy, saying he hoped she had enjoyed the ride and would accept the momento. (It was a copy of the CDR crest which now hangs on our dining wall.) He was obviously delighted we had come - and so were we!

Stranorlar station and surrounds looked quite splendid that morning. Every stone building was painted white. One might imagine Manchester Victoria in this guise! After coffee in the station buffet we were escorted to the workshops and carriage sheds and must have been introduced to almost everyone working therein. This was the 'family tradition' which I thought had disappeared after World War I. So many working in the Shops had relatives elsewhere on the system. Everyone knew the whereabouts of everyone else at a particular day and time; Curran was the Captain of a Crew.

After visiting the big diesel engine which drives the workshop machinery we came to the stores where certain historic vehicles were kept for ultimate display in a projected museum. {These are listed separately at the end of this chapter.] Mr Curran then took his leave and left us to look round the yards, reminding us that we were invited to travel on the Glenties bus at noon as far as Finntown and back.

Among some 'foreign' coaches which were doing service on the CDR there was a bogie carriage off the Ballymena, Cushendall & Red Bay Railway and a train of corridor stock from Ballymena & Larne 'Boat Train' which been given considerable surgery to make the couplings compatible with the CDR. All this additional stock would be pressed into service on Rossnowlagh Excursions, Orangemen's Day, Pilgrimages etc. From an operating viewpoint, the Boat Train carriages were the least popular as they could not conveniently be divided from the set.

The Glenties branch diverged from the Stranorlar-Donegal line where it formed a passing loop between the platforms - in fact the Glenties train had to

THE COUNTY DONEGAL RAILWAYS
JOINT COMMITTEE.

PUBLIC NOTICE.

On SATURDAY, 26th FEBRUARY, 1921,

a number of large boulders were placed on the Railway near Ballinamore
Station on the

STRANORLAR & GLENTIES LINE

to obstruct the passage of Trains, and on the same day, and at a point between
Fintown and Glenties, a rail was removed, the track was torn up, and so
diverted as to result in a Train being thrown off the Line and precipitated
down the embankment into the lake alongside. From information received it
is clear this was the work of miscreants living in the immediate vicinity.

The action of the cowardly criminals who perpetrated the above might
have caused a calamitous accident, and involved the death of the Railwaymen
concerned with the working of the Train, as well as the Passengers, and this is
to give Notice that if there is any further interference with the Railway the

STRANORLAR AND GLENTIES LINE
WILL BE
CLOSED

For ALL TRAFFIC without further Notice.

Any information that will lead to the identification of the guilty parties will
be thankfully received by the undersigned.

HENRY FORBES, Traffic Manager.

STRANORLAR.

stand in what was the main platform of the old Finn Valley Railway terminus opposite the station building as the points for the branch were positioned so as to deny the use of the southernmost platform at all unless a departing train first reversed to clear the points. Such was the state of affairs due to the Glenties branch being the last on the scene and necessitating a sharp curve to carry it over the river as soon as the platform was left.

As Mr Curran left us he pressed two tickets into my hand and told us to leave and return to the bus at any point on the road we preferred. The single-decked CDR vehicle stood in the station yard and the guard showed us seats which he recommended for the best views! I was glad we had taken note of the Glenties branch situation in the station because we could see little of its immediate environs as it left the town. There was one feature however, which could not be ignored, a large steel single-span girder brige carrying the track over the Finn River. We were informed that this structure had been built for a Norwegian railway; it looked quite out of place on the CDR. We intended to see what the road revealed of the railway but, according to the map, some miles beyond Stranorlar the two parted company and did not meet again until our destination, Finntown station.

Such proved to be correct, but it was all worthwhile for the beauty all around. Initially, the railway, river and road were so close as to reveal everything. Each climbed westwards towards the summit near Finntown, almost 2,000 ft above sea level, the mountains on either hand becoming more interesting all the while. The railway, though disused, was quite intact and according to Mr Curran the only reason the service had been withdrawn was the state of the rails themselves which had become thin in the web and could only support railcars. How this could be defied me. It could not be due to wear and tear, but might be due to the prolonged wet atmosphere? As confirmed previously, the CDR preferred to run railcars rather than buses as there was a fuel tax on road vehicles.

Finntown station looking towards Glenties. A remote location.   *Lawrence*

Finntown station, closed but still intact. March 1951. *Author*

Finntown station (currently the centre of a preservation attempt). March 1951. *Author*

County Donegal Railways Joint Committee.

WITHDRAWAL OF RAILWAY SERVICES

Notice is hereby given that the Committee's Rail Services between Strabane and Killybegs, Strabane and Letterkenny, and Donegal and Ballyshannon, will cease to operate after **Thursday, 31st December 1959.**

On and from Friday, 1st January, 1960, Passenger and Freight Services will be provided by road transport as follows :—

(1) PASSENGERS :—

OMNIBUS SERVICES :

Omnibus Services, in lieu of the existing Rail Services, will be provided on the undermentioned r o u t e s, details of which are available at any of the Stations :—

STRABANE-STRANORLAR-DONEGAL-KILLYBEGS;

STRABANE-RAPHOE-CONVOY-LETTERKENNY;

DONEGAL-BALLINTRA-BALLYSHANNON;

BALLYSHANNON-ROSSNOWLAGH.

FARES:—All Rail Fares, including Season Ticket Rates, will be cancelled.

UNEXPIRED RAILWAY TICKETS:

PASSENGERS HOLDING UNEXPIRED RAILWAY SEASON TICKETS SHOULD SURRENDER SUCH TICKETS FOR REFUND. ORDINARY RETURN TICKETS WILL BE ACCEPTED FOR TRAVEL BY OMNIBUS UP TO 31 JANUARY, 1960.

(2) PARCELS BY PASSENGER SERVICES:

PARCELS OR ARTICLES (MAXIMUM 84-LBS.) WHICH CAN BE CONVENIENTLY HANDLED, AND ARE NOT OF AN INFLAMMABLE, EXPLOSIVE OR DANGEROUS NATURE, WILL BE ACCEPTED FOR CONVEYANCE BY THE OMNIBUS SERVICE AT THE APPROPRIATE ROAD RATES.
A SCHEDULED EXPRESS ROAD FREIGHT VAN, SERVING ABOVE ROUTES, WILL ALSO BE PROVIDED FOR PARCELS NORMALLY CONVEYED BY PASSENGER TRAIN.
PARCEL OFFICES WILL BE AVAILABLE IN ALL PRINCIPAL TOWNS FOR THE RECEIPT OF PARCELS.

(3) FREIGHT TRAFFIC:—

SCHEDULED ROAD LORRY SERVICES COVERING THE AREAS AT PRESENT SERVED BY RAIL WILL OPERATE. ALL TRAFFIC CONVEYED BY THESE SERVICES WILL BE DELIVERED TO CONSIGNEES' PREMISES.
REGULAR COLLECTIONS WILL BE MADE IN ALL AREAS AND ANY TRAFFIC OFFERING WILL BE ACCEPTED BY LORRY DRIVERS.
AT LEAST 24 HOURS' NOTICE MUST BE GIVEN IN REGARD TO THE CONVEYANCE OF LIVESTOCK.

(4) DEPOTS :—

THE FOLLOWING ARE THE DEPOTS AT WHICH TRAFFIC WILL BE ACCEPTED, AND TO WHOM ENQUIRIES SHOULD BE ADDRESSED FOR THE COLLECTION OF TRAFFIC.

BALLYSHANNON	('PHONE NO. 10)		KILLYBEGS	('PHONE NO. 35)
DONEGAL	('PHONE NO. 101)		LETTERKENNY	('PHONE NO. 54)
GLENTIES	('PHONE NO. 15)		LIFFORD	('PHONE NO. 61)
STRANORLAR	('PHONE NO. 8)		STRABANE	('PHONE NO. 2220)

THE COMMITTEE ARE CONFIDENT THAT THE TRANSPORT REQUIREMENTS OF THE PUBLIC WILL BE FULLY MET BY THE NEW ARRANGEMENTS. IF ANY FURTHER INFORMATION IS DESIRED, THE PUBLIC ARE INVITED TO COMMUNICATE WITH THE UNDERMENTIONED.

STRANORLAR,
DECEMBER, 1959.

B. L. Curran, Manager and Secretary.

DEMOCRAT BALLYSHANNON

The snow-capped summits closed in more quickly and the waters of Lough Finn ran alongside the railway track for several miles. The guard suggested we had reached the nearest point for the station and our last view of the bus was as it went forward up the pass in a cloud of black diesel exhaust. It was a relief to smell the mountain air, enjoy the silence and be free of the rough ride which the bus gave. A railcar was to be preferred! We wandered down the lonely boreen to the station wondering what we should do if we missed the returning bus.

There was a ghostly air about the discarded station. It seemed to have been deserted as if warned of some cataclysmic disaster and abandoned forthwith. There was a station building, water tank and goods shed. The ground frame and signals were intact and from inspection of the rails, there seemed no reason why a train could not have been accepted at once. Signs of habitation were few and though there were people working on turf bogs high up on the slopes, the land was empty of animals and men. It was sunny yet there was a chill atmosphere and we wondered if there ever had been sufficient population to support a railway? Apparently the railcars provided a frequent service in past times which was well patronised, so we learned. The sun shone down from the other side of the lough, and Aghla (1,961 ft) frowned down on the waters in the shadow. It seemed the kind of place to which railway staff were banished as some kind of demotion!

We stood on the roadside in good time less the returning bus should miss us; we had not spoken to a soul since it left us and the bus was akin to entering a mobile island of civilization except that we were almost the only passengers. The guard was obviously puzzled by our fleeting visit ... A small discrepancy about the spelling of Finntown still remained - and still does.

We had a short time to explore premises at Stranorlar before returning to Belfast and the night sailing to Heysham. It is easiest to record these vehicles as we came across them:

One bogie carriage from the former Ballymena, Cushendall & Red Bay Railway.
CDR 6-wheel Directors' Saloon Carriage.
DRUMBOE (2-6-4T N. Wilson 1907) in for heavy repairs. New boiler on order expected soon.
Railcar No.18 which caught fire in the Bannesmore Gap in 1949, being given new body.
Railcar No. 14 in for general repair.
Wheel lathe suitable for all classes of stock.
Parts scattered around of LETTERKENNY (2-6-4T N. Wilson 1908).
LYDIA (2-6-4T N. Wilson 1907) being repainted after heavy repairs. Is in the running shed but 'due to go out on Monday'.
MOURNE (4-6-4T N. Wilson 1904) not used for 20 years. Being cannibalised for parts.
OWENEA (4-6-4T N. Wilson 1904) out of use following head-on collision with Railcar No. 17 in 1949. Frames bent. Will probably be scrapped.
ALICE (2-6-4T N. Wilson 1912) in for boiler washout.

Chapter Seven

North Donegal Anthology, Part Two, A Hurried Finale, March 1953

During the late Autumn of 1952 there came the unwelcome news via the Manchester 'grape vine', of which I have written earlier, that train services on the Lough Swilly system were unlikely to continue far into 1953. The uncertainty about the closing date made it even more depressing. Our near-recent visit in March 1951 had been practical only because it had been tacked onto the end of a business trip to see our Belfast customers. But a repetition of this strategy was impossible now as the whole situation at the Works had changed with the end of the Government's Utility Scheme for the Clothing Trade. Competition was now keen and I would have to take holidays when opportunity beckoned … and that might be too late!

I made a call to the helpful Mr Whyte at the Londonderry office of the Railway and learned that demolition of the Burtonport Extension track had been resumed near Gweedore (where it had been halted by public unrest) and had now reached a point about a mile west of Letterkenny, only to stop there. For reasons unclear to me over the phone, the locomotive of the demolition train, No. 12 the surviving 4-8-0 tender engine, was now in Letterkenny yard and was said to be unusable.

I had not seen this magnificent engine since 1939; it was the largest Irish narrow gauge locomotive of its type, and unique in the British Isles. Two had been built but only No. 12 remained. Dorothy did not question the quest, save to say she hoped her Mother could look after our two small girls while she came with me. She could and she did.

A further call to Mr Whyte confirmed that he would have the engine pulled out of the shed for us, and with the help of special Easter cheap tickets we took the night-sailing to Belfast. Camera film was still rationed but a friendly supplier rose to the occasion - to have adequate film on hand was a prerequisite for any railway visit - without a supply such a visit would not be worth making.

We took what was now becoming our usual route to Letterkenny via Portadown and the County Donegal system; there was always something new to see. The threat of closure now also applied to the CDR, which made us especially vigilant to make detailed plans of stations about which my notebook had been rather casual previously. Thus Lifford, Ballindrait, Raphoe, Convoy and Glenmaquin (where the signals had been removed) were given a short once-over, the railcar crew having no objection while I alighted and walked along the platform. Such liberties and delays did not seem to arouse the curiosity of our fellow passengers one bit.

What may have interested them more was the condition of my trousers whose state I had overlooked as I walked up and down. I should explain that in Britain and N. Ireland clothes rationing had been introduced on 1st June, 1941 (but not in Eire). To save my clothing coupons it was a good idea to buy good quality trousers (made in Limerick) in Eire, and furthermore, to wear an old pair which were past their best and which could be left behind in the shop. The

Carriage shunting at Strabane. March 1953. *Author*

Walker-built railcar No. 20 at Raphoe. March 1953. *Author*

L&LSR (*right*) with the CDRJC (*left*) alongside west of Letterkenny. March 1953.   *Author*

The overgrown harbour line left. CDRJC (*centre*), L&LSR (*right*), south of Letterkenny. March 1953.   *Author*

Letterkenny engine shed with No. 2 and No. 12. March 1953.

trousers I was wearing had succumbed to the journey and Dorothy was obliged to make repairs *en route* before I was fit to leave the railcar at Letterkenny, or meet Mr Whyte ...

Fortunately the day was still bright when we ran into Letterkenny. I caught sight of No. 12 (4-8-0 Hudswell, Clarke 1905) standing alone in the yard in front of the engine shed, and realised how lucky I was to enjoy the good offices of Mr Whyte. Only years later in Newcastle-on-Tyne did we learn of some other enthusiasts who had also visited Letterkenny before our arrival, and were astonished to find the engine outside as if on display ... I lost no time in reminding them who had occasioned it and suggested they might take us out for lunch!

We lost no time in making our way to the yard. No. 12 proved just as exciting as I imagined and well worth the time and expense of it all. One could see that she was in need of some attention - the smokebox was pitifully thin and its door had several holes, but such was superficial. The tyres were still good for a year at least. I suspected that the boiler inspector had been unhappy at his last visit and maybe had warned that he would only permit 100 lb. boiler pressure and 12 months more active service? None the less, it was a fine machine and worthy of close inspection. Among the features I noted was the absence of flanges on the third pair of driving wheels, the overhead valve chests with their heavily cranked valve spindles, the sanding gear applied only to the second and fourth wheelsets, the steam hooter which must have sounded well amongst the high slopes of Muckish, the Belpaire firebox, the very roomy cab fitted out for right-hand-drive but insufficient to keep out the bitter winds of the Atlantic against which the tender had been given a home-made weather sheet. In my limited wanderings up to that time, I had never seen a 6-wheeled tender before; it was an appropriate appendage ... With Dorothy's help we measured the driving wheelbase; 4 ft 6 in. + 4 ft 6 in. + 4 ft 6 in. Bogie wheelbase 4 ft 8 in. Rear bogie wheel to front driving wheel 3 ft 8 in. Tender wheelbase 5 ft 3 in. + 4 ft 9 in.

There being no further use for the engine, it stood outside until the scrap men called. Although I had been promised one of the large oval brass number plates, it must have been too tempting to send to England and probably ended up as scrap. So our house had to be content with a '12' milepost number on the gate, off the Cork Bandon & S. Coast Railway!

Not wishing to be caught out with another contretemps about our entitlement to share a bed, we had written to the address concerned and booked a room for the night, plus an early meal that day so that we could explore the remains of the Burtonport Extension that same evening. So all was well and we walked along the abandoned track in leisurely fashion as far as Old Town station where the rails petered out. There is something magical about following the tracks of a disused railway, particularly if it is to be for the last time! Daylight was still on our side, for being north and west of home the twilight lingered on. The station was occupied, probably by an employee. I would have been tempted to knock on the door and learn something of the demolition but at such a late hour we should not have been welcome.

In the morning we decided that if our information was to be adequately well-rounded, we needed to add more about the carriages which the L&LSR once

Letterkenny station. No.2 with a Londonderry train. March 1953.   *Author*

No. 2 and train approaches Pluck from the west.   *Author*

used; some were spending their last days in the skeletal remains of the carriage shed and as there was opportunity before our mixed train left for Londonderry, we made a bee-line for two differing rakes of elderly five-compartment six-wheeled stock. From the rubbish lying on the floors (crown bottle tops and half-eaten meat pies) they had been the scene of some last ribald outings to Buncrana. The doors (and some windows) were open but the interiors did not suggest we lingered. The builders were the Oldbury Railway Carriage & Wagon Co. Ltd of Birmingham with axles spaced at 10 ft + 10 ft and a length of 31 ft. There were 14 of them. All had once had acetylene gas lighting but no provision for heat. (Thus both CDR and L&LSR carriages latterly had lighting but no heating which may have been due to doubt about the locomotives being able to supply sufficient steam?) These 14 carriages were reminiscent of my erst-while journey to Burtonport; no 1st Class compartments, wooden slat seats, tongue-and-groove timber partitioning and an all-over one pot, one tin, one brush, paint finish of light gray. There was no lining but the carriage number and the diamond-shaped totem 'LSR' was in light green. A dismal appearance indeed! The L&LSR road buses must have been greeted with unmitigated joy.

The morning working to Londonderry stood in the up platform and we were able to wonder at its length. Surely the news that the railway was about to close must be incorrect? There was one open wagon behind the engine and after it 12 covered vans and the bogie guard's composite in which we were to travel. There was clearly no shortage of business! In front was the Letterkenny-shedded engine No. 2, a Barclay-built 4-6-0 tank, splendidly clean and turned out; its crew greeted us like old friends, as did the guard with whom we travelled. We got the impression that if we were to travel with them more frequently, we would be given the Freedom of the Line, or some such decoration. It gave us a warm feeling.

We told the guard we were anxious to see the abandoned earthworks at Burt Junction, near the Trady embankment. They were well marked as the Lough Swilly tide was low and we were given a running commentary. The land round the sea-girt shore was boggy, low and undulating and the railway rose up and down to suit; the speed of the train seldom varied in the hands of an engine crew who knew their position with their eyes closed. Now and again we dropped the window and looked forward along the rattling, swaying rake of vans. We took in a whiff of stagnant seaweed mixed with the smell of burning brake blocks. Dust arose in clouds from the wheels and grit found its way into our eyes - all the same it was heady stuff.

The train came to stop at Manorcunningham and Newton-Cunningham, seemingly little more than large villages with stations that over-rated their importance. The station buildings were mostly of uniform pattern and gave the impression of a railway which had brought the 20th century into it. There was a passing loop, signal cabin and semaphores by The Railway Signal Co. and McKenzie & Holland. At each station we pulled into the loop and waited but apart from some packages for the guard's van and some long exchanges of gossip, that was all.

From time to time we enjoyed seaward views up Lough Swilly northwards then the land became what I thought resembled the Low Countries with dykes and

A Letterkenny-Londonderry train at Newton-Cunningham. March 1953.   *Author*

No. 2 and train crosses Trady embankment. March 1953.   *Author*

water courses. There was a rattle of wheels as we emerged from a wooded plantation and we felt the carriage take a leftward lunge over the pointwork at Tooban Junction. We recalled the considerable wait we made in the snug signal cabin here when our goods train connection had been held up at the Bridge End Customs. Not this time, however, for the signalman was standing with arm outstretched to catch the single-line staff off our engine as we ran into the north side of the island platform. The Letterkenny goods which we were to pass here had not been delayed at the Customs and had been held for our arrival, its engine crew could be seen sitting in the overhead cabin. The guard warned us, 'There will be a delay here', which in Irish terminology meant there was a tea break in the offing. He collected two mugs from the van cupboard marked FIRST AID and we all repaired to the signal cabin. We should have enjoyed the 'crack' far more if the men had not reverted to their local tongue which I found difficult to follow but which confounded Dorothy completely. Much of it followed the mixed fortunes of the nearby Gaelic Football team, but we nodded at appropriate moments.

The Letterkenny working with No. 15* (4-6-2 Tank, Hudswell, Clarke 1899) left as soon as the preferred team had been 'selected' by those concerned; the train was certainly as long as our own. Shortly we too were off for the short run to Bridge End where, so we learned, the Customs people were overloaded with work and would take their time to check our train which was so long that we had to stand outside the station to keep the road crossing clear.

Ultimately we were called forward into the station and the train was checked. At Pennyburn it would be shunted and the guard recommended we leave it at the level crossing there rather than wait in the van. He said that there was any number of carriages in the sidings there and that after we had seen our fill and looked in at engine shed, we could make our way to the offices where Mr Whyte was expecting us.

He was right about the number of vehicles. There was only time to note some of them but a few odd-looking ones caught my eye, proving to be the bodies of Londonderry horse trams. We looked over the considerable selection. Among them were Burtonport bogie carriages with matchboard planking sides by Pickering of Wishaw and having spoked wheels, and resembling the tinplate toy carriages of my childhood, and a rake of bogie coaches built in 1901 by The Lancaster Carriage & Wagon Co. Ltd. The latter was of keen interest to me as since birth I had been taken to see my Aunt in the Lake District along Caton Road, Lancaster and been fascinated by the big arched gateway of their long sprawling factory: these were the first products I had seen.

The yard was crammed with Burtonport Extension vehicles; pairs of timber bolsters, the odd horse box, bogie open wagons (converted from carriages?). Most were fitted with vacuum brakes in contrast to those of the L&LSR. All gave the impression that when the Burtonport line was commissioned the BOW was lavish with its requirements … all at the British taxpayers' expense.

There was a Clogher Valley wagon in the works yard. The Foreman said that the last van to be built here was assembled from accumulated parts before World War I.

---

* One of a pair of powerful 4-6-2 tank engines specifically built at the Board of Works (BOW) recommendation for working the Carndonagh Extension, and much envied by the L&LSR who 'borrowed' them for the Letterkenny workings. The BOW subsequently took legal proceedings against the L&LSR.

No. 15 and Letterkenny train. Tooban Junction. March 1953.   *Author*

Londonderry train held at Bridge End gates. March 1953.   *Author*

4-6-0T No. 2 with a Buncrana train passing Pennyburn. March 1953. *Author*

Londonderry Graving Dock. March 1953. *Author*

Standing in the shed were parts of No. 14 (Hawthorn, Leslie 1910), the engine involved in the 1925 Owencarrow viaduct derailment; I gathered it had not run since that date.

On our walk to the Office we passed the Board signal controlling the level crossing at Pennyburn. These were an economical type of semaphore board, rectangular-shaped and having a vertical, revolving movement, worked by a hand lever at the foot of an iron rod at the top of which the semaphore was mounted by one corner. When the crossing was closed to railway traffic, the board showed full-face towards on-coming rail movements. The company described this as a 'Diamond' Board Signal although it was not diamond-shaped!

Mr Whyte had gathered a number of documents and drawings for us to examine and commented on them in an engaging manner:

> After Joseph Tatlow was appointed to the Irish Board of Works in 1917 he was given an office in Letterkenny from which he was able to survey the activities of the L&LSR very closely, in particular the movements of locomotives No. 1-4 and 13 and 14 which had been supplied through the Board for specific routes, namely the Burtonport Extension and the Carndonagh lines. Repairs on these had to be carried out under his supervision at Letterkenny (*not* Pennyburn). Envious of the good condition in which they were kept, the L&LSR 'borrowed them' occasionally for other duties especially when it was short of engines. If such matters came to Tatlow's notice, the L&LSR was fined. It was not until Tatlow left that these engines were widely used.

> Nos. 13 and 14 were very good engines but No. 13 was apt to derail when running bunker first. Of the big 4-8-0 tender engines, these were excellent for the job and No. 11, being the better, was most used. The men considered it to be the best engine on the whole system and in consequence it quickly wore out. No. 12 was able to work the wrecking trains on the Burtonport line before it was condemned. They were the most suitable engines we possesed.

> Concerning the Burtonport Extension; the situation was most unusual. Due to the attitude of the L&LSR, no expense had been put into the Burtonport line which slowly deteriorated. Elsewhere the track is good being of heavy ex-GNRI rails with the dropped ends cropped off; the Manager of the Hammond Foundry, Dublin says they form the heaviest narrow gauge permanent way in the country, for instance the line between Londonderry and Letterkenny with its heavier rail is much better than the CDR line between Strabane and Letterkenny.

> I'd like to correct some rumours about the Burtonport line which is said to have re-opened due to the local militance about closure. This was not the case. Although an Abandonment Order was guaranteed, in view of the extreme shortages due to the War (tyres, rubber, fuel etc.), we could not replace the railway with a road service. Nor could the Government rescind the Abandonment Order. Therefore, although the Extension enjoyed no legal authority we reopened it at our own instigation.

Mr Whyte showed us photographs of the special Royal Train which in July 1903 ran from Buncrana to the Middle Quay, Londonderry to convey King Edward VII. It was hauled by No. 7 (4-6-2T; Hudswell, Clarke; 1901) and included an ex-Belfast & N. Counties Railway 'Cushendall Saloon' carriage, all decorated. The engine was named KING EDWARD VII.

(Our visit to Donegal ended here at Pennyburn; it was the last time we saw the L&LSR in action for, true to rumour, the system closed in August 1953. In the next chapter I will describe our later visits to Donegal to examine parts of the L&LSR which closed before this time.)

Chapter Eight

North Donegal Anthology, Part Three, From Rail to Road, November 1961

This chapter concerns two different aspects of how the lure north-west Donegal had claimed on us. The earlier and shorter was an excursion we made by L&LSR bus (the railway having been closed in August 1953) and the latter being part of a longer tour by Land-Rover in June 1962 accompanied by a small party of members from the north-west area of the Talyllyn Railway Preservation Society.

By the time of this second visit the narrow gauge railways of Donegal had closed but such was the interest in them that many Manchester friends were anxious to know more and I gave several talks on the subject.

Dorothy and I decided to combine my next business trip to Belfast in November 1961 with an intermediate weekend in Donegal; we would travel to Londonderry by the NCC route through Coleraine and return to Belfast by the GNRI through Portadown. From Londonderry the plan was to use the L&LSR bus as far as Gweedore station, the terminus of the erstwhile restored Letterkenny-Gweedore train service. Alighting at Gweedore, we could explore the remaining railway artifacts around here until the returning bus. An unknown feature of the district was the existence - or otherwise - of the Gweedore Hotel where Joseph Tatlow had spent his last year in Ireland and written his biography concerning his career as a railwayman in that country. Perhaps the hotel was still open for business and adjacent to the bus stop? Better still, perhaps we could take a meal in its nostalgic surroundings? So ran our thoughts. November was not the best time of year but I was obliged to suit the buying habits of our customers!

(A revised plan came to mind whereby we could take our Land-Rover with us to Belfast and use it to Londonderry at the weekend. We could still use the bus to Gweedore; on the Sunday the Land-Rover could be used to investigate the remains of the Buncrana-Carndonagh railway route. This we did.)

The Land-Rover was duly parked near the Bus Station at Pennyburn and, with rucksack loaded with food as if setting off for foreign parts, we embarked on the bus with indicator stating 'BURTONPORT'. It was a strange experience to be on ground before which we had never been without a railway journey being involved! It was a pity that the day was overcast; the light was poor and I held my lightmeter up to the window and shook my head as its needle rose lazily up the dial. There would be no sparkling pictures of the Donegal Highlands today.

Beyond Letterkenny, where the bus parked on the former railway platform, we were among but a handful of passengers and free to move from side to side to obtain the best views. We agreed that November was not the best time when our views of Muckish and Errigal mountains might be spoilt by cloud. All the same, the bus gave opportunity to enjoy the distant glimpses of the Atlantic to the north and the course of the railway westwards, as a bonus, the bus would leave sight of it to gain some cluster of dwellings which the railway had failed to reach, the best alternative being a station name denoting 'So-and-so Road'.

From Kilmacrenan came a rough, upland hilly terrain, spongey and covered with bog cotton. There was not a tree in sight. Every piece of high ground was

Kilmacrenan, Burtonport direction. June 1962.   *Author*

Gweedore after period as a temporary terminus. November 1961.   *Author*

crowned with crags; here and there were small and bedraggled farmsteads. Where we could see the old trackbed it was ballasted with shingle gravel and near the part-dismantled Owencarrow viaduct to Barnes Gap road and railway clung side-by-side. The poor light emphasised the bleakness of the place. A mile beyond the viaduct came the railway summit and here the sun broke through the clouds around Creeslough and caught the coast below us as the road dropped sharply. There must have been some interesting civil engineering but the bus skiddadled along and I could not take it all in.

I think it must have been Faymore viaduct with its four steel spans. At this elevation we could see how bare the surrounding mountain slopes were; there was nothing to break up the monotony except here and there were signs of turf working and men loading tractor trailers down below us. Other tractors made their way from these isolated turbaries, along rough tracks towards a small turf-burning Generating Station far below us. We could make out other tractors, like small beetles on the mountainsides, making their way, compulsively drawn to the mother-feature which belched out blue smoke from its single chimney. The Station was the only feature which sat uncomfortably in the vast expanse below. Erected with the aims of making electricity from local fuel, absorbing local labour and providing current for use in a very impoverished part of Ireland, such early installations are now amongst the large plants utilising similar practices in the Irish Midlands (Shannonbridge etc.). We regretted not having fieldglasses with us.

Continuing down the hill, the bus conductor alerted us to the shell of a large building on the road/railway side ahead of us. 'That is the Gweedore Hotel' he explained, as if it was still in business. The driver slowed the bus as we passed. It was certainly an impressive ruin and obviously had been the victim of what the Irish term, 'a Burning' - probably in the troubled times of the early 1920s when these parts were sorely inflicted by local disturbances and the railway was a frequent target.

After a short distance the bus pulled up and the conductor advised us that this was our destination. We must have looked surprised; at least it was not raining and there was but two hours until the bus returned … At first it was difficult to make out the outlines of a station. The whole place looked as if it had been the centre of a battle-training ground. The Station House and engine water tank, plus the shells of the platform building had survived. The bus made off so we sat on the crumbling platform edge and cheering ourselves with food, arranged to spend the time absorbing the striking local views and a walk back along the railway to the hotel ruins. There must have been some kind of dump here during the demolition for the nearby river valley, across which there was a spendid stone arch to carry the railway over the Cromore Burn, had been used to unload a pile of steel overbridges. Why? I guessed that the labour of taking them further was not worth their scrap value?

I made a few notes on the permanent way. Gravel ballasting had been done from a pit close beside the hotel for which a siding had been provided. Some outsize stones had been used between sleepers; they were cheaper than gravel but unsuitable for efficient packing … the Extension had become notorious for derailments due to poor track! The track materials included 30 ft rails carried on 6 ft sleepers at 2 ft 6 in. centres. Strange quarter-mile posts were made from an iron disc with a protruding arm. The disc had a number of perforations, but I did not fathom its meaning. Rail fixing had been a mixture of fang and bolt clips and dog spikes, they were not meant to come loose! The loading gauge between parapet walls was 9 ft; this was no Light Railway.

There was also evidence of money well spent on, for instance, Occupation Gates which were of iron carried on robust stone columns and carrying a cast-iron plate reading SHUT THIS GATE OR PENALTY FORTY SHILLINGS. Also noteworthy were the railway company houses with two floors, stone window lintels and decorated by string courses. They were equal to any of like purpose. Were they of this high standard to meet a landowner's conditions? We set off for the walk up to the Hotel ruins. It was as well we had not relied on the evidence of the map for sustinance. Lastly, we met a man who had been the station master. He said lifting as far as Crolly had been temporarily stopped there by an angry crowd but resumed later to just east of Gweedore. The track was restored back to Gweedore again in June 1940 to enable the unofficial service to operate and instal a run-round loop. Fascinating!

The following day we proposed to motor north from Buncrana and follow the site of the Carndonagh Extension in so far as it came near to the road. We would precede this by having a further examination of carriages which we had singled out earlier as being worth further investigation.

It was already afternoon before we reached Buncrana; furthermore my boots had already suffered the rough going at Gweedore and fieldwork near Tooban Junction finally proved they were no longer watertight. Before the day was out I must find somewhere to buy another pair.

Owenboy River bridge at Buncrana. June 1962.   *Author*

The railway articles I had read about the Inishowen Peninsula northward up which the railway threaded did not commend it. Fayle said '… lacking in interest …', but the day was bright and clear and we were prepared to chance it. Buncrana had now become a depressing rail-less station, a dump for old cars; its platforms were used as the bus terminus. Scrutiny of the site emphasised a clear division between the older section eastward back to Londonderry and the younger Carndonagh railway financed by the Government. The latter had been given a separate platform, enhanced engine shed, and turntable. It had its own station building. Its individual signal box (in the same style as other L&LSR cabins) had been appropriated by the local Sailing Club at which it must have seen far more life than in it former role! The lavish provision for the lesser-used Carndonagh-end of the station was illogical but quite typical of other Irish railway locations.

Immediately beyond the station the railway crossed the Crana River by an impressive stone and girder bridge. There followed some miles of upland bog country with commanding scenes of the estuary of the Lough Swilly to the west. From here the railway climbed the western side of Slieve Snaght before descending again. The hill country was bare of trees and the railway course reminded me of that traversed by the Lynton & Barnstaple Railway on the moorland edge above Lynton. Descending the long narrow gorge the railway had been carried along a narrow ledge and through rocky cuttings. There was a high level stone loading bank and siding. Here we lost sight of the Swilly, and photographed a dingle which the railway crossed by the picturesque Meedoran viaduct.

Shortly we reached Clonmany village, with station some way above it. Here all the usual features of the L&LSR had not only survived and, had the track been replaced, were ready to resume business immediately! The passing loop here had been the only one on the Extension. Station house, goods shed and engine water tank were in immaculate condition and testimony of the high specifications to which the Extension had been built: there had been military camps here in World War I.

On leaving, we entered the village, and thinking ahead of a night's lodgings, we spied and booked in at the Inishowen Hotel. The decision was an excellent one for adjacent to the building itself, there was a shop which sold everything (including footwear). So onwards to Carndonagh. There was a further climb over and down into Ballyliffin where the station was a close relation to that at Clonmany and the robust quartzite buildings with yellow brick quoins were far superior to any other locally. There seemed little to attract railway business here - it must have been purely agricultural. This was Ireland's 'furthest north' railway.

To the north there were sweeping vistas of ocean with Malin Head across an inlet to the east. This scene grew more exciting as the railway curved round to its terminus. Between railway and the sea extended a broad sweep of strand on Trawbreaga Bay. Carndonagh station site was little changed from active railway days with evidence of road business in the several score Guinness barrels on the platform. The large station building, engine shed, goods store were of stone in 'as new' condition. The Government had built well!

If there was one feature of Carndonagh station area which surprised it was extragavant amount of land it occupied. Land must have been cheap and buyers

Ballymagon, looking south towards Buncrana. June 1962.   *Author*

Carndonagh Extension Railway, Owenboy River bridge at Bayllymagan. June 1962.   *Author*

Pastoral scene near Clonmany. June 1962. *Author*

Clonmany station, rear. June 1962. *Author*

Ballyliffin, in Buncrana direction. November 1961.   *Author*

Ballyliffin, in Carndonagh direction. A typical example of the fine buildings on the Carn donagh
Extension. November 1961.
                                                                     Author

scarce! The final quarter of a mile of track was laid upon a low embankment through flat farmland. There was a solitary milepost surviving at the platform end, a neat cast-iron oval reading '1/2'. In the tidy waiting room hung two notice boards, the one headed with a cast-iron plate with raised lettering 'L&LSRy.' and the other similarly, 'L&LSRy. NOTICES'. On the doorstep 'L&LSR' had been cast in concrete and every door had its cast-iron plate, 'LADIES WAITING ROOM' (etc.). Obviously, while the Railway Company had other's money to burn, they would not disappoint.

It is said that various L&LSR engines were tried on the Extension and all were found wanting except Nos. 15-16 which were thereon, 'adopted'. Certainly the engine shed had been extended at some stage. Beyond it was a two-arched stone viaduct spanning the Donagh River, and a large gravel pit for ballast. In the middle of the expanse was another cast-iron notice CAUTION DO NOT TRESPASS ON THE RAILWAY PENALTY FOR NONCOMPLIANCE 40/- by Order. We recalled the high degree of illiteracy of those times.

There was a handpump beside the bridge and a postcard in my collection shows this same pump being used to fill an engine tank from the river. Perhaps they had over-spent on cast-iron notices?! So ended our investigations into the narrow gauge railways of these parts. We had not seen them all before it was too late, even if the scrap men were snapping at our heels in the final stages.

And I nearly forgot to tell you about the boots. The Inishowen Hotel was as good as its promise - while supper was cooking I was invited to slip through the communicating door from the dining room into the shop. I chose a Limerick-made pair which were inexpensive and proved a fitting purchase.

Carndonagh terminus, with Guinness barrels evident on the platform. November 1961.
Author

Chapter Nine

A Visit to Ireland Replaces Wales, June 1962

The frequency with which the Boyds seemed to visit narrow gauge railways in Ireland had made us a sick joke. We were either to be envied or pitied. Our colleagues amongst the local members of the Talyllyn Railway Preservation Society were now meeting each other frequently as we made joint visits to the working parties on that railway, and it was not long before a group of us began to visit railway centres which did not feature in the syllabus of the other societies hereabouts. Some of these were not strictly railway-orientated and might include tramways or canals. Therefore, I was not surprised to learn over the bush telegraph that something more adventurous was being considered, to take place during the ten-day Manchester Whitsuntide Holiday break.

This new venture germinated around the Land-Rover with which we had replaced our small family car. We had used it on outings to relatives in Scotland and a holiday in West Cork, and it came to my ear that we might be approached shortly with a wild scheme for a few of us to take the Land-Rover and visit some narrow gauge railway sites in Ireland. To add spice, perhaps some of the trackbed of the Burtonport Extension might be a suitable terrain for the vehicle to traverse ... after all, it was exactly the type of route which promotional advertising for the Land-Rover extolled! Apparently Dorothy and I would do the driving and those involved would pay our expenses and book the accommodation. So, we enlisted the services of mother-in-law to look after the children and asked for more detail. A carload of our friends from Ulster was asked to join the convoy - the more, the merrier. We did not expect them to join us with a car along the more improvised roads!

The plan was to drive from Manchester to Stranraer via Carlisle, and catch a small-hour sailing to Larne. Thereon our route would be:

Londonderry & Lough Swilly Rly	Carndonagh Extension, Burt Junction and Farland Point Tooban Junc.-Letterkenny Burtonport Extension
Co. Donegal Railways Jt C'tee	Surviving vehicles at Stranorlar, Letterkenny, Strabane.
Castlederg & Victoria Bridge Ty	
Ballycastle Rly	
Belfast Transport Museum	

We proposed to deviate if any extraordinary sight caught our eye, but we would have to spend the nights at the places we had reserved beforehand. It will be apparent to the reader that a great part of the visit was already well known to Dorothy and I, but we needed no encouragement to renew acquaintance.

We had not fully comprehended the road distance from Manchester to Carlisle and Carlisle to Stranraer. It was almost the same for each part and it would grow dark as we drove north and light as we drove west! Our passengers were already dropping off as we entered Carlisle but the wretched state of the streets in that city soon had them clutching for a handhold. They were wide awake as we crossed into Scotland and it was quite dark as we began the dreary drive towards Stranraer.

Much later the sun rose behind us and as we approached the south end of Loch Ryan and saw the ship in the distance, we were all stiff and weary. Never again would we use that route to Ireland! But the morning was brilliant and we could not resist a stroll on deck as we negotiated the Loch northwards before making our way to our cabins. It was 4.30 am.

I did not keep a note of the ship's name - was it the PRINCESS MAUD? - but it was certainly one of the pre-World War II railway boats, extremely comfortable and well-equipped. The sea voyage is only 32 miles long but we knew we could sleep on in the cabin until 8 am when the steward would call us to tea. We could rely in the Dining Saloon to give us a breakfast worthy of our night-long exertions. The Irish Sea was like a duck pond and left us with no sensation. The breakfast lived up to expectations and we left the ship in leisurely fashion to meet the Irish contingent (Desmond plus a married couple and their son) with their car on the quay.

By common consent the initial part of the holiday was to be based on the Swilly Hotel at Buncrana, an imposing pile I had spotted some years before and where I felt they would have room for our party of nine persons during Whit week. Bert had offered to make himself responsible for the bookings but some weeks beforehand he telephoned me to say the Hotel had written explaining that all their usual rooms were full as it was their Annual Golf Tournament. Instead they could offer us certain rooms on the ground floor, next to the Ball Room. Would we accept? Knowing the problems of finding rooms elsehere, we were relieved to do so.

We left Larne and headed for Londonderry where the party could make the acquaintance of the Foyle quaysides where once two standard and narrow gauge railways had terminated. Dorothy and I began a week of acting as Tour Guides from here on. Around the site of Tooban Junction the area was obliterated by the the planting of a young forest so we passed on to see the site of the long-gone Fahan Pier. It was interesting to find that the railway embankment here is built up entirely in seashells. There was little to see of this historic landing place except the coal store for landed ships' cargo in the triangle of tracks on the shore. The store was used latterly for stabling the branch engine overnight.

By afternoon and after some time spent on inspecting some of the abandoned stations on the L&LSR between Tooban and Letterkenny (now reverted to private dwellings) we were glad to make our way to the Swilly Hotel as the previous night's journey had caught up with us. The Hotel was deserted and we gathered that most of the guests would be out on the Golf Course until dinner time. We were glad of the opportunity to sleep for two hours. We took seats in the dining room in good time, being very hungry, but were moved to another part of the establishment after being told we had taken seats reserved for the returning golfers. It was the first indication that we were Second Class citizens.

Although I was aware that some of the golfing fraternity were making a night of it, it did not disturb our sleep more than intermittently. However, some of our party said at breakfast that the night-time revels had kept them awake until the early hours, and that if this was to occur again they would ask for another room. We were in agreement with their opinion and spent a glorious day following the Carndonagh line in detail and then continuing northwards. Eventually we stood on the high ground above Malin Head and had a picnic lunch surrounded by wonderful vistas of sea and sky which quite compensated for the interruptions of the previous night. Stretched out in the sunshine on a sandy strand, Alan posed the question, 'James can we discharge the rest of the week's programme by remaining here?' Dorothy and I confirmed that Donegal had cast its spell on everyone and that as so far no one had complained that our glimpses of railways had been minimal.

Our plans for the remainder of our time using the Swilly Hotel as a base were drastically altered by events the subsequent night. Firstly our dinner that evening was delayed because a number of golfers were still out on the links and all the guests had to await their return. Obviously the establishment was geared to the golf schedule and everything else followed suit. We muttered but were in a minority.

Worse was to come. We had only just dozed off when I was awoken by a blast on what I dreamily thought was a cornet. Dorothy, also awoken, said it was a bugle or trumpet and it seemed to come from outside our bedroom door. Then there were sounds of a band striking up and the rhythmic thud of a dance was set in motion. We put our heads beneath the bedclothes and tried to blot out the incessant thumping. We told each other it would die away around midnight but we were over optimistic. The noise never ceased and at length I looked at my watch. Two am. There was a slight pause in the proceedings before it all began again, coupled with much hilarity and stamping of feet.

At length we could stand it no more and I got out of bed and looked out into the ballroom. A great procession of inebriated buffoons was making its way uncertainly round the floor, cheering and shouting and led by a man playing a cornet. It was a rout but I saw a waitress and, though in my pyjamas, found my way to her. 'Where is the Hotel Manager?', I shouted above the din. 'Over there - the man with the trumpet', she said. I knew immediately that our stay at the Swilly Hotel would end abruptly after breakfast.

We had a quick conference over the breakfast dishes. We intended to attend the hotel office *en masse* and ask for the bill. We had no intention of paying for the remainder of our booking and I think the management could detect our determination. As we left we had no idea where we would sleep that night or how our intended programme for the remainder of our stay would fare. Fortunately, Bert had noticed a small Tourist Office as we passed through Buncrana, so we aimed for this and put our troublesome tale of the Swilly Hotel before them. The young lady behind the counter did not seem in the least surprised at our story - we gathered she had heard of everal similar experiences before. She suggested we should try Arnold's Hotel at Dunfanaghy. Would we like her to phone them? In a matter of minutes it was settled and we left in good spirits. It was still possible to use Arnold's as a centre for exploring the railway route to Burtonport without making drastic changes to our schedule.

It was necessary to travel via Letterkenny which, though now bereft of railways, was unvisited territory to all but ourselves. On reaching the station's area we found it a thriving bus station with ample refreshment facilities. We then arranged to meet in an hour. There were still some railway carriages grounded hereabouts and the abandoned CDRJC signal box had not been damaged and was worth investigation! Afterwards we would visit the stations along the Burtonport line until it was time to make our way to Dunfanaghy.

LETTERKENNY SIGNAL BOX (CDRJC) LEVER FRAME

1	GREEN	DISTANT SIGNAL
2	RED	DOWN HOME SIGNAL
3	WHITE	SPARE
4	WHITE	SPARE
5	BLUE	EXCHANGE SIDING POINTS
6	WHITE	SPARE
7	RED	GROUND DISC. PASS LINE TO CATTLE DOCK
8	RED	GROUND DISC. LOCO SHED TO DOCK OR PLATFORM
9	BLACK	POINTS IN PASS LINE/CATCH POINTS IN LOCO ROAD
10	WHITE	SPARE
11	BLACK	POINTS ARRIVAL & DEPARTURE LINE
12	WHITE	SPARE
13	WHITE	SPARE
14	WHITE	SPARE
15	BLACK	POINTS TO DOCK SIDING
16	RED	GROUND DISC. CATTLE DOCK/LOCO SHED
17	RED	GROUND DISC. PLATFORM LINE TO LOCO SHED
18	BLACK	POINTS LOCO RUNROUND CROSSOVER
19	RED	GROUND DISC. CROSSOVER.
20	WHITE	SPARE
21	WHITE	SPARE
22	RED	? (lever plate missing)
23	RED	DOWN STARTING SIGNAL
24	RED	? (lever plate missing)

In due course we found ourselves making for Old Town, New Mills, Fox Hall and Churchill as the railway climbed west and northward from the valley of the Swilly. From pleasant wooded slopes it rose at 1 in 50 to gain the lower reaches of the Donegal highlands where there was no tree to be seen. Old Town had had its passing loop lifted years ago. We failed to find the road to New Mills but encountered Fox Hall which had a small plain building, plus siding and bijou goods shed but no passing loop. At Churchill there were up and down platforms on the loop, the second being a goods feature only. This station had a gated road crossing, goods shed and cattle dock - all revealing it once had been of some status. Also, the station name was still on display by means of a blue and white enamel signboard, used more commonly for stations on the Tooban-Letterkerry section. The empty station house was of the design favoured at level crossings and lacked the attraction of most others on the Extension. All the buildings here were concrete-faced. The waiting room was separate and substantial, and corrugated-iron roofed. We wondered if it had ever been crowded? Standing in one corner was a notice board complete with a timetable for 1936; we felt it had passed its 'Sell-by' date and was too interesting to become firewood. We took appropriate measures.

Approach to Letterkenny station. March 1953. *Author*

BLANCHE shunts Letterkenny yard. The fireman had just added coal! May 1956. *Author*

We passed on to Kilmacrenan, situated in open rough country (which I have mentioned in connection with my 1939 journey), a similar building to Churchill but this time more than fully occupied; there were six boys playing cricket - unusual in Southern Ireland - on the ample approach road. It looked a lively place in what had become a wilder, upland terrain.

It seemed extraordinary that we, nursed on railways with all their facets, should have been focused on one special feature of this abandoned system so far as we had examined its course westwards of Letterkenny. This was the design and quality of its civil engineering. The geology of the terrain lay from south-west to north-east with numerous rivers running through it in that direction, all of which the railway was bound to cross. The topography was such that almost every bridge was a different structure, varying from steel girders, through multi-arched stonework to slender single-spanned stone and brick erections which seemed to leap from one river bank to the other. These last were almost in the pattern of Brunel's famous bridge over the Thames at Maidenhead on the Great Western Railway. To find such high-class work on a narrow gauge railway in a remote part of Ireland was to emphasise the expense the British Government was ready to meet to provide the country with the means to better itself.

Approaching the desolate region and passing through the narrow Barnes Gap, we passed under the adjacent railway as it crossed over the road in this rock-strewn defile by means of a viaduct of three steel spans, whose pillars still stood. It was a formidable setting. A short distance further on, the road emerged from the Gap with the railway's site up on the left. We left the car and clambered up to it; there had been a sharp right-hand curve here where the railway also left the Gap and appeared suddenly on the south-east shoulder of the wide Owencarrow River valley. To me, this sudden opportunity to stand on the threshold of the infamous viaduct here was almost unreal. The long line of its pillars stretched like a staircase before us, and the differing construction of girder spans and masonry arches imposed a slightly comic air, particularly as we had imagined the viaduct to be level wheras it sloped down to the point where it crossed the river than climbed sharply at 1 in 50 over the embankment. Most of the structure was across a flattish and unstable valley floor. Excited by the unusual vista of mountains in the distance and end of what had been a remarkable bridge near at hand, we stayed awhile to capture it all on film.

Eventually, and aware now that it was time to make our acquaintance with Arnold's Hotel, we took to the road again to call in at Creeslough station, six miles before Dunfanaghy. Here there was a passing loop, a goods platform with shed and handcrane, and a station house similar to Fox Hall. A Londonderry horse tram body graced the down platform, which also had a water tower.

It was now the opportunity for our friends in the second car to leave us as they had to be back at work in Belfast the next day. As for ourselves, we carried on from Creeslough northwards, leaving the railway which now turned due west, and as we neared Dunfanaghy we were treated to a panorama such as is all too rare. Before us was Sheep Haven, a wide bay enclasped by a headland to the west possessing fine cliffs, and to the east by Rosguill peninsula. There were several long sandy strands. Dunfanaghy welcomed us with bright evening

Approaching Owencarrow viaduct. June 1962.   *Author*

The desolate valley beneath the viaduct. June 1962.   *Author*

sunlight and charmed us completely. The hotel fitted our needs perfectly and although there was evidence that golf was played hereabouts, a jocular suggestion to the receptionist that there might be a tournament in hand that week brought a relieved negative!

A short evening walk confirmed that we had come to an idyllic place. Later on Dorothy and I were invited to take a glass of Irish Coffee which we accepted with the proviso that we had it in the bedroom … experience had taught us that its effect could be quite sudden. So we lay on the bed and watched a brilliant sunset fill the room with colour before disappearing over the Atlantic horizon. Lulled by the sound of waves breaking on the shore close by, we ended a perfect day.

The plan for the next day was to call at stations down to Burtonport, come as close as possible to the summit of Muckish and see if the railway site offered any opportunity of driving along the dismantled trackbed. There was much to be done!

We took a minor road which led westwards along the railway site and below a gaunt range of mountains with Muckish its highest point (2,197 ft). The line climbed to a summit level of 474 ft here, near the desolate Lough Agher and where the road petered out we were able to drive the Land-Rover onto the coarse ballast. The going was extremely rough. We continued thus and at a suitable point reversed the vehicle to enable us to drive eastwards for extensive views over Creeslough. It was extremely difficult to keep the vehicle on the ballast and with a sudden lurch, it diverted onto the rough ground beside the railway and stopped with the front wheels in a bog. I was able to cling to the steering wheel but the rest found themselves in a heap. Fortunately our speed was extremely low. We were confident that the robust jack supplied by the makers would soon put us back on course.

After some experimental assays with the help of the jack and four men, our confidence was soon blunted. It was not the fault of the jack or the men, but we were soon reminded that all of these could achieve nothing unless the jack was doing its share - it was working correctly but instead of lifting the vehicle vertically, it was slowly driving itself down into the bog. It required a firm foundation to stand on. Where could we find one in an Irish bog? As we searched round for some suitable material I saw that we had an audience; far up on the mountainside a group of turf-cutters had stopped to watch our frustrations. They were too far away to come to our aid even if we had asked them; shortly afterwards they turned away. We could only guess at their comments which were unlikely to have been in English anyway …

Bert had found the railway's boundary wall near by. It was made of round rocks, most of them rather heavy. We stripped off for action and began the slow task of collecting enough to construct a pile of them beneath the jack. They were wet and slimey from bog water, and when crushed beneath the jack they slipped sideways from the pile. We thought of going to look for help from someone with a tractor, but in this wild place we preferred to continue our chosen method. About two hours later we succeeded, managed to turn the Land-Rover round and gained the road again. Stopping at Lough Agher, we took the opportunity to wash and clean up!

Right: Rough going in the summit cutting. June 1962. *Author*

Below: Cleaning up on the summit level after the Land Rover 'de-railed'! June 1962. *Author*

Some of the day had been lost in this futile exercise but we were determined to climb Errigal with its enticing coned shape rising out of a white quartzite rim. There seemed to be no access to the foot except by finding the road to Falcarragh station. After several mistakes we succeeded and found it to be the most carefully restored station we had seen, set in amidst entrancing mountainscapes. We were lucky as the clearness of the air and the brilliant sunshine were in our favour; winter might change our opinion. There was a rough winding track from here to Cashelnagore station, near the highest point on the Extension, 420 ft asl. The station building was akin to Fox Hall and was a complete ruin. The sun disappeared behind heavy cloud and the day became colder and as gloomy as the station itself which, we were told, was the only two-storey building for miles around. We did not linger.

Carrying along this bleak road for a short distance we concluded that it would not take us any nearer to Errigal, so we abandoned the Land-Rover and made across some turf workings to where the real climbing began. Things were not as we had imagined. The quartzite proved to be not the fine sugar-icing we thought it was, but rough lumps of near-white boulders that objected to being climbed-upon; our footwear was more suitable to hill walking and we slid down the sugar-like scree until we had to admit defeat. Standing in this wedding cake senario, we took group photographs and retired, a little disappointed! From here the mountainy track took us to Gweedore station, which looked little different from when Dorothy and I had been taken there by Lough Swilly Railway bus.

I had warned the lads not expect too much of Gweedore station but had to admit its condition was rather worse than before. The stink of spilled diesel fuel which flooded the ground, the empty drums and shattered platform edges, were off-putting but in contrast the view of Errigal rising nearby was superb. We could obtain such a view without lingering, so we moved on. When I reached home I looked up this reference to that part of the old railway which we had traversed that day, as recalled by the contractor …

If we had been treated fairly … allowed to make deviations without the severe restrictions imposed on us, which would have improved the railway without increasing the cost … half a mile of railway disappeared into an underground lake … it was a much more difficult matter to arrange a deviation in Ireland than in Africa … all our united experience and advice was of no avail owing to the exacting terms of the contracts … both jobs resulted in considerable loss to the firm.

The 10 mile remainder of the railway route to Burtonport was not of easy access to the road and we were obliged to guess where the stations had stood, the map being short of this information. We were now out of the Highlands and into The Rosses, a district of small roads which wound their way across granite-strewn hillocks with scattered boulders abounding, interspersed with many lakes large and small, and intersected by rivers and streams. The scenery was a transformation from what had gone before, but similar in that it was treeless. Along the third class and narrow roads we took, we had continuous views of the Atlantic shores along Inishfree Bay to the north.

There was a small single-platformed station at Crolly, with a bijou factory where carpets were made. The building was surrounded by bicycles propped

Falcarragh, looking west. June 1962.   *Author*

Falcarragh. Note the string of courses over the fenestration. June 1962.   *Author*

up against the walls; there was little sight of any nearby housing. We learned that the famous Crolly Dolls were made hereabouts but assumed this was a Cottage Industry. I sought to buy one without success.

The route of the railway through this region reminded me of someone treading carefully across flooded ground while trying not to suffer wet feet; there were instances where the track had been carried over long low causeways through and between the lakes, then it would rise suddenly to plunge into a rocky cutting only to plunge down again onto a further causeway. It was a fascinating piece of civil engineering. It has been said of The Rosses that

> ... they are even more inhospitable than the Burren district further south ... here there is neither earth, wood nor water ... the terrain undulates ... here if ever, there is appositeness in the phrase 'to scratch a living'.

We could see our destination now as the wide sweep of the ocean spread before us. I could recall little of my first railway journey here as the outward run had been made after darkness had fallen, but the the memory of it was clear enough and how I had had the feeling of coming to the end of the world - at least, the western edge of Europe.

We found the Halt, Kincasslagh Road (only opened in 1913) which despite its secondary appellation, was worthy of the name station. It boasted a station house, goods shed and siding, and the title of 'Road' recalled the criticism of the Extension in that the places of such population as there was, were by-passed in favour of reaching Burtonport so that the fish, returning from there, should reach the markets before it went off ... 'fish' was the priority!

Dungloe Road Halt brought the railway near to the only place of consequence though still four miles from the village. It too had a siding, goods shed and station house and was located between two cuttings which must have obscured the sighting of the road crossing from the engine crew. Motoring along the narrow spit of land between Lough Meela and the sea, we caught sight of a railway and pulled up quickly thinking it must be a branch of the Burtonport line which had escaped notice; on inspection we found signs of a narrow gauge railway connecting a quay on the Lough with a stout stone jetty and boat house on the foreshore. Further examination showed there to be the skeletal remains of a large sea-going ship stranded there. Between lough and shore the narrow gauge railway passed through a rock cutting 15 ft deep! Intrigued by it all, we called at the Priest's House and learned the system had been installed to ship minerals quarried near the lough to coasters beached on the shore. It would have been good to know more but time was short; so we came to Burtonport which had been, and still was, an anti-climax.

Actually, it was rather better than we had feared having told everyone about my first disappointment, especially with its limited vistas of the open sea. But we had all had such a wonderful feast of superb scenery that we were in a forgiving mood if Burtonport was to fall slightly short. Unexpectedly, the little harbour had received a face-lift from the Irish Government in the name of the fishing industry. Slipways and quays had been repaired and warehouses built. Two new and large clinker-built motorised fishing boats were tied up, white and freshly painted. Remarkably, all the surviving railway buildings which

Bridge between Falcarragh and Cashelnagore. June 1962.   *Author*

Kincasslagh Road, Letterkenny direction. June 1962.   *Author*

The relics of Burtonport station. June 1962.   *Author*

Burtonport station has made an attractive house. June 1962.   *Author*

The siding along Burtonport harbour wall has been retained. June 1962.   *Author*

Burtonport. The railway has gone but fishing has returned. June 1962.   *Author*

The Atlantic shore's well-protected anchorage, Burtonport. June 1962.   *Author*

The surviving vehicle at Burtonport is a useful trolley. June 1962.   *Author*

were there in 1939, remained untouched as if a Preservation Order had been placed upon them. Clearly, most of the boats and men were out at sea for there was a number of parked cars, each suggestive that there was money to be made hereabouts.

A hint of former days was a robust railway line which stretched the length of the old station and along the shore. Along this a well-used trolley was being employed. Altogether it was a place of prosperity enjoying a lease of new life. Dorothy and I wandered up into the village, thinking there might be some reminder of the cottage that had housed me all those years ago. It was useless, except that I realised how very small the place was and how in this present narrative I have not set out some of the happenings of that occasion. It is better thus.

We all sat on the side of the slipway and discussed the day's events. We must leave Arnold's in the morning and once again I was aware of the hold the Irish west coast had taken of me. If this was the proverbial 'Congested District', it certainly had the power to cast a spell, railway or no!

On 16th June, 1962 we left Dunfanaghy with great regret; the Lough Swilly Hotel at Buncrana had done us a great favour! Our next port of call would be Strabane where there was a number of CDRJC survivors which had been retained for shipment to the USA to join the private Cox Collection there. We thought that a journey to see them before they left Ireland was prudent. (In retrospect, it is worth noting that, for reasons which escape me, they never left Ireland.)

The abandoned station precincts at Strabane were a curious sight; the items reserved for Dr Cox had been left in an otherwise-empty set of sidings somewhat as a small child leaves his toys scattered on the nursery floor when summoned to tea. There was a considerable number of coaches which hinted that Dr Cox intended to operate a passenger service. Apparently all the locomotives were not here, but I eventually listed MEENGLAS (Strabane), COLUMBKILLE (Stranorlar carriage shed), ERNE (Letterkenny). As there was only one locomotive here and the lads were not as curious as I was about carriage matters, we moved a few miles south along the GNRI line to Victoria Bridge station. In former days, this had been the exchange point for the Castlederg & Victoria Bridge Tramway (C&VBT), a lesser-known 3 ft gauge system connecting the places in the title. We did not expect to find much of historical interest here but took the Land-Rover along a road where formerly the tramway had run at its side.

The station sign still read - correctly - 'Victoria Bridge Change for Castlederg' and there survived a narrow gauge platform and a corrugated-iron transfer shed for goods. There was little else to stir the imagination. Candidly, none of us knew much more about the tramway except that it had closed in 1933 and its rolling stock was sold either to the Clogher Valley Railway, as garden sheds or broken up. We pursued the roadside course with a grim determination that there would be nothing to see after 30 years. In any case, we did not know what we might be looking for; the C&VBT had not been a prime seller on the railway bookshelves and I had not done my usual 'homework' before we left on holiday.

Along the road one had to use imagination to pick out where the rails had lain. Obviously there were several stretches where it had been necessary to raise the track considerably above road level to reduce some extreme gradients but generally the route was free of hills and curves. There had been three intermediate stopping places in seven-odd miles between the termini, correctly 'tram stops' (Fyfin, Crew, Spamount). Castlederg had been the hub of the tramway, an agricultural centre once suffering greatly in the famine years of the late 1840s. Victoria Bridge had had little traffic to offer save that it was the nearest transhipment point for the GNRI.

We could pick out the sites of the three stopping places for even after much road improvement, there had been much noticeable widening there. The tramway had entered - more correctly quitted - Castlederg in clandestine fashion through a gateway at the streetside in the town. Here, the tramway's imposing brick station headquarters were easily distinguisable and made the visit worthwhile. The style of the buildings was exactly in the pattern of the Clogher Valley Tramway which I had visited in 1939 (*see p. 19*).

On our return to Victoria Bridge we espied a small goods shed with a platform beside the line at Crew. Altogether we had not learned very much but there was the satisfaction of having been there! After a night in Ballycastle, the next day we followed the former Ballycastle Railway route (3 ft gauge) up to Ballymoney on the NCC line from Belfast to Londonderry with its small stations at Dervock, Stranocum Armoy and Capecastle. The line was without a passing loop at these places. It was good to find that two of the original Ballymena, Cushendall & Red Bay Railway coaches Nos. 16 and 21 had survived on their bogies at Ballycastle as camping vehicles. These were unusual; fitted with Fox's Patent Pressed Steel Underframes dated Leeds Forge 1894. These bogies had spoked wheels, outside frames with coil and transverse leaf springs. The coaches were 40 ft 3 in. long on 4 ft 10 in. wheelbase bogies; they were 6 ft 4 in. wide. For me at least, these rare vehicles were worth anything else we had seen on the holiday! Regrettably, the original saloon-style interiors had been lost in the conversion.

The last day of the holiday involved going back to Heysham on the Belfast sailing, so we incorporated the Belfast Transport Museum on the way. As this is still open on a new site, I feel it is not an appropriate diversion for this Saga! One that is, is the discovery we made that Northern Ireland holiday-makers will not enjoy themselves if their doctor does not allow them to eat 'rasher and egg'. We were offered this fare at every meal in fact, I was sorry I did not keep a numerical record. In this and every other respect, the trip was a success, even to the unfortunate sojourn at Buncrana ...

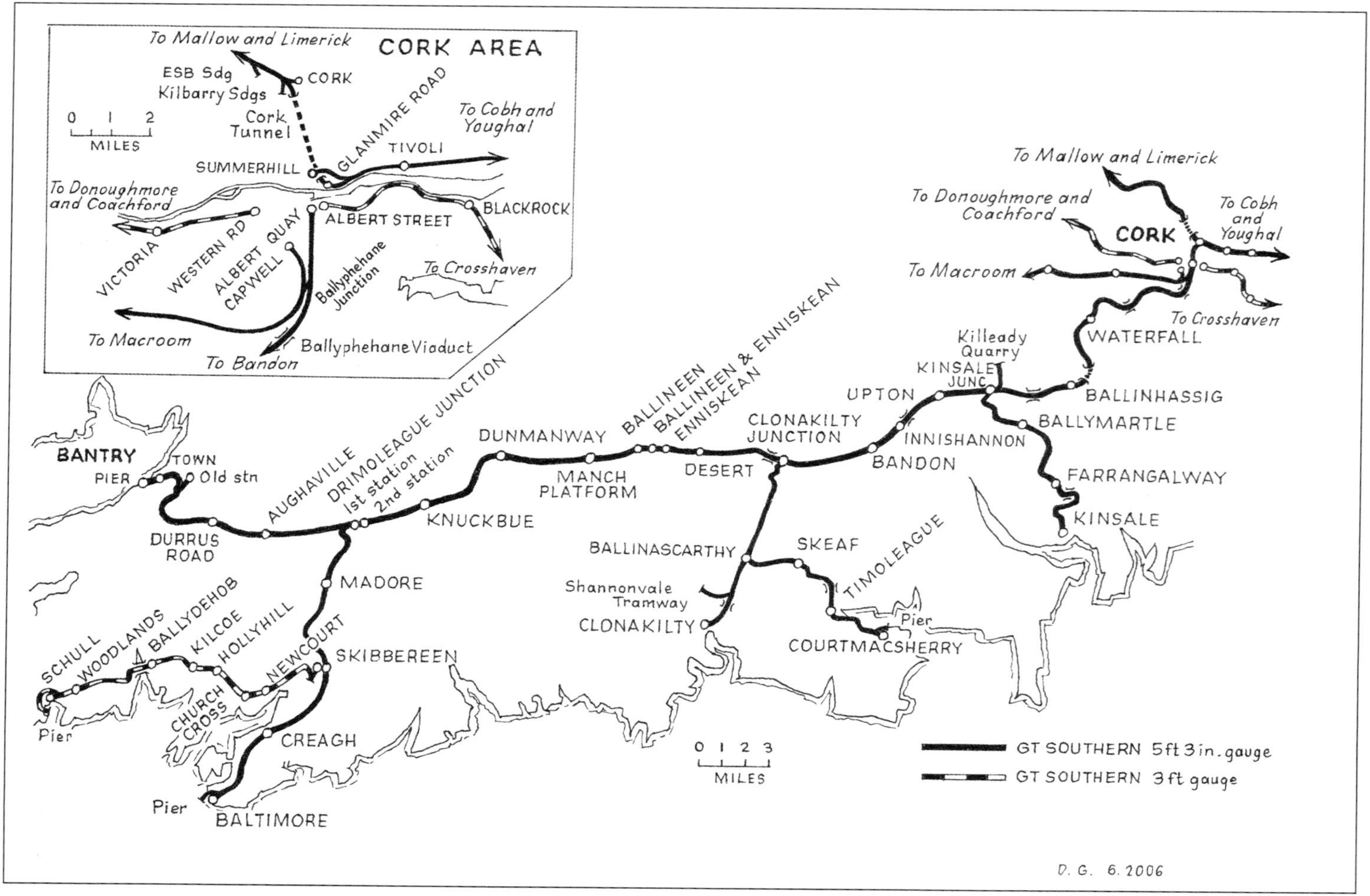

GT SOUTHERN 5ft 3in. gauge
GT SOUTHERN 3ft gauge

D. G. 6. 2006

CORK

To Mallow and Limerick
To Cobh and Youghal
To Crosshaven
To Donoughmore and Coachford
To Macroom

WATERFALL
BALLINHASSIG
BALLYMARTLE
FARRANGALWAY
KINSALE
Killeady Quarry
KINSALE JUNC.
UPTON
INNISHANNON
BANDON
CLONAKILTY JUNCTION
SKEAF
TIMOLEAGUE
Pier
COURTMACSHERRY
DESERT
BALLINEEN & ENNISKEAN
DUNMANWAY
MANCH PLATFORM
BALLINASCARTHY
Shannonvale Tramway
CLONAKILTY
KNUCKBUE
DRIMOLEAGUE JUNCTION
AUGHAVILLE
1st station
2nd station
MADORE
SKIBBEREEN
NEWCOURT
HOLLYHILL
KILCOE
CHURCH CROSS
BALLYDEHOB
WOODLANDS
SCHULL
Pier
CREAGH
BALTIMORE
Pier
Pier

0 1 2 3
MILES

BANTRY
PIER
TOWN
Old stn
DURRUS ROAD

CORK AREA

To Cobh and Youghal
BLACKROCK
TIVOLI
GLANMIRE ROAD
To Crosshaven
CORK
ALBERT STREET
Ballyphehane Junction
Ballyphehane Viaduct
To Bandon
DRIMOLEAGUE JUNCTION
To Mallow and Limerick
ESB Sdg
Kilbarry Sdgs
SUMMERHILL
Cork Tunnel
ALBERT QUAY
CAPWELL
WESTERN RD
VICTORIA
To Macroom
To Donoughmore and Coachford

0 1 2
MILES

Chapter Ten

A Long Walk in West Cork, The Schull & Skibbereen Railway, April 1953

Like many others in the late 1940s and early 1950s, I viewed with dismay the shrinking railway map as systems which were deemed to be uneconomic were ruthlessly abandoned and torn up. Like them also, I learned of the fast pace of such policies and wondered if I should ever enjoy the privilege of a personal visit and whether it would become a race against the calendar and disappearance at the hands of the men with the bulldozer. It was quite impossible to contemplate even the most modest of strategies and the best solution was to list a limited number of places which could be reached before it was too late. As my interest in Irish lines was uppermost, they took priority but had the disadvantage of being further from home and would therefore require extra travelling time and involve added expense.

At this time our Manchester business was going through one of its difficult phases and passing out of the post-war problem of rationing to one of more generous supply, if only one could trace adequate sources. In the immediate period to this, it was comparatively easy to tell our customers what quantity we could allow them and trust our own suppliers would not let us down. It was also possible to sneak a long weekends absence from the works!

My personal list of chosen Irish railway destinations included those which could be readily reached by extending a visit to the premises of those customers who were nearest the railway, so killing two birds with one stone. A number of them must have wondered why they were especially favoured! Of course, these times did not last and having covered my Irish list I was left with what remained at a time when this useful ploy had quite evaporated. What had survived?

The 3 ft gauge railways which were accessible by train and on foot from Belfast were visited by extending my regular business calls over a weekend but my sights were set especially on the still-extant Schull & Skibbereen (S&S) section of Coras Iompair Eirann (CIE) which, if 'the grape vine' was reliable and although seeing its last train in January 1947 had since that event lain dormant, its track and equipment mouldering. The need to visit West Cork was imperative but it was April 1953 before an opportunity came to take ship (the term 'ferry' had not yet come into use) for Dublin, the train thence to Cork and, by changing railways in Cork which by then had lost its passenger trains across the River Lee into West Cork, using the former Cork, Bandon & South Coast Railway (CBSCR) section to Skibbereen. It would require a night on the boat, and all the following day on the 5 ft 3 in. gauge lines to reach my destination.

The journey was made more difficult as the Irish railways were then suffering a most acute fuel shortage and CIE trains had been cut to the minimum. There was a train from Dublin to Cork with connection off the boat, but the CBSCR section had but one train, Cork-Baltimore-Bantry, daily (not Sundays). Skibbereen was on the Baltimore line and the daily train left Cork at 4.30 pm, being the same train which had arrived from Bantry the same morning. I had several hours to

Cork Albert Quay station showing level crossing onto river bridge in foreground. August 1969.

Author

Albert Quay station. The train shed. August 1969.

Author

wait in Cork city so I decided to arrange to meet my good friend Walter McGrath and spend the time until 4.30 pm in his informative company.

To avoid absence from work it would be essential to catch the 10.15 pm Holyhead train from Manchester Exchange (or what was left of that station after the Manchester blitz) on a Friday night. I should then be in Skibbereen in the evening of the following day. I proposed to walk the length of the S&S line and spend the night in Schull, hiring a car there on Sunday morning to take me to Bantry where the early morning once-daily train would return me to Cork and hence to Dublin. My contacts in the International Hockey world gave a good lead to accommodation in Schull where the Misses Symes would look after me and arrange the critical link with the hire car, for it would be impossible to leave Schull on a Sunday otherwise unless on foot or by bicycle.

The Bantry visit would enable me to ride the Bantry-Drimoleague section of the CBSCR and also explore Bantry's original, now abandoned, terminus there. All the foregoing would seem to make the most of the lucky opportunity and considerable expense!

I met Walter at his favourite hotel in Cork for a late lunch; he was on intimate terms with everyone, being editor of the *Cork Evening Echo*. He told me he planned to travel on the train with me as far as Enniskeen & Ballineen station so we should have a longer time together. He would then leave me to catch the Skibbereen-Cork bus which would return him to Cork at a late hour. (Many weeks later he confessed he had missed the bus, and walked many miles along the roadside before being picked up by a van in the small hours. (Owing to the petrol crisis he was fortunate indeed.)

The 4.30 pm train for Skibbereen had a generous selection of vintage CBSCR bogie and six-wheeled carriages. Being the only train it was carrying much mail and baggage so that station stops were prolonged. Our engine was one of the Beyer, Peacock CBSCR 4-6-0 tank engines which made heavy weather up the long drag out of the city. Walter explained every inch of the way as, not being a car owner, he knew the route well. In due course he left the train. Little did he know how long it was to be before he saw his bed that night!

The West End Hotel in Skibbereen was of that basic commercial variety found all over Ireland, and adjacent to the CBSC and S&S stations. I had little inclination to look around as it was almost dark when I arrived. It was a relief that in the morning I should need to waste no time in finding my way to my objective.

Breakfast was served 'en famille' at a large communal table with the proprietor, his matriachal mother, any quests ranged around. 'Herself' sat at the table head behind a large tea urn, from which she dispensed. The other guests were all known to her being regular visitors and though they talked together they ignored me. I hurried through my meal and so out with rucksack and camera; it was a beautiful morning for my walk of almost 16 miles, assuming I did not leave the railway track at any point! The main line station was deserted; the platform had lost its overnight stabling of the Baltimore train, which had left earlier for that place as an Empty Stock working. It would then run as a Mixed Train Baltimore-Drimoleague to make connection with the daily Bantry-Cork train which left Bantry at 8.30 am, to which the stock would be attached. The engine for this unusual schedule was stabled each night at Skibbereen, almost

A Drimoleague-Baltimore mixed train at Skibbereen.   *Author*

No. 6s was the last engine to work on the Schull & Skibbereen Railway, it stands forlorn outside Skibbereen shed. 1953.   *Author*

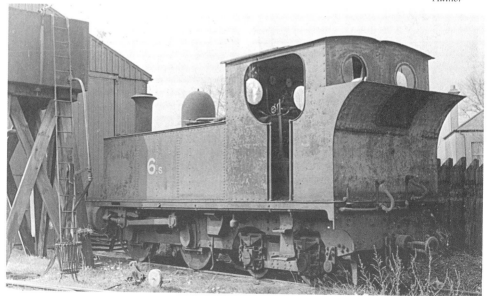

under the large overhead water tank which had done duty as an 'engine shed' ever since the small shed at Baltimore had been abandoned.

In the S&S side of the station stood rows of forlorn rolling stock, as if abandoned when the final whistle blew. The scene reminded me of that at Portmadoc Harbour where, as here, grass grew from roofs and much was obscured by growing vegetation. Hearing sounds within the building, I decided to make myself known before going further. The station master, for it was he, greeted me warmly. No one had ever called with the same mission as mine, and he clearly had the time to talk.

West Cork at that time was a very depressed area and enjoyed few visitors; the tourist trade as later encouraged was unknown and I was considered to be something of a curiosity. The standard greeting was always courteous but included the initial phrase 'Wer yar fram' (Where are you from?) but seldom, 'Where are you going?' I must have been so addressed by everyone that day without exception. I showed the station master my railway ticket and said I hoped he did not want to collect it as it would be a nice souvenir. He expanded when I told him how long I had been coming to Ireland and he made reference to MANCHESTER on my ticket. 'I always buy my ties from Manchester ' he said, flicking out a rather dog-eared tie end from his waist coat. I added that my wife used to work for the firm on the label, Tootal, which was further along the same street as our works. 'They are good value for a shilling'. I agreed - it was a small world.

Our conversation continued and I was fearful the morning would be over before my quest had begun. I began my farewells but he protested, 'I must give you a souvenir from the tram' he said and disappeared, returning with a battered length of tube to which a length of heavy chain was attached, on the end of which was a monstrous key. It was all a very home-made affair and had been used many times as a blunt instrument. 'You will know what it is; it won't be needed again. You must have it.' It was the Single Line Token and the key for the Ticket Box for the Section 'Skibbereen-Ballydehob'. I accepted the battered object with due reverence but was dismayed by the added weight I should have to carry!

I was encouraged by the sight of the river on my left but further along the road rose above it as moved south towards the sea at Baltimore. The road continued westwards until it reached Church Cross and began a long climb. The tramway track looked in good shape and capable of much further use. The rails especially were but little worn on the head and I noted their ex-GNRI origin. Rumour was that the track was going to the Irish Turf Board for use on its bogs in the Irish Midlands. The sleepers, too, were largely in good condition; a few were rotting around the rail fastenings but it had been a very dry winter and many were starved of the creosote they had not seen in recent years and reminded me of the parable of the Dry Bones they were so white! There was, however, an almost complete absence of ballast and when the occasional car went by, everywhere was clouded in dust due to the sparse amount of tarmac applied. The side roads were quite untreated.

The countryside had lost some of its charm hereabouts but cheered up beyond Church Cross where I could see the river estuary to the south, islands, church and a ruined castle, Hollyhill station came next; it had a basic station building and the remains of a poster announcing the cessation of the train

Schull & Skibbereen Railway carriages Nos. 6s and 7s, and a number of cattle wagons stand at Skibbereen station.   *Author*

Kilcoe Halt and crossing keeper's hut in 1954. The track had been lifted six months previously.   *Author*

service. There were the beginnings of attractive mountain views ahead and for the first time the tramway left the roadside and swung into rocky and hummocky ground to the right. It rejoined the road some way down a long hill and crossed a river and made a very steep climb to Kilcoe station. The extreme gradient fascinated me. The wonderful views over Roaring Water Bay compelled me to stop and sit on a wall for this again was the Ireland which I had envisaged, remote, rough, windswept and little known to the Englishman. At that time I was largely ignorant of the Great Famine which had swept this part of West Cork in the late 1840s and of how much the country might tell. It was as well; I had a long way to go and time was pressing on. Again there was a bare concrete platform beside the road with a small corrugated iron waiting shed thereon. This was Kilcoe and, here again, there was scant evidence as to where the tramway sourced any passenger traffic.

Once again the the tramway and road parted company and I was obliged to follow the rails down a steep and winding fall to Crooked bridge, where they crossed the river. There was a water tank beside the bridge, water being pumped up from below for locomotive purposes. The supporting pillars of the tank were contrived into a rough shed to conceal a hand pump with an oversize operating wheel. Beyond the bridge the track climbed steeply to restore it to the level of the roadway again; I could picture the labouring engine as it pounded up the curves here, filling the quiet countryside with sound and the air with smoke! There was a Board of Works cottage here beside a level crossing, the first such house I had seen. It was clearly occupied and I was tempted to knock on the door to speak to someone, but once again I resisted as I knew that I was falling behind on my schedule. As road and rail came together, the tramway had to occupy a deep and curved cutting to reach the roadside.

At the top of the hill the road stretched ahead of me; I could see its course a long way ahead. The mountains beyond this viewpoint beckoned me forward and I enjoyed the long steady fall towards Ballydehob which was below me and still out of sight. A car drew up beside me and the expected opening came out, 'Where are ye from?' And then another, 'We can fit you in'. The car was packed with impedimenta, crates, bundles and the like. Overall, there was the strongest of bovine smells within. I thanked them but it was an effort to persuade them that I was walking for the pleasure of seeing the countryside. They had possibly never heard that before. I realised that I had walked nearly nine miles from Skibbereen and this was the first vehicle to stop; perhaps my refusal to accept a lift was ill-considered!

I did not regret my decision, following this delightful route. Another BOW lineside cottage marked a level crossing where the rails suddenly crossed the road to its south side to plunge out of sight towards a charming creek which, as I drew nearer, became a considerable river estuary. The large village of Ballydehob rose up the hillside on the far shore. The rails followed a precipitous course above the water, clinging sinuously to the hillside. Along this stretch, for the first time, the route had succombed to the mild climate and in places the jungle was taking over. Years afterwards I read in the Working Timetable that in locations such as this there was an 8 mph speed restriction. I estimated that the railway was falling at 1 in 25; there must have been quite a cloud of smoke from the hot brake blocks.

The station itself stretched out from the foot of the hillside and from here the line assumed a level course. On way down to it one could see it was laid out on a high embankment leading high and above the estuary. The tide was clearly out and there were vast areas of mud flats leading out of sight towards the open sea. It was all laid out like a model railway on a table top. Beyond the station the various tracks converged into a single line heading to the top of a stone-built viaduct of many arches and, after the somewhat monotonous walk along the roadside, the varied scene filled me with delight; the sea, the little harbour, the woodland and the mountain background with its Paul Henry-painting hues were completely to my taste. And the station too offered further discoveries.

It was soon obvious that the station itself was something of an anti-climax. Disappointingly, it had been cleared of everything and when the last train had left, it had taken every remaining vehicle with it whereas I had nursed the hope that, as at Skibbereen, further stock might have been stored these last months. Worse, I realised then that if the clean-up was as thorough as it now appeared to be, the chances of finding anything on the rails at Schull were slim. And so it proved to be!

The place was a workmanlike establishment. No frills. As at Skibbereen all the points were operated by ground levers. The buildings were quite empty - no chance of finding the odd souvenir in the form of a printed waybill or wagon label! Whoever had cleaned up had made a first class job, you could have eaten off the floors. I suspected that the last person in charge (who lived in a small house nearby) had been told by his wife to leave the premises spotless. There was still an uncanny feeling about - a sunny Saturday afternoon, no one to be seen and the low moan of the wind on this elevated site, plus the sound of a trickle of water overflowing from the loco water tank on the platform. It was almost reassuring to see a few people about on the road below.

I completed my notes sitting on the platform edge eating chocolate. Why was it that Irish chocolate tasted so much better? The tea and Guinness were the same …

The map told me that over the viaduct the railway climbed the hill to the south-west and rejoined the road further on. I decided that this would save me about half a mile and I could explore the viaduct and quay before tackling the steep village street; I thought I would be able follow the railway's progress by eye from the road until it met up with me again. (How wrong I was. It was several years before I learned what I had missed!)

Down on the quay a man told me that the former station master lived at the first bar on the right up the street. I set off in high hopes but 'Himself is away just' I was informed and not wishing to wait, I continued up the steep hill. For the first time, my rucksack felt heavier! At the top of the rise I realised that on my left there was a hill which obscured the view I had expected of the tramway coming towards me, and it was some way along the road that I discerned it on a low embankment carrying it diagonally across an adjacent meadow. The embankment was much obscured by boscage but the route of the line reaching this point showed that there must have been some severe curves and impressive climbing in the meantime. I somewhat regretted the short cut I had chosen through the village.

The railway joined the road to my left by a noticeably fierce climb, followed by a road crossing at an acute angle which, coming together, must have made for tricky control. The geography of the site would have prevented the existence of crossing gates and there was no evidence of a former crossing keeper's cottage. Again, I was seeing evidence of the operating skills of the trainmen involved. With the tramway to my right now, I set off for Schull with slightly depleted energy. At the top of the next rise I could see the 'white bones' of the track up to a point where they suddenly disappeared to the south; I assumed they made a bee-line for Schull Bay from here. But the view ahead - mountains and hills excepted - was of the railway and road passing through an extremely dreary piece of country. To the right was an extensive bog bordered by scrub-covered hillocks. To the left some low hills prevented any view of the coast beyond. I knew that there was a Halt somewhere along here and my curiosity to see it quickened my steps.

When I reached it my surprise was heightened. It was merely a nameboard alongside an iron gate. Of any kind of habitation there was nothing. Strange that the title had survived. How did the driver pick it out in the dark, or perhaps it was seldom used? (Later I learned that it was often used between here and Schull, but as a Mancunian this fact seemed unbelieveable to me. I had much to learn about Ireland.)

I was photographing this simple subject when a car drew up. It was a rather better-looking vehicle than any of the few I had seen earlier, well cared-for and clean by local standards. 'Can we be of help?' a lady's voice enquired. I replied, 'Yes please. Can you tell me why this abandoned railway station is named Woodlands as there is hardly a tree in sight?' The lady seemed a little perplexed by my question. Now having a moment to take in the situation I realised that I must have been an object of curiosity standing in the road with a camera.

It seemed that the car contained four nuns and mountains of luggage. They had been 'up in town' and were returning to Schull, and were obviously excited to find me. I was politely questioned and when I told them I had come from England specially to visit West Cork and the tramway, their interest sharpened. This encounter would be the talking-point of their day. The youngest of the four was at the wheel but it was an elderly member in the passenger seat who did most of the talking and I gather owned the car. The Mother Superior had given them leave 'to go to Skibbereen for the messages' (the local term for 'shopping') and they were literally bubbling like girls out from Boarding School. They insisted that I joined them in the car ... they would drop me close by Grove House ... their Convent was near Schull station, etc.

I saw little of the tramway route until I begged to be put out when road and railway reached the edge of Schull Bay, as I had to carry several of their impedimenta and my rucksack on my knee. To judge from the cardboard boxes they had called at Skibbereen Cathedral (RC) to collect candles and the like. They would not drive away until I had given them my complete itinerary for the rest of my stay in Ireland. I think I was forgiven for spending the night at a Protestant household in Schull as I had told them of my links with the *Cork Examiner*. We parted in excellent spirits; I was quite exhausted.

Schull Bay was at its most attractive in the early evening sun over the sea southwards towards its many islands, terminating in Clear Island. I determined that, even without the railway location, I must come again! The cliffs round this large bay were not as high as I had expected but their setting was superb. There were several large local fishing boats at anchor, bearing their licence number prefixed by 'S'. The tide was high and the waves came ashore on the small strands which lay between the sea and the road. To the south-east I picked out the chimneys of several abandoned mines on the hill top while some of islands clearly had houses on them, presumably connected to the mainland by boats serving Schull pier which I could pick out further west along the bay.

I walked beside the track where it lay between the road and the shore. On coming to Schull station, it forked. To the left it passed through a gate and entered the station precincts; to the right it crossed the road on the level and, after continuing on the right-hand verge for a short distance, terminated in a substantial concrete stop block. Exploring the station first I found it was quite the most impressive on the system, being mostly given over to the station master's residence. Washing ballooned out from a line over the platform and the now empty carriage shed alongside was draped with further drying garments in the manner military banners are hung in the nave in Manchester Cathedral. They made a brave sight.

Beside the platform a wooden stage and shed had served for goods purposes but had also succumbed to the pressures of domestic needs, so I went eagerly to the turntable and engine shed, the latter set unusually at right angles to

Schull terminus, engine shed and goods shed, showing the protective sea wall. 1953.   *Author*

everything else. The shed door was securely locked but visible within through its many unbroken windows. As at Ballydehob, the place had been swept clean. It was something of an anti-climax.

I set off from the station towards the stop block where the rails had come to an end on the roadside opposite its frontage, feeling that the best was probably over. I judged there was less than half a mile to the pier where the S&S ended. The curious manner in which the track disappeared before the railway reached its destination was puzzling me.

Shortly beyond the stop block, the tramway had crossed the road - the rails were still in place under the gravel and presumably there were crossing gates at some date - and continued downwards along rough open ground to the edge of a stony strand. For protection, the tramway site was walled in as it took up a sharp bend which carried it openly onto a substantial stone-built jetty. This was clearly the shipping point on which the connection to the many islands, some inhabited, was centred, as evidenced by the many domestic items lying around, along with farm equipment. All these gave me fresh insight on the former importance of this extension from the station. Of the track along the pier there was little trace and I assumed it had become disused before the tramway had closed.

By good fortune, a man leaning against a stack of fish barrels nearby, and as surprised to see me as I was of him, told me the railway down to the pier had been purchased by the Schull station master, and had been lifted and the material sold. It had all taken place when the line to Skibbereen had been abandoned. He could remember an occasional engine hauling fish vans along the pier but the catch had been carried by road direct to Cork for a long time now. His strong accent made it difficult to understand him and feeling I had made the best of a long day, I set off to walk to Grove House, my brain full of aspects of the day, my notebook of hastily scribbled notes and my camera of precious exposures. It was to be 1956 before a legacy of £100 from an executor of my Aunt Mabel (who, in fact, was still very much alive), persuaded her that as my young family was hoping to go on holiday to Ireland with me, a partial execution of her Will would be of enormous benefit ... etc., etc. In this way, much of the August 1956 saw me back at Grove House again and in those days when inflation was low, the legacy comfortably covered all our expenses! Furthermore, several useful personal contacts answered some of the questions riased during my walk. Luckily we had the use of our new Land-Rover - then a rare sight in Ireland - and could roam the Tramway from end to end. It was a disappointment, however, to find some uncharacteristic urgency had caused the thorough disappearance of the track and rolling stock in the meantime. This was due to the dire shortage of fuel in the country and the urgent need to develop the turf bogs to supply the power stations. Additional railways on the bogs were part of the enterprise and the S&S system was an obvious target.

As for the mystery of the Schull Pier Extension, the astute Schull station master had ascertained that it formed a separate undertaking from the main system, and that an offer for its materials might be accepted by CIE. It was. His daughter now enjoys recalling the affair.

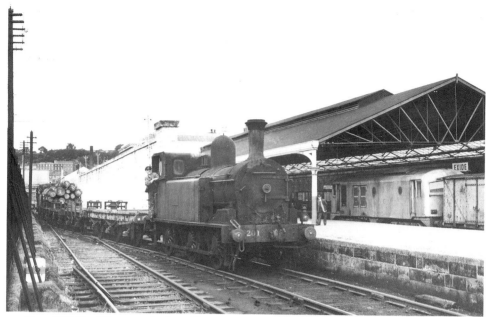

Class 'J11' No. 201 on a train from Glanmire leaving Cork City Railway to enter Albert Quay station. May 1960.　　　　　　　　　　　　　　　　　　　　　　　　*Author*

Class 'B4' 4-6-0T No. 465 carriage shunting at Glanmire. July 1963.　　　　　*Author*

Chapter Eleven

Political Intrigue in Bantry,
The Cork, Bandon & South Coast Railway, April 1953

To make the most of the opportunity to be in West Cork, my ambition was to combine the walk along the Schull & Skibbereen line with a journey over the ex-Cork, Bandon & South Coast Railway section of the former Great Southern Railways of Ireland The missing portion of this plan was the Bantry - Drimoleague length, i.e. that part of the main line between Cork and Bantry which I had not covered on my journey to Skibbereen two days previously, interesting in itself as being not opened until July 1881, four years after the original line had reached Skibbereen (the town which is always considered to be the 'capital' of West Cork). This meant that by ending my walk at Schull on a Saturday evening, I should have to travel north between Schull Bay and Bantry Bay on a Sunday in order to catch the once-daily train from Bantry to Cork the next morning. Luckily my kind hostesses at Grove House were influential in hiring a car to take me between Schull and Bantry after hearing about my idea of hiring a bicycle for the 14 mile interval.

I had done a certain amount of homework in preparation for the CBSC line. In those days each May issue of the *Railway Magazine* was devoted to Irish subjects and I was particularly intrigued to learn of the background to the amended route of the Bantry branch which had originally terminated at an isolated terminus some distance above the town; this arrangement did not reach the harbour with its potential for the fishing trade and a lucrative tourist business by means of the newly-formed Bantry Bay Steamship Company. There was obviously much to unearth about Bantry which the brief article in the Magazine did not disclose; it should keep me fully occupied on the Sunday! I would investigate the original station first and then carry on along the newer 1½ mile which had opened on 7th May, 1893 as the Bantry Bay Extension Railway. Half its cost was paid for by the Government, which included a new pier beyond Bantry station.

It was another beautiful morning and the driver of my car was extolling the wonderful view of Bantry Bay and the distant Caha Mountains beyond as the car came down the hill towards the town. He was taken aback when I interrupted him in full flow and said that I wished to be carried no further, preferring to alight and walk the rest of the way. I had some difficulty insisting that I realised there was some distance to go before we reached the town, but guessed that the best way to find the original station would be up a wooded escarpment which climbed steeply eastward from the side of the road. I thought that the less I said about this unorthodox route the better involving, as it must, some trespassing through the private Bantry House Estates.

I must have looked hot and fairly dishevelled when, after giving the House itself a wide berth and so surmounting the escarpment, I left the wood and came to a large pleasant clearing. I paused to brush myself down and absorb the scene. Below me was a long, narrow and attractive stone building, fronted by a long terrace also faced with stone. Surrounding all was a well-manicured grass

Clonakilty Junction, looking east. August 1951.   *Author*

A Sunday excursion to Courtmacsherry entering Clonakilty Junction with No. 463. August 1954.
                                                                                   Author

lawn. To find such a well-tended property in Ireland was not common and it was a moment or two before I realised I was looking at the former terminus station which had been abandoned since 1893, the impressive building with platform and the area of the tracks.

I was caught unawares by the voice and presence of a girl aged about nine. 'Hello', she said brightly, 'I expect you have come to see my Daddy', as if she had been expecting me. I tried to display a similar composure and she led me along the converted platform into the house to meet Paddy O'Keefe who, from local lore, was clearly 'Mr Bantry'.

It would take too long to describe how we spent the next two hours, talking and listening intently but I took tea on the terrace and promised to return for supper after I had walked the Extension Railway and booked some accommodation in the town.

The Extension forked left from the old course prior to the old station and took a great swathing, contoured clockwise curve following the hillside above the town, dropping 74 ft as it did so. The old station had been reached by a steep access road. The line had terminated abruptly just beyond the platform end and alongside a small engine shed whose remains had been put to domestic use. The whole site was on raised ground with steep sides and later Paddy told me how a passenger train had failed to stop and ploughed through the buffer stop to plunge down the slope. He enlarged the story by maintaining that Charles Parnell, the political activist, and his paramour, were travelling incognito on the train and had be pulled from the crushed carriages. (I had no means of telling whether it was just an example of the 'local Blarney' which pervades West Cork but I have failed to substantiate the date.)

The old station building was a more lavish affair and should have been a simple structure as at Skibbereen, but the contractor thought otherwise! Following abandonment by the railway it had become a Police Barracks and was burnt out during the Civil War. It was then converted into two houses in which two prominent local families lived, the O'Keefes and the Briggs.

On my way from the old station I joined the new Extension. There was a disused siding and platform to a Barytes Mill *en route* and as the line reached the edge of the town (descending at 1 in 80) it crossed the main road to the north by a plate girder bridge. It passed behind the Parish Church and, coming down to street level now, flanked the north side of the market square to enter a single platformed station on the edge of the harbour. Beyond a long platform the running line extended onto a wooden, three-span jetty, sufficient to berth a ship on each of its three sides. There were also extensive sidings in the market square and a single road engine shed containing 4-4-2T No. 31; I suspected this engine worked the Bantry-Drimoleague-Baltimore services: on the Skibbereen-Baltimore section (the Baltimore Extension Railway) the heaviest CBSCR 4-6-0 tank engines were not permitted.

All the signalling was supplied by the Railway Signal Co. of Fazakerley, Liverpool and the neat little signal box was sited so that the frame was 'athwart-ships' to the running lines. As common on the CBSCR, there was a turntable - it seems that this company, which had no tender engines, had a dislike to running its tank engines bunker first.

Home signals at Dunmanway. June 1960.   *Author*

Drimoleague, looking west. August 1956. *Author*

Baltimore, looking out to sea. August 1954. *Author*

Baltimore from the buffer stops with class 'F6' 2-4-2T No. 34. August 1954.   *Author*

Baltimore: the 2.10 pm for Skibbereen. 19th August, 1954.   *Author*

The arrangement of the piers was unusual and had been created by a simple adding-on construction to accommodate the Admiralty which had funded the work.

Anxious to secure a bed for the night, I went a short distance up the street to Vickery's Hotel which was deserted on a late Sunday afternoon. I had to go into the back regions to arouse the hall porter who found me a single room for one night and told me there was no one else staying in the place. I dropped my rucksack in the room, explained that I must catch the early morning train to Cork, and would want a suitable early call and breakfast. I was assured of his attention but neglected to proffer a tip, probably a mistake as it happened. Then I set off unburdened to return to the O'Keefe household and supper in the former refreshment room.

Paddy had had time to consider my visit and was ready to fill me with information. He had strong views about the former CBSCR Company which was 'staffed by firm Church of Ireland adherents' while 'Freemasons had all the plum jobs'. The Bantry station master's house was in this old terminus, so Paddy was his next door neighbour. But its first occupant had been Bill Johnson, the CBSCR locomotive superintendent. No wonder Paddy was so well informed!

Of other matters on which he had much to say was the Schull & Skibbereen; Harry Jack, an Englishman, cut up the early engines which had stood disused in Skibbereen yard for a long time. Some years afterwards I made enquiries for the whereabouts of Jack, to no avail. Also discussed were the strange events concerning the Achill Branch of the former Midland & Great Western Railway, notable in that its first and last trains had conveyed the coffins of local people who died in tragic circumstances away from home - moreover that these events had been forecast years previously!

Bantry shipping was very important to his business as a merchant with a large warehouse in the town; he detailed the competition given to all railways in south-west Ireland by the Clyde Steamship Co. which called at all the small harbours of Co. Cork and Kerry with utmost regularity, once a week, notably the VALENTIA. There were three steamers in the Bantry Bay Steamship Co. The company had strong commercial links with the CBSCR. It was the practice for cargo boats to load maize at Bantry and sail direct to Liverpool for the Corn Exchange.

The evening passed quickly and it was dark when I found my way back to a deserted Vickery's Hotel. Luckily the front door was open but the premises were as deserted as they had been in the afternoon. I lost no time in going to bed.

I must have slept soundly as I heard no morning call. Luckily I was not too late and there were sounds of stirring in the dining room. In due course the same hall porter appeared bearing a boiled egg; I assumed this was all I might expect at such an hour ... the Irish are not given to early rising. After a quick breakfast I was ready to leave. Despite some repeated hammering on the brass bell inside the hotel office window, there was no one to answer and I left hurriedly without paying a bill.

A huge cloud of black smoke hung over the station; No. 31 was in the platform with a short mixed train which had stood there all Sunday. The engine

The original terminus at Bantry showing the platform side. April 1953.   *Author*

Bantry pier extension *c*.1920.   *Vickery, Bantry*

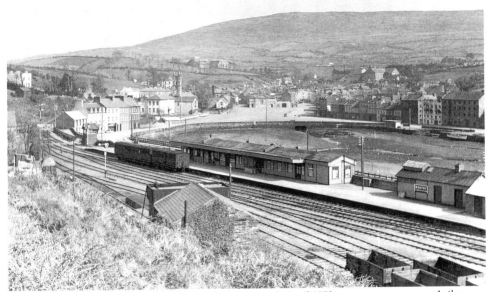

Bantry station, with the engine shed in the foreground. April 1953. *Author*

Sunday in Bantry, not a wheel is turning. August 1954. *Author*

was well loaded with a mixture of poor coal, slack and brickettes - hence the smoke - and the fireman had the blower on full; there was a long pull uphill out of Bantry and we should need plenty of steam. I deduced that an earlier working that morning had provided a Baltimore-Drimoleague connection with my train to Cork, perhaps also using No. 31? I had no copy of the skeleton timetable current in those difficult days and have omitted to enquire since then!

There was little activity on Bantry station and though the train was moderately loaded, the main business seemed to be around the parcels vans. Departure time came and went, seemingly there was no hurry as we were the only train on the line and had no connections to make. It made for a strange atmosphere. Friends in Bantry told me that the service was so scant that unless one was going up to Cork for an hour or so and returning on the afternoon train, the railway had no attraction, people preferring to pool their rationed petrol coupons, overload their cars and reach Cork by road. Anyway, my journey gave no trouble, we did not have to stop for want of steam and I had plenty of time at Cork Glanmire station for bite to eat. At the head end of the 3.15 pm Dublin train were two engines to lift us up the renowned gradient through the Glanmire tunnel; No. 503 (class 'B1') 4-6-0 with No. 20 (class D17) 4-4-0 as pilot. It was worth the weekend to see these two stalwarts!

My Boat Train from Dublin Kingsbridge was hauled by a small ex-Dublin & South Eastern Railway No. 423 (class 'G1') 2-4-0 Tank engine, short enough to be accommodated on the limited Dun Laoghaire Pier line. As it pulled round the stiff curve to the buffers, there was a frightful tearing noise and the end of the first coach was wrenched away. The train stopped suddenly and I got out to find the vacuum brake hose on the engine was supporting much of the woodwork of the end carriage, which dangled helplessly in the air. Obviously the coupling between the engine and train had failed - it was a spectacular finish to my Irish excursion!

* *

During the next half century my family and I came to know south-west Ireland intimately. It is now cynically dubbed the 'Irish Costa Brava', so popular has it become. But in the time described Co. Cork was a depopulated and deprived area.

The railways of West Cork are now but a memory yet in the period before they closed I was able to familiarise myself closely with their fascinating features, and ultimately to drive the steam trains in their melancholy task of lifting the CBSCR main line. That time was a saga in itself, and is recalled in Chapter Nineteen.

Chapter Twelve

The Cavan & Leitrim Railway, A Remote Delight, March 1949

Our Manchester business was keen that I should become familiar with our suppliers and customers to endorse our family continuity. Many of them called regularly at the factory but meeting them on their own ground gave a special insight into the local requirements and an opportunity to familiarise myself with the relations they had with our agents. Such visits involved careful planning as there were times and seasons when visits to customers would be inappropriate and unprofitable - such as Grand National week in Liverpool, Whitsuntide in Manchester or 12th July in Belfast. There were minor limitations too (Wednesdays were always avoided). The time arrived in 1949 when it would be useful to familiarise myself with the Belfast scene, where no one had called since 1937.

The additional possibilities such might offer were not lost on me, but there was no opportunity that year for a trip to the Cavan & Leitrim (C&L) 3 ft gauge section of the former Great Southern Railways (GSR), whose doom seemed close at hand. In the event the useful combined arrangements I had prepared for this had to be postponed for commercial reasons, and instead my wife agreed to spend the long Whitsuntide week-end holiday solely for the purpose of a railway visit; it would be her first acquaintance with Ireland and apart from the risk of a rough sea passage, she relished the idea which involved two days and a night in Ireland flanked each side by a sail from Holyhead to Dun Laoghaire and back. We could leave Manchester on the Thursday evening as Whit Friday was a religious holiday in that city.

Those readers who cannot recall the dreary years during World War II - and after - will not imagine our excitement at going to a country where food rationing was scarcely noticeable, where shop windows displayed items like clothing and footwear not available here without coupons ... my wife had already started a Shopping List such as nylon stockings and shoes for herself (and trousers for me) plus food supplies such as a piece of beef, some Irish butter, sugar etc. Any one of the latter was on ration at home. If word got about that nylon stockings were at so-and-so's shop, Dorothy would jump on her bicycle to reach it before meagre stocks ran out. We were unsure how food would travel in the ship but intended to sit out on a cool deckside seat and hope for the best ... the return voyage would be back in Holyhead before midnight. So we hoped to have prepared for any eventualities. It will be clear that the visit had several other motives besides railways!

In those days there were several routes from Manchester to Dublin. The one chosen by us was that of the old London & North Western Railway. We would take the train from Manchester Exchange to Holyhead (changing if necessary at Chester), the Mail Boat to Dun Laoghaire, and a through train from the Pier station to Westland Row. From there the down Sligo Mail would carry us north-west to Dromod, the place of interchange with the C&L line to Ballinamore ... we could be on the narrow gauge by lunch time, having left Manchester at 10.20

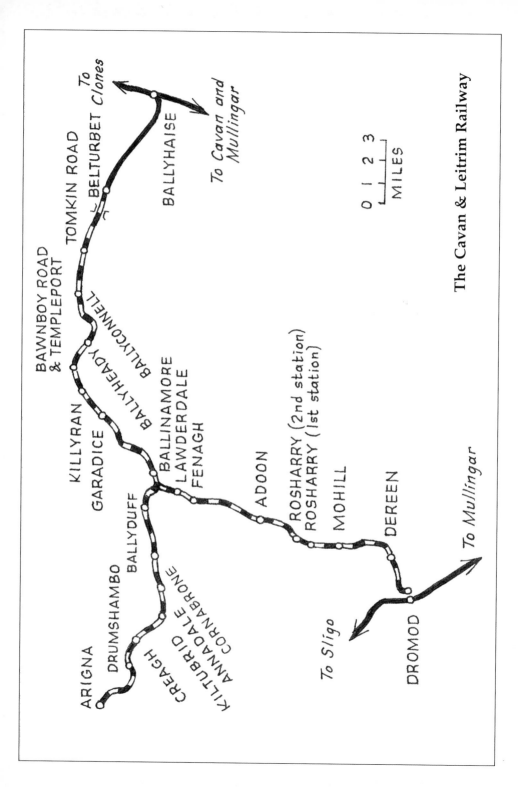

The Cavan & Leitrim Railway

pm. By wartime experiences, this was wonderful. A further bonus was the short sea crossing about three hours compared with five via the Liverpool boat.

The children were left with 'nanny' who stayed at our house for the purpose; we departed on the local electric train for Manchester and walked cross the city to the post-blitz shambles that had been Exchange station. In our rucksacks the contents had been carefully packed to save chaos and time should the Irish customs be enjoying one of their occasional forays and wanted them all out on the tables at 5.30 am. Included in this assortment was the precious store of camera film, a commodity equally unattainable outside Irish cities, maps, measuring tapes, notebooks, toilet paper and the like. We were equally careful not to bring in items which *The Post Office Guide* said were banned in Ireland such as 'contraceptives, Elm Trees...'!

Luckily for us, the Manchester train arrived in Holyhead before The Irish Mail from Euston, and we were able to take a leisurely walk from the train, across the nearby platform and straight onto the gangway of the steamer alongside. There was a fairly merry throng aiming for the adjacent gangway which served the Steerage portion of the ship, but as we were travelling Saloon and held the mandatory Sailing Tickets, we found seats near to a deck opening, free from the fug of the inside saloon. So the first of our problems passed trouble free and we crossed the infamous Irish Sea in good fettle and snatched some sleep in comfort.

We could anticipate the scrum through the Customs at Dun Laoghaire as the London passengers would have joined us together with those from Steerage, but we were not yet knowledgable in Irish matters enough to know that many Irishmen would be returning home at the end of Whit Week. They would be the worse for wear! But the Customs people did not regard us as a profitable target, peered into our rucksacks, scrawled some hieroglyphics on them in green chalk and waved us through. So we passed the second problem point and were learning fast. There was a train of elderly ex-Dublin & South Eastern Railway (DSER) bogie carriages in the sharply-curved platform on the pier; it was newly painted in two-tone CIE livery and to impress, the brass doorhandles had been exchanged for chromium. It was bursting with humanity but I found a seat for Dorothy and went to check our engine which was ex-GSR No. 673, a Bazin-designed Inchicore product of 1933, one of class 'I3' 0-6-2 tanks, built for suburban service. After a confusing 10 minutes a porter came along and locked all the doors ... they certainly intended us to reach Dublin! Then, with a prolonged warning screech of whistles, we lurched forward at 7.35 am. There was no opportunity to gaze out; the compartment was crammed with standing passengers and the atmosphere stiff with second-hand drink, not a good introduction to the South.

Thank goodness the journey to Westland Row is relatively short, being along the edge of Dublin Bay and on the site of the early Dublin & Kingstown Railway which was atmospherically worked. Writing of atmosphere, one of our number managed to open a window and we received fresh draughts of sea air which revived the party a little - a few souls had simply fallen forward in an effort to sleep. Then there was a sudden application of brakes as we approached the terminus. Those standing grabbed the luggage rack but we were all so tightly packed there was no actual damage. After what seemed eternity a man came along and unlocked the door. Probably the driver of No. 673 applied the brakes in this rough manner to assist the platform staff in emptying the train in quick time ...

We had time before the Sligo Down Mail to stand and watch the Dublin scene arrive for business by train. Most trains terminated here, hauled by bustling ex-DSER 2-4-2T or 4-4-2T, coming in from the south, Bray region especially. The station work was very smart. Chromium door handles were much to the fore, but compartment illumination was still largely by gas, and the station reeked of it.

The worst of the coal shortage was over by 1949 and the days when GSR (now CIE) steam engines had to make use of tomato boxes, turf or Arigna coal were over, although train services were still limited. Dublin local trains relied on supplies of South Wales brickettes which were a mixture of coal slack and cement. The train crews were delighted with them. They certainly burned better than the rubbish which was delivered to our house which was a commercial robbery. At Westland Row I asked a fireman if he had experience of Arigna coal. 'Yes. If you put a shovelful of the stuff in the box while you were running, it was immediately lifted off the shovel and up the chimney before it touched the firebars'.

The Sligo train departure was at 9.10 am and we learned we might travel in the Dining Car throughout to Dromod, which was contrary to English practice where passengers had to sit elsewhere unless they were actually eating a meal. The empty stock came in behind ex-Midland & Great Western Railway (M&GWR) 4-4-0 ex-GSR/CIE No. 542 class 'D6' built 1911, an impressive beast to my eyes which amply filled the generous Irish loading guage. The main train consisted of three elderly bogie carriages (including the Dining Car), a six-wheeled guard's parcel van behind the tender and a jamboree of six-wheeled parcels vans at the rear. The aforementioned stock was all in the new CIE two-tone green livery. Our engine was in black and had lost its GSR-fitted Crewe-type number plates in favour of large yellow-painted numerals and the CIE 'Flying Snail' on the tender. I thought the engine and train lived up to my expectations exactly, and the memory of our uncomfortable arrival was quickly effaced!

Up to our departure and afterwards, we were the only people in the Dining Car. The attendant laid up for breakfast and shortly afterwards we left Dublin with an enticing smell of frying bacon and eggs wreathing about us. The attendant placed a large stand of fancy cakes before us and disappeared. It was all too much. As we rumbled slowly above Dublin and round the west side of the GNR Amiens Street station temptation overcame us, and though it was still early morning we began to demolish the cakes. Before breakfast itself was to be seen, they had all disappeared ... obviously the smells which had so entranced us came from the staff cooking their own breakfast.

Beyond Amiens Street we were back on the metals of the former M&GWR main line westwards, once double-tracked but since GSR formation in 1924 had been singled from seven miles out of Dublin. For much of the first part of our journey the railway was to keep very close company with the Royal Canal, on its way to join the River Shannon, together crossing the great Bog of Allen which is such a feature of the Irish Midlands. The city was soon behind us and we rushed through tall hedgerows in the lush green countryside, a green-ness which has no counterpart in England. Then, from the comparative 'English-ness' of the Dubin hinterland, the scene changed gradually to poorer farmlands and farmsteads, so to Mullingar, the important junction where the Sligo line truncates north-westwards from that to Galway and the west. Here some passengers nipped quickly off the train to the refreshment room during the 15 minute stop. The engine took water; we had arrived early. One or two joined us in the Dining Car and, at last, breakfast arrived commencing with porridge then 'the fry', bacon and two eggs. The attendant made no comment as he removed our already empty cake plate; it was probably a deliberate ploy to keep us quiet until Mullingar! We had not had a square meal since leaving home the previous evening.

After Mullingar we ran closely along the shore of Lough Owel for a time; here the water lapped the sleeper ends. The scenery now was bleaker with many miles of turf bog which contained woodland growing in clusters within it. Dorothy commented that 'She was seeing more donkeys and blue bells than ever in her life'. So past the remote Inny Junction, outpost of the erstwhile M&GWR branch to Cavan; here the points were now worked remotely from Multyfarnham. I recalled that this south end of the branch was now closed but we passed at a brisk pace and I failed to take it all in. Looking through the open window I could see that the train was being followed by a tremendous cloud of white dust, no doubt due to the continuing dry weather.

We duly arrived at the county town, Longford, a frontier post so far as the train service was concerned. Our counterpart, the up Morning Mail, was already standing in the station. The engine crews and guard swopped trains, so allowing them to return to their home depots the same day. Not so lucky were the Postal and Dining Car staff. The latter had insufficient time to take stock in the Bar, which must be done for Revenue purposes, and secured by lock and key afterwards. None-the-less the Longford stop was an extended one; I had time to note the signalling arrangements, how like at other stations there was a well-attended garden and the station name board was surmounted by a smaller board showing the mileage (76.22) from the original M&GWR Dublin terminus at Broadstone. I approved of this useful feature!

It was 11 miles from here to Dromod which we reached at 12.19 pm; it had been a journey of great contrasts between the English and Irish landscapes. The latter was much to our liking. The manner in which the train was worked was fascinating. At stations there seemed to be a leisurely stoppage as goods was exchanged between platform trolleys and vans, and the customary green baskets used by the Post Office. I could see the apparatus for exchanging the mail bags at speed, attached to one of the vans, but had no note of where or when it was used. Writing of exchanges, in the case of Single Line Tokens, this was carried out while the train was in the station so there were no 'hairy moments' as on the GNRI! Between stations, the train sped through the countryside and our high-wheeled engine could be glimpsed pounding along as if making up for lost time.

Dromod at last, and prospect of pastures new. We crossed behind our train at a rail-level foot crossing, following a few other passengers who also ignored the footbridge. Expecting the site to be on the same scale as narrow gauge stations elsewhere I had come to know, the size of the place came as a surprise. It lay to the east of the down main line which had long siding parallel to it which served a substantial goods transfer shed; narrow gauge features were all to the east of this. There was nothing diminutive at all; it was simply a well-endowed junction where one side of the business catered for a railway of different gauge. (Tynan had been like this (p. 19) had I had the time to inspect it all!) My impression of the Irish narrow gauge would differ from now on - it was on the scale of the Isle of Man Railway not of the Festiniog or Talyllyn Railways, and clearly the architecture of the brick-built station building here at Dromod (and elsewhere as I would discover) had the same source as the Clogher Valley Railway (CVR). There was an engine shed of stone with 24 ft turntable without, and a large elevated water tank. I learned that Dromod water was unkind to boilers and that the engine shedded here would be regularly sent to Drumshanbo where the water cleared out the ill effects. There had been a carriage shed. A six-lever ground frame was near the yard throat. The platform had a lengthy run-round loop on which stood our train for Ballinamore led by No. 12C, a balcony-ended bogie coach, over a dozen vans and a small passenger brake van in the rear. One more of the ex-Cork Blackrock & Passage Railway (CB&PR) 2-4-2 tank engines, No. 13C, was in the yard (these had been brought here from Inchicore in 1934 when the coal traffic from Arigna was developing and more powerful engines were needed). With their 4 ft 6 in. driving wheels they were said to be the fastest narrow gauge engines in Ireland and their crews told me there was no train too heavy for them. They were popular too (with the original 4-4-0 tanks 'getting rough' and in need of constant attention), but were confined to the C&L main line. Of the four brought from the CB&PR, three were still serviceable.

Finally there was the important transhipment siding at which all wagons loaded with Arigna coal were unloaded by hand into broad gauge wagons and conveyed away for locomotive or power station use.

There was plenty of seating in the saloon-type carriage; we departed at 12.25 pm but noticed that the sliding doors at each end were left open to encourage some fresh air within; we questioned whether there might be an objection if we sat on the balcony steps outside but when the guard came through he obviously concluded that our Passes, signed by the Traffic Manager in Dublin, were authority to do as we pleased. So we enjoyed a spanking departure, a quick view of coal and cattle changing trains and in no time we were out in open country. The going was exhilarating. The fall-plate* was pulled up and rattled against the balcony rail, the buffing heads of the buffer-couplings nudged against each other noisily and their rocking pins and chains swung carelessly from side to side. An occasional lump of ballast kicked up and rattled against the underside of the coach. Hemmed between the rear of the bunker of No. 12C and the end of the coach, we could peer along the winding track ahead. Sometimes chewing grit between the teeth, we came to Mohill.

---

* Fallplate. A hinged steel plate which could be lowered to cross and cover the gap between two coupled vehicles, so enabling the staff to pass through a train so equipped. When not in use it could be raised into a vertical position and secured there by means of a chain and hook on the adjacent vehicle.

There was an extended stop here during which there was an opportunity to inspect the fine station garden while train and station staff came and spoke to us. Perhaps our presence and the Official Pass we had shown had broken down their reticence. Off again, we were immediately taking a curvaceous course around and beside numerous lakes. The land between was rather poor and the farmsteads reflected this. But it was all fresh to us! The train did not stop at several small stations, each with its level crossing; such gates could be in charge of a small girl who waved a green flag high above the tall grasses as soon as she heard the oncoming whistle of No. 12C. Dorothy commented that each wore the current fashion of 'The New Look', which had reached the wilds of County Leitrim before it was commonly seen at home; it looked quite incongruous in this faraway setting. My thought was that at that age the child should be at school!

Whilst in England one would expect the person in charge of a station to be in the signal box or station master's office; it appears that in the case of minor railways in Ireland, an outhouse, convenient to the kitchen, serves. Here the various flags etc. are hidden away behind the half-door which gives a clear vista of the adjacent line. On the C&L system, it was from there that these up-to-the-minute-dressed Irish colleens appeared when summoned for duty by the train driver's whistle, to close the crossing gate by hand, and do their flag waving.

As the train neared Ballinamore, the hills to the north-west drew nearer. These were the Iron Mountains and looked most interesting, being the first high ground (c.2,000 ft) we had seen since reaching Ireland.

We concluded we were approaching a place of the utmost importance when our engine began a series of elongated shrieks on its whistle which persisted for several miles. So much so that I wondered if a herd of stray cattle was wandering on the track. But no, we were simply giving ample warning of our approach to Ballinamore with its level crossing at the entrance - and not conveying the Pope! We ran alongside the Arigna branch which came in from the west and accompanied us for some distance to the station. Heeling over on the super-elevated curve here we continued at a brisk pace to clatter over the level crossing and reach the platform. A spirited finale.

Ballinamore, the hub of the system, did not disappoint. It was on a par with Douglas (Isle of Man) in its facilities. The station building was again of CVR parentage. There were two main platforms linked by footbridge and a bay used for the branch. We realised that there was no time to look around as our connection was already standing in the bay. Suddenly the station master was at my side, asking if we were Mr and Mrs Boyd? He thrust a large envelope into my hand, hoped we would enjoy the ride to Arigna and said he would see us on the following day. 'I have booked you a room at the hotel in the main street for two nights', he added.

The Branch train runs but once daily in each direction as a mixed working; our train had one of the original C&L engines, No. 8L, a 4-4-0 tank still with the cutaways to the cab rear sheet, a balcony-ended bogie coach, a goods guard's van and a rake of covered and empty open wagons. The last-named were being returned to the coal mines beyond Arigna station. Once more we chose to ride on the balcony steps of the coach which was well filled with folk returning

Ballinamore station towards Dromod. An empty coal train bound for Arigna has just left. May 1949. *Author*

Ballinamore station looking towards Belturbet. May 1949. *Author*

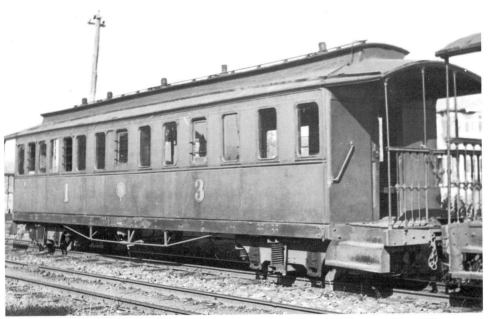

Saloon-type carriage No. 7 still in Great Southern Railways livery, Ballinamore. May 1949.

Author

Horse box No. 2L at Ballinamore. May 1949.   *Author*

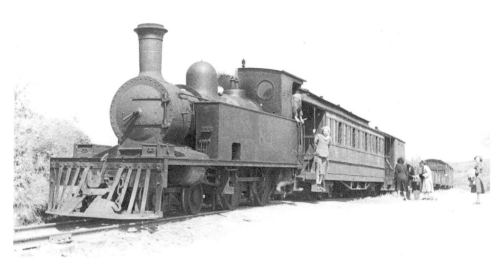

A wayside stop on the Arigna branch. The road alongside is hot and dusty. May 1949.   *Author*

A mixed train for Arigna stands at Creagh. Locomotive No. 8. May 1949.   *Author*

home to Drumshanbo. Seated here, we were almost on the engine's footplate but considerably cleaner and more roomy.

I noticed that the train on which we had travelled from Dromod had crept away silently to Belturbet. We also left without any ceremony or whistling and for the first 400 yards or so ran alongside the Dromod line. Then away down a steep embankment, along the side of the abandoned Ballinamore & Ballyconnell Canal (now more like a river than ever in its neglect). The guard - who never asked to see our Pass - told us that the canal often flooded to the extent that train services had to be stopped until the level dropped. 'Boats?', I asked. He had never heard of any.

As far as Ballyduff, three miles from Ballinamore, the Branch is a railway proper, but from here it assumes the guise of a Tramway laid out at the edge of the adjacent road except where that road makes a sharp turn. At such places the tramway abandons the roadside and is given its own independent course only to rejoin the road again further along. Sometimes, these 'railway only' sections were hedged and the points where tramway and road parted company or vice versa were often obscure. We agreed that road users had to be vigilant. No. 8 took these locations with what I thought was gay abandon, but the driver tugged the whistle cord for the whole time we were on the diversions. It was very hard on the ears! For the nine roadside miles we saw no motor transport.

There were a few horses and carts and an occasional donkey accompanied by a very small child. The road itself was unmade westwards from Ballyduff and in the present dry weather even pedestrians threw up the dust. Children on bicycles - usually two or more per machine - were covered in white dust from waist downwards. Most were barefoot and their overall appearance was of angels in a school Christmas Nativity Play. Official stops were marked solely by a bi-lingual enamel sign in the hedge. At several of these passengers left the train and set off across open rough country towards unseen dwellings; at other points they would drop off the balcony steps regardless of the speed of the train.

(The experience of a ride along this Tramway was the epitome of our journey to Ireland and the remembrance of it remains very vivid; it was last survivor of several broad or narrow gauge roadside Steam Tramways that existed in Ireland. The interplay between road and railway as they crossed each other's path was an unforeseen bonus and the absence of collision a miracle!)

About 12 miles from Ballinamore we reached Drumshanbo, a place equal in size to the former. Here the carriage emptied and we were left alone. Off the road now, there was a proper station with passing loop (disused) and the site of a engine shed. In busier days, an engine was shedded here which brought a coal train down from the mines to Ballinamore before breakfast. No. 8 took water and then did some shunting with the whole train attached as it did so.

The run after Drumshanbo took us across the boggy valley of the River Shannon, which rises in Lough Allen, a large sheet of water near the coal deposits. The river is narrow at this point and we crossed it by girder bridge. A little further on we crossed the ultimate length of the canal where it links with the expanse of Lough Allen.

In contrast to the previous convolutions of our progress, the train now ran along a straight roadside for almost a mile before curving to the left and

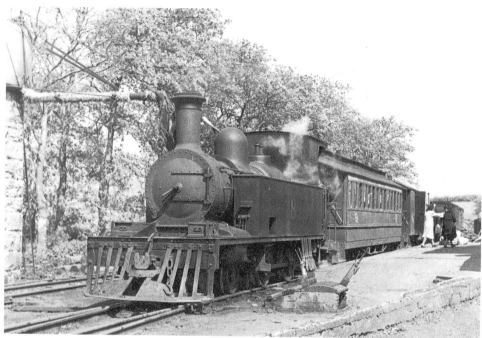

No. 8 is the usual engine for the Arigna branch, seen here at Drumshanbo. May 1949. *Author*

A loaded coal train returning to Ballinamore at Drumshanbo. May 1949.   *Author*

entering the precincts of Arigna station. On this previous length our speed had increased considerably, possibly to 35 mph. The Rule Book gave a limit of 12 mph for the Tramway but presumably this could be overlooked on the straight sections. The dust cloud behind us had grown to enormous size so we retired into the coach and kept door and windows closed.

Arigna station proved to be a delightful setting in a grove of large Alder trees. The passenger station was a single platform on one side and the track extended beyond to a goods shed. A lengthy passing loop was carried forward from the platform face and curved away to end in a turntable. Numberless wagons were stabled on it throughout. At the further end of the platform, prior to the trackage just described, the C&LR proper ended and the mineral line to the iron and coal mines began. It left the Tramway on a sharp right-hand curve, and crossed a road by a gateless level crossing before heading off for Aughabehy. The guard told us that our coach was not taken up the railway to the mines but we could travel in the four-wheeled van attached to the empty coal wagons if we wished. So we again chose the balcony of the little vehicle but soon went inside as coal dust blew all round us as the train started.

The course of the mineral line was to follow the valley of the little Arigna River northwards to the coalmines' area. This railway had been built as recently as 1920 and was well graded and in good condition. It snaked along the left-hand bank of the river in a picturesque setting between closely fitting hills on either side. It was hard to imagine a place less likely to reveal a coal mine! Tempted by this pleasant setting we resumed our position on the van balcony rather than miss the experience. It would lead to trouble later!

In due course our progress halted and the guard uncoupled the van from the train. The engine ran ahead with the empty wagons. The guard explained we could stay in the van if we wished or walk up towards the coal loading point where the engine would pick up a train of loaded coal wagons, and run down past the van with it, thus allowing the van to run by gravity onto the rear of the train. So in this remote spot we watched this little spectacle and wondered how many curious Englishmen had done the same. There were only two coalfields in Ireland. This was the bigger and each had been connected by a new railway about the same period. We caught no sight of any mine, the coal being brought down from adits on the hill above in tubs suspended by a wire ropeway. Once over the empty wagon siding, the tubs tipped over and their contents fell into the vehicles below.

We set off for Arigna station at a sedate pace. Although the timetabled return to Ballinamore was as a mixed train, there were no potential customers in sight. Meanwhile the train crew had other things do. The train was one of the permanently-coupled made-up sets which trundled up and down between Arigna and Dromod and vice versa. Each had a C&L wagon at each end to facilitate coupling to the locomotive. In between there might be wagons from any of the former Irish narrow gauge systems which had closed and whose open wagon stock had been drafted to the C&L to assist in the national need for coal. Such wagons might include those from the Cork & Muskerry, West Clare, Clogher Valley, or Cork, Blackrock & Passage lines. Owing to lack of standardization, there was no consistent pattern of coupling between them but the C&L workshops had devised a linkage which, though not a perfect marriage, was sufficient for the purpose. To these the guard gave his attention and with the aid of a hefty sledge hammer was driving home any coupling which seemed unlikely to secure the train in one rake as far as Ballinamore!

Meanwhile the driver was walking along the train and choosing selected lumps of coal from off the wagons which he put into a sack. This was laid carefully onto the wagon next to the engine presumably for Domestic Consumption. We had given the coal a quick examination ourselves. It was small, slack and crumbly and would hardly be categorized as 'domestic grade' in the austere conditions at home. But Irish power stations had to accept what they were sent.

A curious machine standing off the track beside the station had caught my eye. Its origins were in a pushbike designed for two riders seated alongside each other. Each had his own pedals and the whole contraption was fitted with flanged wheels suited to the 3 ft gauge. We had no difficulty in encouraging two of the staff to mount for a photograph and we left Arigna in lighthearted mood. (I never saw a similar design until many years later when I found one in Drimoleague engine shed on the Cork, Bandon & South Coast Railway section. It was, of course, for the 5 ft 3 in. gauge, and must have been a heavy and clumsy machine to pedal. Were these used for more than track inspection? I wondered if they were the fruits of some travelling salesman's visit to Ireland; although they looked ancient they were probably fairly common from c.1880 on railway backwaters.)

No. 8L collected the waiting bogie coach and shunted it onto the wagons. Its one patient passenger left us at Drumshanbo. Dorothy had had a shock when she saw herself in the small vanity mirror from her pocket. She looked at me; we were peppered by smuts and soot but, despite them, resumed our ride on the carriage balcony from which we watched the little engine before us snaking its way from curve to curve, across and again from one side of the road to another like a demented cat pursued by a determined dog.

Inspection cycle at Arigna. This was in regular use. May 1949.   *Author*

At length we heard the attenuated whistle for the approach to Ballinamore; the Dromod line took up its position beside us and we crossed the now deserted street through the village. We had decided the day had been long enough to do more than locate the hotel further down. In the stillness of the evening the street was full of turf smoke from many chimneys. The hotel bore no obvious name* so we chose the most significant building, entered and stood in the small hallway for some signs of life. A woman came through from the back regions. We explained we were the couple the station master had booked in. She looked at us very strangely; we must have looked like a couple of windswept chimney sweeps. Rather than be refused a bed we explained our appearance. It seemed there had been other people before us who had patronised the hotel because of its convenient location near the station and our reservation through the station master proved to be a trump card. After a thorough cleansing and an excellent High Tea we were all on the best of terms. We now faced another problem.

I must now explain our problem with regard to photographs. I have mentioned earlier that these were an essential outcome of our visit but the universal shortage of camera film posed difficulties. We had managed to bring what we thought would be sufficient for the weekend but the C&L system was proving so attractive that my self-imposed rationing schedule had already been breached before we returned to Ballinamore. I had anticipated such a crisis by buying a few 'home-made' films from a friend who cut up ex-RAF sheet film into camera-size strips and sold them on the Black Market. He warned me that the resultant rolls were not always light-tight on the spools and to avoid the film being spoilt by light getting in, recommended I should store them in a light-tight tin and load them into the camera in a darkened room or inside a Changing Bag. (A bag inside which all handling could be done in daylight.)

I had purchased such a bag and kept a few RAF films in it. Now that we were ensconced in the hotel I decided to load one into the camera. The bedroom was by no means dark enough to risk it, and even covering myself under the bedclothes was unsatisfactory. Dorothy tried shutting me in the wardrobe but the doors would not close. Ultimately, I mastered the art of using the bag anywhere; it was cheap, light and took up no space. So we set off for Ballinamore station the next day with adequate film and made a beeline for the yard and engine shed.

Firstly we paid the station master a visit to thank him for the hotel accommodation and the courtesies we had been shown on the journey to the mines. He suggested we look at the withdrawn vehicles in a long siding nearby, and the contents of the engine shed. On the siding three bogie coaches of the type in service were to be seen; they were only fit for scrap. The axle box covers on the bogies were embossed CL&RR (Cavan, Leitrim & Roscommon Railway). All were built by the Metropolitan Cariage & Wagon Co. Ltd, Birmingham.

Outside the engine shed were two of the Tralee & Dingle section engines (Nos. 3T & 4T) which had been brought over here to work the coal traffic. We learned that they had been adapted to burn Arigna coal - whatever that meant. They were not permitted on the main line but suffered severe flange wear on the branch line curves, 'their wheelbase is too long'. They were popular with the men, No. 4T being the favourite.

* 'Central'.

The locomotive position was as follows:

1L	Class DN2	4-4-0T	Recently sent away for scrap
2L	Class DN2	4-4-0T	Dromod shed
3L	Class DN2	4-4-0T	Ballinamore shed
4L	Class DN2	4-4-0T	At Inchicore for repair
8L	Class DN2	4-4-0T	Ballinamore shed
10C	Class FN1	2-4-2T	Dromod shed
12C	Class FN1	2-4-2T	Belturbet shed
13C	Class FN1	2-4-2T	Dromod shed
3T	Class KN2	2-6-0T	Ballinamore shed
4T	Class KN2	2-6-0T	Ballinamore shed

We returned to Dromod by the afternoon train and were entertained by the troop of Scouts who sang all the way. The up Dublin Mail was hauled by No. 537 4-4-0 of class 'D7' built Broadstone in 1912 (scrapped 1953). The train crews exchanged at Longford again and we took the night sailing to Holyhead from Dun Laoghaire. It had been a most successful weekend.

The envelope given to me by the Ballinamore station master contained several Accident Reports, of which this one is typical.

16 February 1892 Charles Macguire of Ballinamore supposed to have intended travelling by train leaving Ballinamore for Dromod attempted to jump into the train while in motion and at a distance of about 200 yards from Ballinamore station close to first level crossing and fell & got run over by the Guards van receiving instantaneus fatal injuries.

The train consisted of 2 carriages next engine, Guards van & two waggons in rere & was brought to a stand in a space of 60 yds after Guard found shock crossing the body.

Deceased was trespassing on railway but it is supposed with the intention of jumping into the train when passing after its having started from station. He had no ticket entitling him to travel.

Accident arose from want of caution on part of deceased who recklessly jumped against train while it was running. That Charles Maguire came to his death by shock occasioned by his attempting to enter the train whilst in motion and we strongly recommend that there should be an interval between the starting of two trains which usually leave the station together to better ensure the public safety and that we desire to express our sympathy with the father & relatives of the deceased.

Chapter Thirteen

The Cavan & Leitrim Railway - Revisited, July-August 1951

My business visits to Northern Ireland now took on a regular annual pattern and I proposed to break a week-long stay with a weekend on the Cavan & Leitrim section, and acquaint myself with the Belturbet-Ballinamore line which we had not seen in May 1949. Once more I had learned from Manchester colleagues that there was a cunning method of contriving this from Belfast. It had to be put into operation because reaching Belturbet in the Friday evening was not feasible by GNRI train; Belturbet was on a GNRI branch from Ballyhaise. I could reach Ballyhaise by a connections from Belfast but the Belturbet branch train closed down early each evening and its last train would have left Ballyhaise before I arrived, thus stranding me there. The recommended ruse to overcome this was as follows:

1. Before leaving Belfast, to telephone the station master at Ballyhaise and have the call transferred to the signal cabin.
2. Ask the signalman there to ring his colleague at Belturbet signal cabin to run down to the garage at Belturbet and order a car to meet me at Ballyhaise station off the train from Clones. The car would then take me cross-country to Belturbet in time to catch the evening train on the C&L section to Ballinamore.

A difficulty might arise when I used the phone in our Belfast office because I knew that our agent there would express strong feelings if he realised I was speaking to a number in the Irish Free State with a view to going there. Luckily I made arrangements whilst he was out of the office but when I explained my weekend plans he nearly exploded - 'You will get a knife in your back by going over the Border'. I told him to expect me at the office on Monday morning. I was as good as my word.

The weather proved to be exceptionally hot and sunny and I knew that it would be useless to try and do any business after lunch on a Friday so I caught the 1.45 pm railcar No. 605 from Great Victoria Street station on 31st July, 1951 to Clones where I would have to change for the connection to Ballyhaise. I was able to find a seat at the front of the railcar where the glass panel gave me an uninterrupted view of the line ahead.

This once important main line was double-tracked towards Armagh but singled at Rich Hill. Afterwards we had a protracted stop at Tynan for Customs examination. I duly changed at Clones to a type of train formation which I had never encountered in England - it was headed by a small boilered 0-6-0 tender engine (number not noted) with one bogie coach, two open goods wagons and a goods brake van - a charming ensemble.

This trundled down the Cavan branch at a leisurely gait to Ballyhaise where I left it and anxiously scanned the entrance for signs of some well-used garage hack which would take me to Belturbet. My heart fell when I discovered none. But there was a smart-looking brand new green Morris Minor whose driver saw me searching and hailed me with 'Would ye be the gent who ordered a car?' The system had worked perfectly!

No. 10C pounds up the gradient into Ballinamore with whistle screeching, heading a train from Dromod. August 1951.

I enjoyed that car ride as much as any I have taken since. My loquacious driver clearly knew his way along a miriad of rural boreens which took us through rough woodland, dilapidated farmsteads and a gypsy camp which I thought had only survived in 18th-century oil paintings - a battered caravan, numberless ragged and bare foot small children, scraggy-looking horses tethered to trees and a huge fire whose thick heavy smoke caused my driver to make his way carefully in case some errant child should appear without warning ... All were camped out on the wide verge beneath a canopy of venerable elms.

Our arrival at Belturbet station gave me sufficient time for a stroll round. The arrangements were similar to those obtaining all over Ireland. The GNRI line ended in a single-lined platform with all-over roofed building; the narrow gauge flanked the other side. There was a useful and large roofed goods shed covering an island platform for mutual use. The small GNRI engine shed housed the branch engine No. 96 2-4-2T which had been put to bed, in fact the entire GNRI premises were deserted and lifeless. At the platform stood its train of carriages, also waiting for the dawn.

On the narrow gauge side of the business ex-Cork Blackrock & Passage Railway 2-4-2T No. 10C stood simmering quietly awaiting departure time. It had the customary bogie saloon carriage with a tail of covered vans behind the bunker, and in the rear one of the small brake vans. The driver said the load was the maximum for the route and, almost as an afterthought, 'Come on up, there's plenty of room'. He must have known it was my birthday!

Although it was now late afternoon, there was still a brilliant sun and, as we were travelling west, it made for difficulty in seeing against its glare. We soon reached a spanking speed and like all engine drivers making for home, arrived at Ballyconnell early and we were obliged to stand for a while until our time was due. The run so far had been hectic for 10C was not in the best of health. There was a hole in the smokebox large enough to pass a cup and saucer through it and worse, the boiler cladding had come adrift and as we ran it flapped up and down like a wounded bird. The noise was dreadful but the driver assured me that the engine steamed well and they would fasten the cladding back at Ballinamore. We continued to Bawnboy Road where there was another protracted wait. The fireman made a careful inspection of the fire to see if we needed further coal before we finished. I could see the grate was almost bare but he seemed satisfied. There would be less clinker to clear!

It was like coming home to be back at the small hotel again. I had written to book a room, so I ignored the front door bell and went in. The rambling rear regions were empty and I spent some time in rousing a tweenie; the place was incredibly hot and I assumed that such staff as they had were taking the weight off their feet somewhere. Despite my footplate trip I was considerably cleaner than when we arrived last time. Worse than the heat, all the windows at the back of the building were open so allowing ripe smells from the adjacent cowsheds to permeate everywhere.

The tweenie led me along a lengthy upstairs passage. Obstructing one end was a young man seated at a small table, closing one end of it. He was bent over a large ledger in which he was drawing, by dip-in pen, diagrams of individual

A Belturbet train standing at Ballyconnell with locomotive No. 10C. August 1951.

Author

conifer trees. I concluded he must be recording the number the Forestry Commission had planted during July. I wished him a 'Good evening' as I squeezed by but he seemed too engrossed in his work to notice me. Was this an Irish method of creating full employment?

My allotted room had been overlooked by the over-zealous window-opener and though hot, was not bovine-perfumed. There were three of us at a large communal table in the dining room for High Tea, two men who were together and my arborial acquaintance who sat aloof. The men soon fell into conversation with me and suggested we adjourned to the bar. I in turn suggested a later meeting and hinted I wished to go down to the railway station while it was still daylight.

Down at the station a night-shift of cats was prowling about but otherwise there was no movement. As the next day was Saturday I decided to make an early start at the station. I had taken the precaution before leaving for Ireland of writing to the powers-that-be at Kingsbridge station for a Footplate Pass for the C&L section and Working Timetable. It permitted me to travel by any train.

I took an early breakfast alone - the Irish are not early-risers - and then, armed with the useful authority to go where I pleased, absorbed the goings-on at the station. There was an empty coal train for Arigna leaving at 9.30 behind 9L but I learned it would be delayed by 8L which would leave first with a train of wagons containing ash and clinker cleared from the engine shed pits. This would carry a permanent way gang who would spread the load on the track between Drumshanbo and Arigna. I resolved to travel on the permanent way special and pick up the train bound for the colliery Extension at Arigna.

No. 8L ran nonstop to Drumshanbo where it took on water and stopped on the long straight roadside stretch beyond. The gang had found seats in the brake van, leaving me to enjoy a balcony ride; on the way from Ballinamore we had passed through a very heavy rainstorm which had the effect of damping down the dust in the wagons. At the allotted place the gang jumped out, dropped the side doors on the wagons and shovelled the contents onto the roadside track. They must have been but poor benefit but at least the engine shed had somewhere to dispose of them.

Meanwhile the empty coal train which was following us had been held up at Kilturbrid and Drumshanbo. Our own train moved in stages along the line until the wagons were cleared and then ran forward into Arigna station, to be overtaken shortly by the coal empties. This following train went into the yard, 9L was detached, turned, and with me in the van we ran up the Extension to the siding and overhead conveyor. It was very hot and there was no escape from the dust and grit. My eyes and ears were full of debris. I shook out my clothes as best I could and decided that a restful afternoon would be be appropriate.

Back at Ballinamore again I had a chat with the men about the Arigna Extension. They explained that the 3 mile branch from Arigna station to Governor's Bay, where the C&L Company's own colliery was located, was closed and lifted in 1927-30. The present rails on the Extension weighed 60 lb. yd. All this made me keen to explore the abandoned coal and iron mines and railways north-west of Arigna, a project I was able to fulfil some years later!

There was some activity here. The mixed working had left for Arigna at 1.50 pm with 2L. It had two bogie coaches plus vans but I forgot to ask why. Already departed was 13C with a ballast train for Bawnboy Road where it would be put into the loop to allow the passenger train to pass. It seemed that proper stone ballast was being used on the main line while the branch had to make do with ash and clinker!

In the engine shed were Nos. 12C and 5T, the latter recently arrived from an Inchicore overhaul. It was the Dingle line's largest engine, of 2-6-2T arrangement and a local favourite. Nos. 3T and 4T, which had been here on my last visit, had been sent to Inchicore. It was said that 3T would return but 4T might be scrapped - 4T had 'ended its days on the Dingle section working the Castlegregory branch as it was unsuitable for anything else because the fire choked'. (I had not heard this story before.)

Also on shed were 3L, 4L, 8L; 4L was under the lifting tackle as its wheels had gone to Inchicore. No. 3L still retained the maker's brass plates 'No. 2612 Robert Stephenson & Co. Engineers NEWCASTLE ON TYNE 1877'.

There was no particular oddity among the signalling. It had all been installed by Saxby & Farmer and every needful location had its ground frame, that at Ballinamore being set in the middle of the main platform where it was accessible to all. Ballyconnell had a frame at each end of the station but there was no up starting signal alongside the level crossing.

The younger saloon bogie coaches were divided into three, 1st, 3rd non-smoking, 3rd smoking ; the 1st had individual seats on one side and a perimeter seat on the other; the 3rd had perimeter seating throughout - it was of wooden slatted type and passengers were known to bring a generous handful of straw with them to ease their discomfort! In the later design one end was given over to a guard's compartment but the remainder was arranged as in younger style.

The proportions of non-smoking to smoking and of 1st to 3rd Class were similar to that provided in similar vehicles found on other Irish narrow gauge railways and suggested that a goodly number of patrons would be travelling 1st Class and that smokers were prevalent (which they probably were!). If the examples on the C&L section were any guide, the fenestration lacked ventilation and we preferred to ride on the balcony as the atmosphere inside was atrocious. I think a blind eye was given to regulars who occupied 1st Class seats without a suitable ticket … or any ticket at all, for that matter.

I paid a brief visit to the sidings full of condemned wagons then, hot and tired, made my way back to the hotel. Feeling better for a wash and rest, and completing my notes for the day, I went down for high tea and was accosted by the two fishermen who were curious to learn what I had been doing. The fact that I was interested in the railway and moreover, came from England for the purpose, completely baffled them and they turned the conversation to the next day, Sunday. How would I spend Sunday, when they doubted any trains could be running? They appeared to want a further talk after Mass in the morning but when I said I was not an adherent of the Church of Rome, they came to the point at once. Would I like to go fishing with them?

I had no plans for the Sunday other than to explore the Canal, and when they added that they had a car and boat nearby I was innocent enough to accept their invitation. The couple had a quick conversation with Herself from which I gathered that whatever we caught she would cook for our tea, and we set off for Lake Garadice in a well-used van. It was a lovely day and the countryside was at its best. We skittled along, winding between various small lakes interspersed with hills in a very attractive setting. Squashed in the back of the van along with fishing gear, rods, nets, coats, boots and tackle, I made the best of it. But the road became a track and the van's suspension had passed its sell-by date. When a large sheet of water came alongside I was relieved to know it was Lake Garadice. The road became a rough track and the contents of the van jostled about around me. Suddenly we turned sharply and stopped in the middle of a thicket. My companions jumped out and released me through the back doors. Then they disappeared into a jungle of undergowth to drag out of the boscage a long flat-bottomed punt with squared ends. It was full of brackish green water which was ladled out with a rusty can. So this was the boat!

From inside the van came two unequal poles with flattened ends; I gathered they were the oars. After some conversation I agreed to start rowing while they fished. We would then change places. As there were no seats I was recommended to sit on the floor. There were no rowlocks but 'some dowelling out of the van would do' instead.

We took our places without capsizing and with difficulty I found room for my feet among the impedimenta we had taken with us. I could imagine Dorothy's horror had she seen me; I always insisted on wearing lifejackets when out sailing. Worse, I was too well-dressed even though my business attire was back in the Belfast hotel. No wonder these men were so keen I should come with them.

There was some excitement just after we left the shore. The punt rocked violently and took on some water over the side. This rapidly filled one of my shoes. and dampened what little enthusiasm I had. I could not see exactly what was happening but there was a thump and a splash. Something hit the floor and slithered towards my feet. It was large, evil-looking and did not look like the kind of fish which could be used for our supper. I was informed that it was a pike and would return with us to feed the cats.

We continued to drift over the lake and I kept the punt moving as best I could. By now the seat of my trousers was fairly damp and the uncomfortable sitting position was becoming impossible. Suddenly I felt a bite on my foot and looking down saw that the wretched pike had come to life and had grabbed me by the toes with its viscious teeth. With my other foot, I kicked it clear. By good fortune my outdoor shoes were stoutly made and the bite did not penetrate the leather.

It was suggested that we changed positions but I recommended that we pull into the shore first. That done, we spent a tedious hour or so moving round the water. We caught four or five smaller fish which were reputed to be edible but, thankfully, no more pike. My colleagues agreed we had had enough and in due course we returned to the hotel without further mishap. I declined their invitation to accept one of the fish for supper. A little puzzled by our early return, our hostess was told we wished to go to Evening Mass.

I spent the evening walking along the bank of the canal; there was a proper tow path here but where it crossed the lakes, steam power had to be used.

On the Monday I took the morning train to Belturbet 'on the cushions' and the little GNRI branch train to Ballyhaise; our through connection to Belfast was headed by one of the recent small 4-4-0s. At Clones I spoke to the driver and cautiously mentioned my Pass for the C&L. 'Come with us now, if you like', he said. It was a nice change to be on the open footplate of a tender engine and I could compare the experience with those I had recently had on the Altrincham-Chester line of the Cheshire Lines Committee over which ex-Great Central Railway Pollitt 4-4-0 tender engines were often used. (They were shedded at Trafford Park where my friend Mr Rickards was in charge. Verb sap!)

I made the most of the journey, well aware that before the working day was out I was due in our Bedford Street office again and could testify by evidence that I had returned to Ulster without harm! Just before we reached Tynan the driver reminded me that there would be a longer stop for examination by the Northern Ireland customs, and did I have sugar in my tea? As we stood at Tynan platform which was crowded with folk who had been into the Free State to buy goodies not obtainable in the Six Counties, three mugs of tea appeared. I had hardly had a sip of mine when a Customs officer nipped onto the footplate and asked me to accompany him to his office. As we walked down the platform every head on the train hung out to learn why I had been detained. Once in the Customs office the man put his hand on my camera and asked to see it. Where did I buy it, how much did it cost and could I recommend one? Finally, where could he buy one? A few heads were still hanging out when I returned to the engine, and as I was not in handcuffs they were disappointed. So was I. My tea had gone cold.

Mr Hunter was waiting for me. He asked me nothing about my absence, either then or later. Clearly I had evaded the knife in my back!

A Belturbet coal train awaits departure from Arigna. May 1958.   *Author*

A coal train bound for Ballinamore taking water at Drumshanbo. May 1958.   *Author*

Chapter Fourteen

The Cavan & Leitrim Railway - Arigna Extension, May 1955

Geoffrey Naylor telephoned to ask when I was next going to see our Northern Ireland customers. He was in the dyestuffs business and thought a visit from their Manchester head office would be timely. Should I care to join him on a convenient weekend over there, he would be hiring a car for a fortnight and I could recommend some railway venues to visit. I readily agreed to the idea and we chose the last weekend in May, he to meet me outside our Bedford Street, Belfast office.

The use of a car would give us great flexibility and by a prompt start on Friday evening, we might reach Ballinamore and so have the Saturday to travel on the Belturbet and Arigna lines of the Cavan & Leitrim section of CIE. Furthermore, we could use the car on the Sunday to explore the abandoned railway beyond Arigna station.

We took the road through Keady where the unfinished Ulster & Connaught Light Railway (3 ft gauge) of 1899 conception passed under the GNRI yard there by means of a long tunnel. The tunnel was easily discerned and encouraged us to learn more about this ambitious project which was never completed. (Life being what it is, I was never able to study the subject further.)

Then, we were back at the Central Hotel, Ballinamore which like all similar hostelries in that part of Ireland, seemed changeless in its fittings and staff. The position was much the same next day at the station where four engines were in steam daily. In evidence were 2L, 3L, 4L, 8L, 10C, 4T with 3T standby. No. 4T was still unpopular, being 'too small firebox for Arigna coal'. No. 12C was in the back workshop, 'either for heavy overhaul or scrapping'.

We travelled by the 9.30 am empty coal train and learned they were still sending approximately 100 tons of coal out to Dromod each day. Geoffrey, perfectionist as he is, was very critical about the mechanical state of engine and train - he had a lot to learn about Irish standards! The train was made up of ex-CB&PR wagons entirely so Geoffrey was not entertained by any heavy hammering. All the couplings matched. He approved of the adaptors at each end of the rake. We rode up to the loading siding but decided to leave our walk up the abandoned section until the next day when there would be more time.

No. 2L was our engine returning from Arigna with the loaded coal wagons and a string of vans; the engine was clearly overloaded and slipped incessantly. At Drumshanbo the driver attacked the sandpipes with a heavy hammer. He was certain they were blocked. To obtain a good run up the bank into Ballinamore, avoid more wheel slip or being brought to stand if the road crossing gates were not open for the railway, the driver brought us to halt. As soon as the home signal cleared he yanked open the regulator, held down the whistle cord and we climbed the gradient in fine style, careening over on the curve. With whistle screeching we were still going like hell when we crossed the main street; now I knew why we had entered Ballinamore like this on our first visit. It was as though no one on the station would move to open the crossing gates until he was certain the driver meant business! Once on the station level the vacuum brakes brought us to a rapid stop and the safety valves lifted as in a great roar of triumph. Even Geoffrey smiled.

In the afternoon we went to Belturbet and back. I travelled in the new Inchicore-built bogie coach built out of bus components, and was not impressed. Obviously the weary-looking saloons had given up the ghost. We spoke to the driver of the Belturbet train, telling him of the heavy loading we had just witnessed. 'Ach', he said, 'the load limits are 100 tons for the main line and 80 for the tramway - determined by someone in an office in Dublin who has never been here'.

While awaiting departure time here we had a good browse around the station; the GNRI side of the business was deathly silent - as I found it last time. The engine crew warmed to us when we returned. 'Come on up. There's no place like the footplate for getting an idea of the road'. I let Geoffrey go alone so that he could learn about Irish railways at first hand. I noticed he was less abrasive afterwards!

The next day, Sunday, we drove the car to a deserted Arigna station and walked up the Extension. We knew that an older tramway had been a forerunner of the line built in the 1920s. Hoping it would become apparent we began our search at the north end of the Arigna Colliery yard (east side), alongside the church wall. The course followed a lane, climbing the while, and there were two considerable embankments. A third came near the old terminus at Aughabehy.

The modern line follows the west bank of the Arigna River valley, then turns inwards on the mountain where it ends with a number of parallel sidings and a run round. There is a stone-built loading platform. From here an incline rises up

Arigna Extension: overhead loading sidings at the coal mine. May 1958.   *Author*

Arigna. A coal train has the couplings checked before leaving. The variety of wagons is noteworthy. May 1958.   *Author*

the mountain-face. The connection between the terminus and incline foot is unclear. The incline was worked on the balanced principle and a vertically-mounted winding-drum survives. At the top the colliery was sited between the incline and the road, there is evidence of a vertical shaft, now filled in. On the hilltop stand two boilers, one vertical and one locomotive type; near them is the site of a winding engine.

The track on the incline would appear to have been less than 3 feet gauge. At its foot were several stone block sleepers drilled for iron pegs. It was a puzzling situation. We returned to the car and drove along the road at the incline top through a bleak and uninviting piece of moorland. There were a number of rude dwellings; through the uncurtained windows primitive accommodation used by the miners could be seen - iron bedsteads, wash stands, broken chairs and ragged blankets.

I made a note of what I thought were non-passenger vehicles from the time of line opening, all built by Metropolitan:

| Roofless cattle vans | Open wagons | Timber bolster wagons |
| Covered vans | Open wagons (High sided) | |

Exceptions were a number of similar types supplied by the Bristol Wagon Works Co. Ltd. 1889. Wagons noted were all in a series Nos. 80110. Painting was light grey with black ironwork: on the central side panels in small white characters - C&LLR.

The Cavan & Leitrim Railway, Patrick J. Flanagan, 1966 (published by David & Charles, Newton Abbot, Devon) contains additional information especially regarding the Arigna Extension.

A Belturbet train at Bawnboy Road with carriage composed of motor bus components. May 1958. *Author*

Belturbet. The GNRI line lies to the right of the platform. May 1958.   *Author*

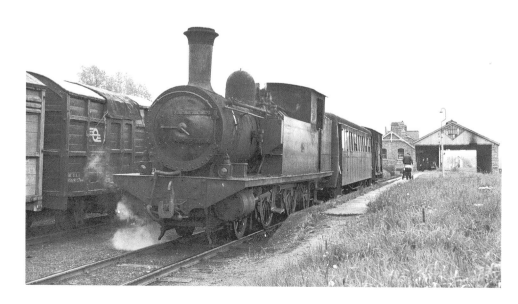

Chapter Fifteen

Just Passing By, Ballinamore Again, May 1958

It had become the custom for a group of us to make an Irish tour each Whitsuntide. There were bargains to be had. It was still possible to buy a Monthly Return from Manchester to Dublin for £1 10s.; even better CIE offered unlimited rail travel for seven days for £10.

Taking advantage of this bargain, our itinerary for 23rd May, 1958 was:

Saturday-	Dun Laoghaire-Kingsbridge	Steam
24th May	Kingsbridge-Limerick	Diesel
	Limerick-Ennis	Railcar
	Ennis-Kilkee (West Clare section N.G.)	Railcar
Sunday-	Kilkee-Kilrush-Kilkee	Walk
Monday-	Kilkee-Ennis (West Clare section N.G.)	Railcar
26th May	Ennis-Athenry-Galway	Diesel
Tuesday-	Galway-Clifden-Galway	Bus
Wednesday-	Galway-Ballaghaderreen	Bus
28th May	Ballaghaderreen-Claremorris	Steam
	Claremorris-Manulla Jc.-Ballina	Diesel
	Ballina-Manulla Jc.	Diesel
	Manulla Jc.-Westport	Diesel
	Westport-Westport Quay-Westport	Walk
Thursday-	Westport-Castlerea	Railcar
29th May	Castlerea-Ballinrobe	Bus
	Ballinrobe-Kilfree	Steam
	Kilfree-Collooney	Diesel
	Collooney-Sligo (goods train)	Diesel
	Sligo-Ballinamore	Bus
Friday	Ballinamore (C&L section N.G.)	Steam
30th May	Arigna-Belturbet-Dromod	
	Dromod-Longford	Diesel
Saturday	Longford-Athlone	Bus
31st May	Athlone-Kingsbridge	Diesel
	Kingsbridge-North Wall (ship)	Bus

(Some short hired car journeys are not shown).

(This shows what could be achieved with some intermixing of bus and hired car journeys. What it does not show is the accident to our bus between Longford and Athlone; ours was a moderately sized group but I was the only casualty! I shall only cover the C&L section of our visit in this chapter.)

Dorothy and I were the only people who had been to this part of Ireland previously, so to make the acquaintance of a steam-worked narrow gauge railway which had such an interesting down-to-earth commercial use was attractive in itself. At Ballinamore the C&L locomotive picture was depressing. Of the original 4-4-0Ts, only No. 4L was in steam while 2-4-2T No. 10C worked the main line passenger trains. However, it was all a rare novelty and the character of the railway was refreshingly different from the West Clare section

199

A busy scene at Ballinamore as ex-Tralee & Dingle Railway No. 8 draws in with a coal train. May 1958. *Author*

Mixed train leaving Ballinamore with empty coal wagons and No. 8. May 1958.　　　*Author*

No. 10 makes a fiery start from Ballinamore with a Dromod train. May 1958.   *Author*

Ready for the off! A Dromod train stands at Ballinamore headed by a well-used No. 10 sporting
express passenger train lamps. May 1958.   *Author*

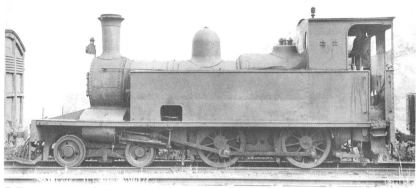

Ballinamore yard shunting engine, in poor mechanical condition and with no identity number on the side tank. May 1958.

Author

with its near-new diesel locomotives which we had seen earlier in the week. Furthermore, the Central Hotel had only been able to accommodate all our party by putting a number of beds into the former retail shop section of the premises. This proved to be the highlight of the trip as four members had their beds in full view of the street through the empty and bare large plate glass windows. It was the main talking point of the week!

Of certain other ventures of the week, I shall make reference elsewhere. We never saw the C&L again before it closed on 31st March, 1959. Years after that we looked for Arigna station again only to find it had all disappeared - railway, station buildings and trees ... everything!

However, my notes make reference to other aspects of the railway which should be mentioned. Concerning the working of the single line:

Staff & Ticket: Dromod-Mohill; Mohill-Ballinamore; Ballinmore-Bawnboy Rd; Bawnboy Rd-Ballyconnel-Belturbet.
Staff & Tablet: All the original main line. Ballinamore. Drumshanbo: original C&L Tramway system in use viz: When a train from Ballinamore reaches Ballyduff, the guard phones Ballinamore. A following train may then leave Ballinamore. At Kilturbrid the procedure is the same between Ballyduff and Kilturbrid. Drivers phone for information on preceding train at each station.

The railway used Wise's System of Train Staffs. It was not commonly found, the best known user being the North Wales Narrow Gauge Railways.* The Tablets are fixed to the Train Staff, two at each end of the Staff; the Tablets are released from the Staff by a key kept in the Booking Office. The whole is a heavy and clumsy affair, not easily mislaid on the footplate!

Mileposts; these are similar in style to others used elsewhere on routes in Ireland.

Quarter mile	Rectangular board set on one corner
Half mile	Triangular board
Three-quarter mile	Inverted triangle
Full mile	Rectangular board often showing the number

Numbers were only painted on full mile boards, remaining boards were distinguished by outline.

Distances measured: Dromod-Belturbet: Ballinamore-Arigna.

* Also West Clare.

Chapter Sixteen

Antrim and the Ballycastle Line

It was my preference to stay at the Strand Hotel, Bangor while working from our Belfast agent's office in Bedford Street. This would give me a pleasant few nights by the seaside and enable me to travel in and out of the city daily by the Belfast & Co. Down Railway using Queen's Quay station which was on the far bank of the River Lagan from the office. There was much to see while walking between the stuffy office and station; the city trams were still operating and they terminated inside the perimeter of Queen's Quay station in a glazed double-tracked bothy. A nice touch, but I preferred to walk. Another homely touch was that the Strand Hotel used the same patterned crockery as my mother had ... 'Indian Tree'!

I had calculated that if I deferred my return home I could make a railway visit on a Saturday and sail home to Liverpool the same evening. So it was that I found myself on 26th May, 1948 taking the train to Ballymoney from Belfast's York Road NCC station. Ballymoney was by now the closest place to Belfast where the NCC still offered a 3 ft gauge passenger train service. This operated on what had once been the Ballycastle Railway, an independent concern which ran from the former Belfast & Northern Counties Railway station at Ballymoney to Ballycastle. It had closed in 1924 but had re-opened almost at once under the NCC umbrella. Although most of its native Ballycastle Railway features had been replaced by the NCC, it was a desirable venue for my extended working-week visit, especially as rumour was that closure was nigh.

Always ready to squeeze more into the time, I had left Bangor early that Saturday morning in order to spend an hour or so wandering round the precincts of Queen's Quay station, having already gleaned from local sources that one could prowl round the outer fringes without hindrance. So, at 9.15 am I had them to myself. There were many 6-wheel carriages off-duty, mostly built by the Ashbury Carriage & Wagon Co., many still gas lit and painted in LMS red. The 1sts were five compt, and the 2nds & 3rds had six. The last two classes carried an enamel notice in each compartment 'PLEASE DO NOT SPIT IN THE CARRIAGES. IT IS OFFENSIVE TO OTHER PASSENGERS & IS STATED BY THE MEDICAL PROFESSION TO BE A SOURCE OF SERIOUS DISEASE'. I assumed this was mainly directed at ship-yard workers, who were not usually found in the 1st class compartments.

In the yard were bogie saloon carriages with clerestory roofs, converted from steam rail cars. There were no other bogie carriage vehicles in sight. Did the B&CDR have any, was my thought?

Around the engine shed one could sense the same circumstance as with carriages - the demand for either must be at a low point on a Saturday morning and many locomotives which would be in service Monday to Friday were stabled here. Beyer, Peacock had been the chosen builders of B&CDR motive power for many years and it was difficult to spot an exception among those on view. 4-4-2 tank engines were the type preferred and they were represented by

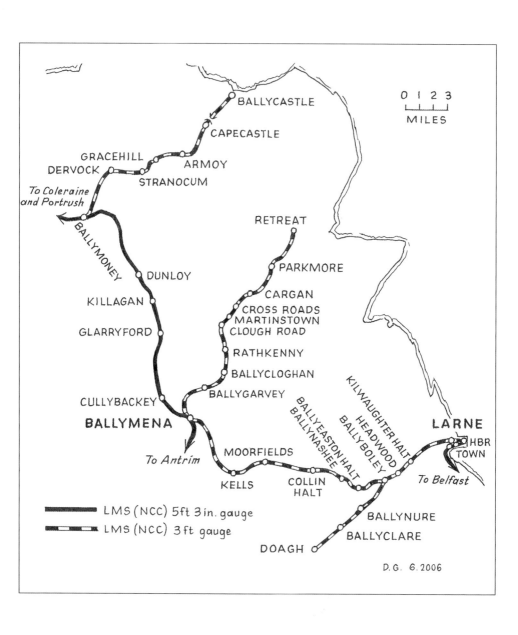

BALLYCASTLE

CAPECASTLE

GRACEHILL
DERVOCK
STRANOCUM
ARMOY

To Coleraine
and Portrush

BALLYMONEY

RETREAT

DUNLOY

PARKMORE

KILLAGAN

CARGAN
CROSS ROADS
MARTINSTOWN
CLOUGH ROAD

GLARRYFORD

RATHKENNY

BALLYCLOGHAN

BALLYGARVEY

CULLYBACKEY

KILWAUGHTER HALT
HEADWOOD
BALLYBOLEY

BALLYMENA

LARNE

BALLYEASTON HALT
BALLYNASHEE

HBR
TOWN

To Antrim

MOORFIELDS

To Belfast

KELLS

COLLIN
HALT

BALLYNURE

LMS (NCC) 5ft 3in. gauge
LMS (NCC) 3ft gauge

BALLYCLARE

DOAGH

D.G. 6.2006

0 1 2 3
MILES

Queen's Quay station. Approach from the east. 1948.   *L&GRP*

No. 8 Beyer, Peacock 4-4-2 tank.   *L&GRP*

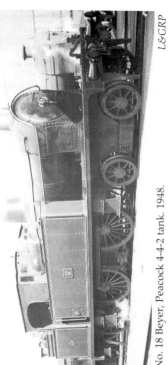

No. 18 Beyer, Peacock 4-4-2 tank. 1948.   *L&GRP*

Withdrawn Beyer, Peacock 4-6-4 tank. September 1954.   *Author*

No. 7 Beyer, Peacock 2-4-2 tank. 1948.   *L&GRP*

Withdrawn locomotives in Queen's Quay engine shed. September 1954.   *Author*

Standard covered van. March 1964.

Author

All third class compartment carriage. Queen's Quay. September 1954.

Author

Standard open wagon. Adelaide yard. October 1959.

Author

Ballast brake van. Queen's Quay. October 1959.

Author

A Belfast train near Ballymoney headed by class 'W' No. 94 MAINE. March 1950. *Author*

A Londonderry train near Ballymoney headed by class 'W' No. 96 SILVER JUBILEE. March 1950.
Author

the youngest and oldest, all, it would seem, in running order and commendably smart and clean. For me, one of their four massive 4-6-4 tanks was especially noteworthy - curiously, despite their size they were never superheated and on the road did not live up to their apparent potential. Even my quick visit served to show how different were the traffic requirements on the B&CDR compared with anywhere I had been at home. Also, the sight of rows of locomotives all sired in Gorton, Manchester was evidence of profound satisfaction and loyalty.

It was time to move on to York Road, so I took a tram which conveniently terminated in the station, and the next train for Londonderry. Looking back on my notes I recall they are so spartan because I found the NCC system resembled the LMS at home and was unworthy of close attention. I saw our locomotive was No. 96 SILVER JUBILEE, one of the modern (1933) 2-6-0 Derby designs class 'W' for the NCC. More to the point, that lunch was available on the train and I succumbed to the suggestion. The menu offered Sausage and Mash, Ice Cream and Coffee all for 2/6d, and there was plate of Soda Bread with much butter to fill in the time between courses. (A reminder, food at home was still rationed.)

My meagre notes suggest my eyes were more on the plate than outside the window but I noticed that unlike the Bangor line, the track had singled from a distance beyond Belfast and we were stopping at major stations. Although there was a passing loop at some of these places, where we were not due to make a pass the train took the 'wrong side' of the loop; again this appeared to me a strange procedure but I concluded that although we were travelling on one of N. Ireland's major routes, business in these parts was insufficient to demand all the railway's equipment all the time - hence economy was the watchword.

The NCC branch from Cookstown Junction was being worked by GNRI class 'T' 2-4-2 Tank engine No. 67 on a short passenger train, and the goods was shunting in the yard with GNRI 0-6-0 No. 153 of class 'QS'. Knowing that Ballymena had once been an important interchange for the Ballymena & Larne (B&L) narrow gauge system, I left the table to hang out of the window but was some years too late to spot anything significant! I was to have better luck another year. There was some time to spare on arriving at Ballymoney; before the Ballycastle train left, I wandered round the yard and made some interesting finds. In a shed was Portrush Tramway engine No. 84 built by Kitson and apparently stored awaiting formal preservation. With it was an ex-Ballymena Cushendall & Red Bay Railway 'bogie' saloon coach, transferred by the NCC for use on Lammas Fair Day traffic when business was too great for existing capacity. It was No. 306, vestibuled with end verandahs, sliding gates and long slatted perimeter seats. The bogies were unlike others I had seen. It had been painted in NCC red and must have been a poor second choice for would-be passengers.

It was time to take a seat in the Ballycastle train made up of two ex-B&L 'Boat Train' coaches with black-painted NCC No. 43 at the head. There was an all 3rd and a 1st/3rd and two ex-B&LR four-wheel brake vans in the train. The corridor connections and the wc had been removed. I thought that this was the smartest narrow gauge ensemble I had ever seen, and on entering the coaches this impression was confirmed. But firstly, the locomotive; what attractive lines it had! Beyer, Peacock was a leader in locomotive design and in these 2-4-2 tank

No. 41 at Ballymoney. Main line *left*, Ballycastle bay *right*. March 1950.   *Author*

2-4-2 tank No. 41 and train approaching Ballymoney. March 1950.   *Author*

engines the drawing office had produced a winner - there was grace in every line. They were good performers too, for after the first had been delivered, a repeat order was placed. For some duties the bunker capacity was inadequate, and certain engines carried an extended version which did not spoil their pleasing lines. Unless one viewed them from the front and saw the two oddly-sized cylinders, they looked conventional enough but they were two-cylinder compound machines of which the Belfast & Northern Counties Railway (B&NCR) had long experience. On starting from rest, they take high pessure steam into both cylinders but by means of a jockey valve, they could be converted to compound working at the behest of the driver. On the footplate (on which I rode the following day) it was possible to detect the change from the sound of the blast from the chimney. Also, when running compound there was a slight uneven surge in progress - or did I imagine it?!

The interior of the carriages was no less attractive for they were still of 1928 'Boat Train' category. Each section was divided into roomettes with thick well-upholstered seats - so much so that I thought they had been demoted from 1st class. Furthermore, the track was well-maintained and the riding qualities of the stock second to none. I enjoyed my ride to Ballycastle ... it remains an outstanding memory.

Ballycastle station lay on high ground behind the town. The day had been bright and the view eastwards over the Irish Sea drew my attention constantly; the Mull of Kintyre and the Scottish coast beyond, the nearer Rathlin Island and the further Scottish Highlands beyond were bathed in sunlight. Ben Nevis to the east and Muckish to the west were on the skyline and the scene remained as I climbed the main street to the Marine Hotel and booked a room for the night. The weather looked promising for the following day so I determined to leave my inspection of the station premises until the next day.

The Marine Hotel looked very smart from the street but seen from my bedroom window out at the back there was a cluster of yards, sheds, clutter and disarray with washing hanging out. I thought of the old adage, 'Queen Ann front and Mary Ann behind' and deduced it must have originated here. For all that it was very comfortable and the breakfast excellent; The dining room waiter wore a newly-laundered white linen jacket whose effect would have been complete had it not been for the fact that it was a mass of holes from the waist downwards. We fell into conversation and on telling me he was the organist at the Church of Ireland here, discussed church music until breakfast was over. And it was a true Irish Break Fast, porage with cream, rashers, eggs, potato cakes, liver, kidney and that Irish delicacy made from sea-weed scooped from the water at low tide! I thought I had better not disclose any of this when I reached home.

I spent most of the morning making notes but determined to come again with my camera. No. 41, newly painted in UTA livery, returned the train to Ballymoney and I caught a stopping train to York Road where I had left my suitcase in the left-luggage office. There was time for meal in the railway hotel before making for the night sailing to Heysham. The extra day given over to Ballycastle had been a profitable exercise. On the next occasion I would try to see something of the NCC narrow gauge lines around Larne before going north

2-4-2 tank No. 41 and train descending to Ballycastle. March 1950.   *Author*

Ballycastle. The approach from Ballymoney. March 1950. *Author*

Ballycastle station. March 1950. *Author*

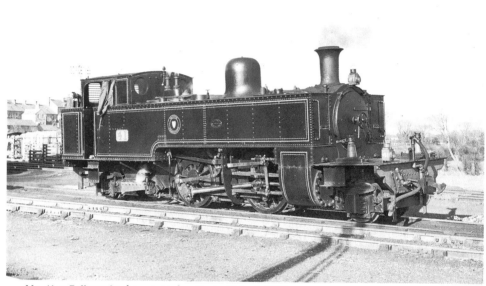

No. 41 at Ballycastle; the paint is hardly dry! March 1950.   *Author*

No. 42 newly-painted in UTA livery. Ballymoney. March 1950.   *Author*

Train ascending from Ballycastle with 2-4-2 tank No. 42 in 1950.　　　　*Author*

2-4-2 tank No. 43. Ballymoney. March 1950.　　　　*Author*

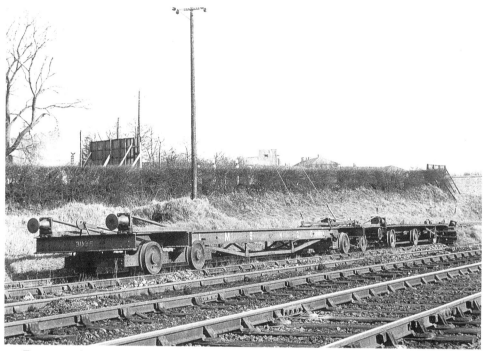

Transporter bogie wagons for carrying 3 ft gauge stock. Ballymoney. March 1950.   *Author*

Luggage/brake vans. Ballymoney. March 1950.   *Author*

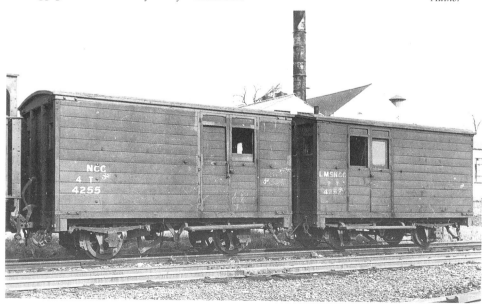

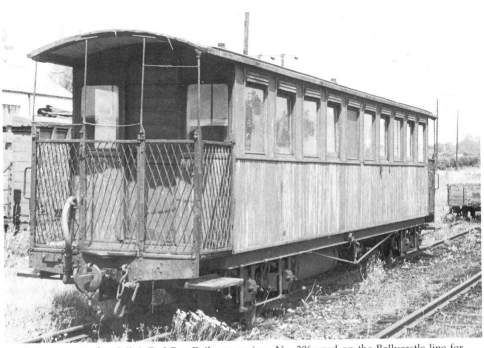

Ballymena, Cushendall & Red Bay Railway carriage No. 306 used on the Ballycastle line for Lammas Fair Day. June 1950.
E.M. Patterson

'Doagh Bogie' ex-B&NCR No. 328 converted to a camping coach in 1937. Ballycastle. June 1962.
Author

'Doagh Bogie' ex B&NCR No. 327. Converted to a camping coach in 1937. Ballycastle. June 1962.

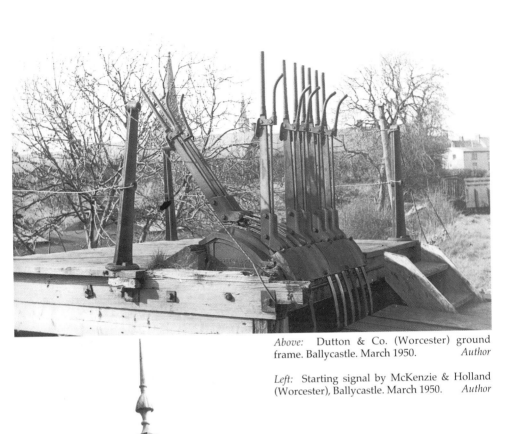

Above: Dutton & Co. (Worcester) ground frame. Ballycastle. March 1950. *Author*

Left: Starting signal by McKenzie & Holland (Worcester), Ballycastle. March 1950. *Author*

Larne Harbour station with mixed gauge tracks. June 1948.   *R.E. Tustin*

Three foot gauge approach to Larne Harbour. June 1948.   *R.E. Tustin*

to the Ballycastle branch again. Here the mixed gauge tracks had already caught my eye.

My next opportunity was on 25th March, 1950; to be nearer my goal I opted to make my business visit based on the NCC hotel at York Road station and on a Friday took an after-breakfast train to Larne. The NCC Ballymena-Larne line was now reduced to a working to supply the paper mill at Ballyclare with coal for the boiler house and a return with paper products to Larne. This ran daily but called for only one engine and brake van, both based on Larne. Obviously a skeleton operation and I learned it ran at times 'As required', so if I walked up the line from Larne westwards I hoped to make its acquaintance. I calculated it was about 12 miles from Larne to Ballyclare (beyond which the railway had been lifted) along the track, and in fact I accomplished this and returned to York Road for the night.

The narrow gauge yards west of Larne station were full of wagons ... and one steam locomotive. At their full extent the railways - of both gauges - intermingled and crossed as they made their way to Larne Harbour and station. To the south-west of here the ex-B&L line made its way a short distance to Larne Town station, the 'business end' of the system where the workshops, locomotive and carriage works were situated. Here the broad and narrow gauge railways, which had contributed to several intriguing track formations hereabouts, parted company and set off in different directions. The large collection of wagons above-mentioned included many which were the property of the Aluminium Works adjacent to the north side of the yards, as was also the solitary locomotive. This was No. 1 of the British Aluminium Co., built by Peckett & Sons of Bristol, works No. 1026 of 1924 and the last survivor of three similar machines.

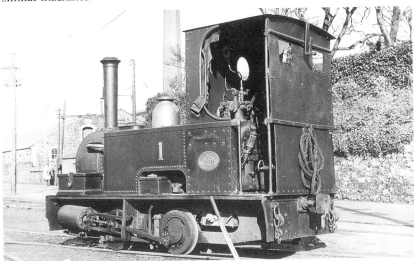

0-4-0T Peckett of 1904 No. 1 British Aluminium Co., Larne Harbour. Gauge 3 ft. March 1950.   *Author*

Larne. Disused station *far left*. March 1950.   *Author*

Larne Town looking east.   *Real Photographs*

Larne Town station, disused. March 1950. *Author*

Larne works and engine shed with locomotive No. 13 just visible. *Real Photographs*

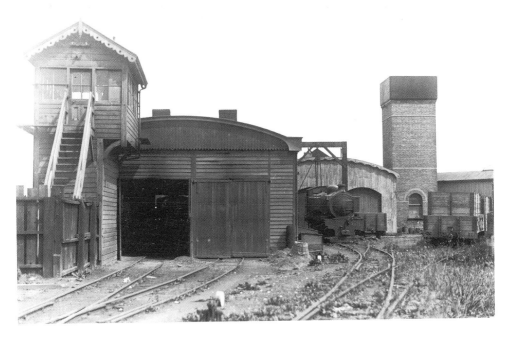

Course of the line out of Larne. March 1950. *Author*

Ex-Ballycastle Railway 4-4-2 tank No. 113 with a coal train climbing out of Larne. *Photomatic*

There was nothing attractive about the complex, littered as it was with immense quantities of errant paper which had escaped from wagons collected from the Mill. It was a perpetual eyesore. To make matters worse, the surviving B&L buildings were all built of timber and these were in such a state of dereliction as to remind me of pictures of the Low Countries during the Great War which had fascinated me as a child. Seldom had I seen a railway in such a wretched state.

The line climbed steeply (1 in 36) as it made its way to the pitiful remains of the Town station. There was clearly some activity going on here as there was a cloud of blue smoke and the sound of someone hammering the last breath out of an innocent metallic victim. Through the smoke I perceived a man who stood encircled by large chunks of what had been a railway locomotive. The object of his exercise was an inner firebox and I realised that this was a vital part of a Beyer, Peacock 2-4-2 tank engine which, had I been here a day or two earlier, I could have photographed entire. A Knacker's Yard indeed! The man's brogue was so broad that I lost most of what he told me, but I gathered he had no recollection of the engine's number. He was not a railway employee but a scrap iron contractor. I trudged on with a heavy heart, the litter of oversize confetti continuing all the while. In due time, I left the environs of Larne behind me, and the litter.

The railway course was pleasant but not beautiful. The track still remained but its course had been stripped of everything non-functional. In due course I came to places where there had been stations but were now unrecognisable as everything had been removed down to the bare ground. This was disappointing. An exception was the little station of 1896 and platform at Headwood which was now occupied and looked very smart; nearby was the only signal I saw, a somersault-armed specimen protecting the nearby main road level crossing with a continental-looking 'blob' on the and of the arm. The distinctive finial revealed its Worcester origins.

Plodding on I came to the site of Ballyboley Junction where the Ballymena and Doagh lines had divided. Little remained of the station except the water tank but the passing loop and a siding were intact and in first-class condition. Furthermore, I had run the daily train to earth - I had already despaired of locating it. Headed by 2-4-2 tank No. 42 it had a number of sheeted open wagons followed by a brake van. There were about five men in all - they seemed surprised to see me in this lonesome place, and had clearly been enjoying an extended lunch break. They shortly set off for Larne leaving no evidence of a Paper Chase in their wake!

Determined to see how the railway ended I continued through open country to the site of Ballyclare terminus, with its Paper Mill siding. The station platform and a run-round loop survived. Eventually the track petered out in a buffer stop. It was all well cared for and the weed-killing train had recently done its business. But I had to use my imagination to recreate the busy little hubbub of yore.

I could now feel I had thoroughly covered what little remained of the B&L line. It was certainly bare of artifacts and though my legs were tired I sat on a grass bank and removed a picnic from my rucksack, well satisfied with the day's work. Tomorrow, I would take the train to Ballycastle again … this time with a camera. There were still wagons at Ballymoney (including the unique

Left: McKenzie & Holland signalling looking towards Larne harbour. March 1950.   *Author*

Below: Headwood level crossing signal, sole survivor. March 1950.   *Author*

Headwood station, occupied by the gate keeper. March 1950.   *Author*

The site of Ballyboley Junction with the course of Ballymena line right. March 1950. *Author*

Remains of Ballyboley station looking towards Larne. March 1950. *Author*

2-4-2 tank No. 42 with the daily paper train at the site of Ballyboley Junction. March 1950.

Author

No. 42 with the daily paper train leaving Ballyboley for Larne. March 1950.   *Author*

six-wheeled transporter used to convey narrow gauge vehicles by broad gauge to Belfast for repair, etc), the camping coaches at Ballycastle and a more detailed look at the premises there. I would have to return to York Rd in good time for the Heysham boat; a full day could be anticipated.

When I returned to the hotel from my B&L walk I ventured to ask the young lady at reception if she could apply some First Aid to my holiday trousers which had been caught in a barbed-wire fence and if I sat in a public place wearing them, I would certainly have to keep my legs crossed … She was kindess itself and admitted there was a first time for everything.

Next morning the engine on my Ballymoney train was NCC No. 66, a much-rebuilt four-coupled tender type of class 'A1' BEN MADIGAN, very distantly related to the Derby-built steeds of that arrangement which I had known on the Somerset & Dorset line during my days at School. The Irish version was a delightful hybrid which did its work in a most placid manner quite suited to the limited demands of the NCC. I was intrigued by the considerable space between the high-pitched boiler and the frames, also the small tender whose springs were positioned outside the tender body above floor level; the whole effect of engine and tender put me in mind of those Bavarian-built large-scale clockwork models advertised in the model railway catalogues of my boyhood. It was an unexpected gem and I was pleased to learn later that a similar machine had gone into the Belfast Railway Museum.

I had a leisurely interval at Ballymoney and was able to photograph such features as I had been denied on the last occasion, including trains on the main line. And so down the Ballycastle branch to do the same there, but there was so much to fill my note book that I had to leave the Camping Coaches for another

Ballyboley station in happier times!   *Real Photographs*

Former Larne Boat Train stock introduced by NCC, Ballymoney. May 1948.   *Author*

Larne Boat Train coaches at Strabane for use on the Co. Donegal system. Note the height of couplings. May 1956.   *Author*

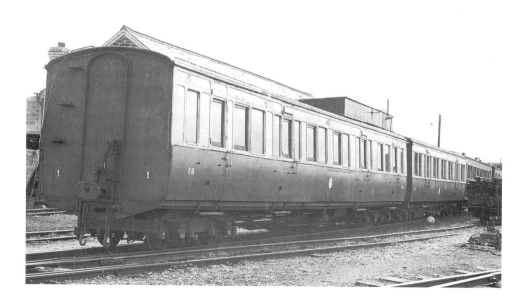

Ballyclare station.   *L&GRP*

The site of Ballyclare station. March 1950.   *Author*

occasion as I had an invitation to travel on the footplate of No 41. By chance these vehicles outlived the railway surrounding them and so on 17th June, 1962 on returning from Castlederg we found them in newly-painted condition and with help to hold the other end of the tape measure, recorded details of these two historic carriages. These were described by E.M. Patterson in *Ballymena Lines* as 'Doagh Bogies' of 1895 which were converted to camping coaches Nos. 16 and 21 in 1937 and 1938, ex-B&NCR Nos. 327 and 328. They had been built as third class 'tramcars' and carried plates stating they had Fox's Patent pressed steel underframes and bogies, built by the Leeds Forge Co. founded in 1893 by Samuel Fox who had developed a technology of steel pressing by hydraulic means suited to making strong but lightweight railway wagons. These coaches were 40 ft long, 6 ft 4 in. wide with seats for 42 persons. They were vestibuled with end doors and fallplates but due to conversion the original interiors had been lost. They were used on the Ballymena, Cushendall & Red Bay Railway section of the B&NCR and in their present location looked good for some years to come.

The end of the line at Ballyclare paper mill. (Site of the line to Doagh behind the camera.)
March 1950.   *Author*

Chapter Seventeen

Once Daily and Once Monthly, The West Clare and Tralee & Dingle sections of the CIE, 27th-30th September, 1950

Our enthusiasm for the narrow gauge lines of Eire had been increased by our journeys over the Cavan & Leitrim section in 1949 and we decided to use an autumn break in 1950 to visit the West Clare (WCR) and Tralee & Dingle (T&DR) lines before they too fell under the hammer. Other than the C&L, they were the only two narrow gauge survivors from the former Great Southern Railways which were still operational. The former ran passenger and goods trains but the passenger service on the latter had been suspended since April 1949. Owing to coal shortages, there was only one through passenger train daily on the Clare line whilst on the Dingle an outward empty cattle special left Tralee monthly for Dingle and returned, loaded, the following day. These special workings ran in connection with the Dingle Fair, and on all other days the line was closed. After much thought, we ascertained two appropriate days for the Clare line whilst we obtained the necessary days, times and Passes for Dingle. With these very limited timetables we would have to spend two days covering Clare (with an intervening night at Kilkee) whilst we could only travel out from Tralee to Dingle by train and would have to use the CIE bus back to Tralee. It was all quite an adventure!

More detail came our way. The Dingle section cattle trains ran in two parts, each double-headed and following each other half an hour apart. The train crews slept in Dingle overnight and equipment for men and machines would have to travel with us.

The run across to Athenry on the former MGWR main line was without note, there being ample stops at Mullingar, Athlone and beyond to Athenry, the great area of bog landscape stretching as far as eye could see to north and south. It differed but little as we travelled further west.

At Athenry the MGWR line is crossed by the ex-Waterford, Limerick & Western Railway (WL&WR) which became part of the Great Southern & Western Railway system in 1901 by which the GSWR obtained access to Sligo and the north-west - much to the chagrin of the MGWR. Here we left the Galway train and changed into the daily working from Sligo to Limerick, an unhurried caravan of three ex-MGWR six-wheeled carriages and a newly-upholstered ex-GSWR bogie coach, quietly snoozing in a bay platform. At our head was No. 96, an ex-GSWR 4-4-0 class 'D14', vintage 1885. We chose a six-wheeler!

In an hour we were in Ennis after 60 minutes of travel through pastoral but unspectacular country. The route had a special appeal. It was very much a secondary artery, with a few quite expensive earthworks and a curvaceous course at times as if the contractor had been warned not to overspend. At the same time, the surroundings had a lonely feel. There was only one major station at Gort. Our carriage ran along with that peculiar motion given to six-wheelers and the particular sound which is given when passing over flat-bottomed rails.

We had a wait of three hours in Ennis which allowed us to see the station and yards thoroughly, and then go into the town for a meal and some essential shopping. First, to exchange my time-expired trousers for a pair of Limerick-

The West Clare Railway

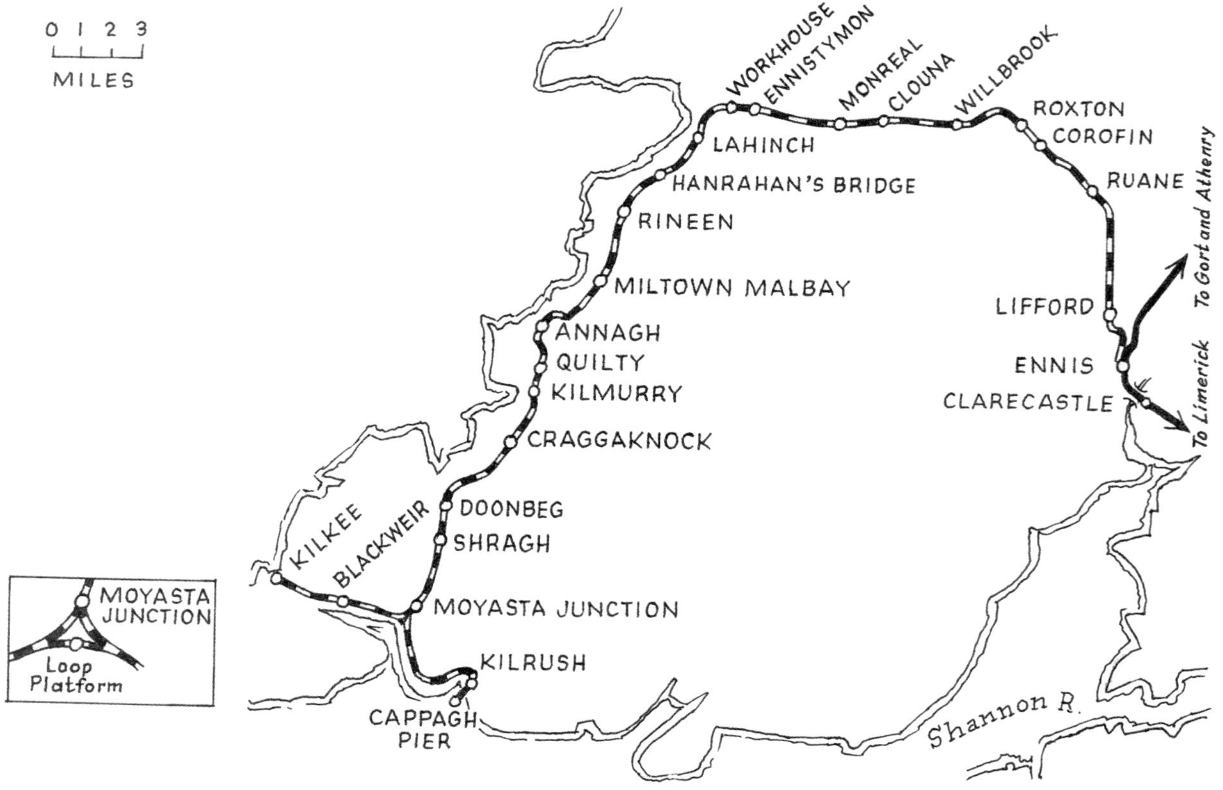

0 1 2 3
MILES

MOYASTA JUNCTION

Loop Platform

To Gort and Athenry
To Limerick

RUANE
COROFIN
ROXTON
WILLBROOK
CLOUNA
MONREAL
ENNISTYMON
WORKHOUSE
LAHINCH
HANRAHAN'S BRIDGE
RINEEN
MILTOWN MALBAY
ANNAGH
QUILTY
KILMURRY
CRAGGAKNOCK
DOONBEG
SHRAGH
MOYASTA JUNCTION
KILKEE
BLACKWEIR
KILRUSH
CAPPAGH PIER

LIFFORD
ENNIS
CLARECASTLE

Shannon R.

made ones for which I would not have to surrender any of my precious Clothing Coupons. Dorothy was so impressed with the quality and value, that she was tempted too which meant her rucksack had to bear an extra parcel. The other impression of Ennis was that its proximity to Shannon Airport might give it the title of Little America if goods in the shops were an indication. But down at the railway yard there were no flamboyant ties or suede shoes to be seen at the offices, works and sheds of the West Clare system, situated to the north-west of the station. The narrow gauge terminates on the west side of an island platform, with the main lines to the east. There was an imposing slightly ecclesiastical stone building at the northern extremity of the narrow gauge which I concluded was a legacy of the former Limerick & Ennis Railway.

Outside the more mundane corrugated-iron repair shops was a number of the six-wheeled third-class saloons used for tourist traffic during the summer. At this time of year they are stored but the first-class vehicle had been purloined by the yard foreman for his office. The remainder were six-wheeled six-compartment stock, built for the opening of the line in 1887 by the Bristol Carriage & Wagon Co. The carriages were illuminated by carbide gas, supplied by a plant in the guard's van. Most carriages were now painted in CIE green with its Flying Snail totem, an exception being a small Ford-engined inspection car, still in GSR livery with coat-of-arms. It was built for the Tralee & Dingle line but had been at Ennis for some years. All the Clare coaches had a long wheelbase with six wheels but fortunately there were no sharp curves. Additionally there were some bogie coaches from the T&D section stored at Kilrush. They were lit from batteries for which there was a charging plant at Tralee station as T&D stock had no dynamos. Consequently, they could only be used on the Clare section in summer!

Engine No. 5 was in steam in the yard (0-6-2T by Dübs of 1892) and No. 10 (4-6-0T by Kerr, Stuart of 1903) was on shed nearby having new brake blocks fitted. This engine was unusual as the valve gear was arranged forward of the leading driving axle between the frames. The valves were driven by rocker arms to the valve chests outside the frames. Maker's plates had been removed and replaced by small 'home-made' substitutes fixed to the footplate valance; they contained several curious spellings.

The locomotive repair shops where all but the heaviest work was done, were up beside the wider gauge goods yard. Here were to be found: No. 1 (4-6-0T by Hunslet of 1912,) No. 9 (2-6-2T by Green of 1898), No. 7 (4-6-0T by Hunslet of 1912), No. 11 (4-6-0T by Bagnall of 1909). No. 3 (4-6-0T by Hunslet of 1922) was out on a goods train and No. 6 (as No. 5) was at Kilkee for the shuttle working to Kilrush. The locomotives were used turnabout as available. The heaviest turn was the goods working which often ran to 20 wagons. Noted how the 4-6-0T arrangement predominates. Further enquiry revealed that No. 11 had Baguley-Price valve gear between the frames, No. 9 had transverse motion in the axleboxes of the pony trucks and that its rear driving axle passed through the ashpan in a 'tunnel'. The story goes that after it was blown off the track by a gale so frequent in these parts, the wheels were reduced in diameter!

Derailments due to high winds were common here and 56 lb. iron weights were put under the carriage seats to prevent this. (For the same reason, concrete slabs were to be found under the side seats of T&D carriages.)

Ennis station. *Left*: West Clare train just arrived. *Right*: Limerick train due to depart. *Centre distance*: WCR engine shed. September 1950.   *Author*

Ennis station with West Clare train at interchange platform. January 1961.   *Author*

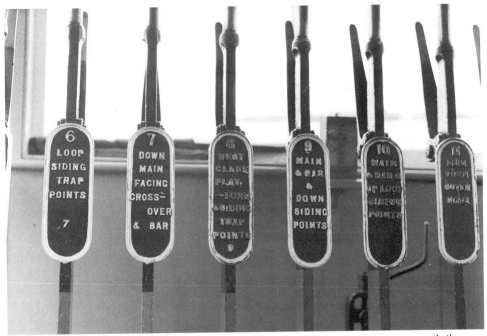

Ennis. The lever frame serves both gauges. June 1963.

Author

Ennis. Signalman Martin Crotty in Ennis signal cabin. June 1963.

Author

Ennis ground frame with locking key. January 1961.

Author

Walker-built railcar leaving Ennis. January 1961.   *Author*

Inspection car inside Ennis workshops after transfer from the Tralee & Dingle section. January 1961.
                                                                               Author

We left the station at 4.55 pm with No. 5, two five-compartment coaches and a Dingle bogie guard's van. There was time to measure the van's cute little T&D bogies with their 3 ft wheelbase; their bodies were 28 ft long. The compartment was well filled by those who had come into town for the day and we sat tightly together. It had just about stopped raining but the atmosphere was damp and the windows steamed up so we could see little of the passing scene. To make matters worse, the wet clothes of our fellow travellers gave off a very bovine pong. This became so obvious that most of the young women lit cigarettes while men pulled out a well-used pipe and relit its plug embers. The atmosphere was atrocious.

Northwards from Ennis the two gauges run side by side but on different earthworks and they cross the River Fergus on independent bridges before the Clare line swings westwards. Our impression of the setting was of a bleak wet landscape almost immersed in water. Farmsteads were mainly roofed in thatch and in their flooded yards bedraggled cattle stood inches deep in water. It must have been raining for days while the waterlogged ground was so lowlying it would not throw off the flooding. We had not seen this desperately poor part of Ireland before and it made a lasting impression on us. Now and again a crumbling stone ruin of some worth and set upon higher ground would pass. On our return in better weather we recognised these as castlelike fortified houses found hereabouts.

We made a brisk run to Corofin (8¾ m.) and I estimated our speed was about 40 mph. No. 5's connecting side rods thrashed up and down as the engine whistled continuously but the carriage ran most smoothly even though it was not the acme of comfort. The compartment was only 6 ft 6 in. wide inside which I compared with the same figure on the Festiniog Railway with its 1 ft 11½ in. gauge. Why was the Clare stock so narrow?

There was a long wait at Corofin while we waited for an oncoming train to pass us. Our train effectively blocked the level crossing and soon a menagerie of donkeys and scraggy horses pulling two-wheeled carts piled with turf had collected. I took the opportunity to surprise our companions by cleaning the windows with the *Irish Times*.

Beyond Corofin the line rises consistently to its highest point and the watershed. We made a request stop at Willbrook (11¼ m.), simply a platform and then ran over a twisting portion across barren high ground to Ennistymon (18½ m.) the largest intermediate point. Here was No. 3 on a considerable goods train. It passed us as we stopped for water. It began to rain again, pitilessly and straight off the Atlantic Ocean only a few miles away to the west. To complete our discomfiture, the compartment had filled with more wet bodies and my newly-wiped windows had steamed up again.

A short run brought us to Lahinch (20¾ m.), a small seaside place with a station above the beach. There were peculiar signals here governing the passing loop, one arm being fixed to the other on either side of a common post. The clear position could only be shown by each arm alternately, denoting which side of the loop was set for through running.

From Lahinch the railway runs above and beside the sea. The hinterland is poverty-ridden, rocky and infertile. The cottages were ill-roofed and a damp sea mist drove in restricting visibility to a train length. The men glared through the

River Fergus bridges north of Ennis. January 1961. *Author*

Ballygriffey Castle, looking towards Corofin. January 1961. *Author*

A typical bi-lingual station nameboard. January 1961. *Author*

Corofin, looking towards Moyasta. January 1961. *Author*

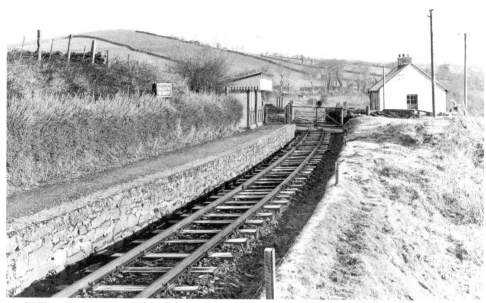

Willbrook looking back towards Ennis. January 1961.   *Author*

Ennistymon from the Ennis direction. January 1961.   *Author*

Kilkee train at Ennistymon with No. 5. September 1950. *Author*

Morning train for Ennis at Ennistymon with No. 5. September 1950. *Author*

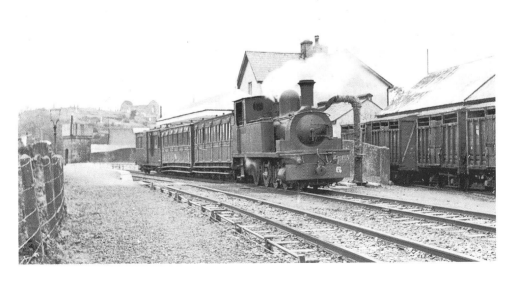

Ennistymon, looking towards Moyasta. January 1961.   *Author*

Railcar leaving Ennistymon for Kilkee. January 1961.   *Author*

Lahinch looking west. The signals only indicate the setting of the passing loop. January 1961.
Author

Lahinch. Dorothy examines who is sending what and where? January 1961.　*Author*

Daily goods train passing Lahinch with new Walker 0-4-4-0 diesel-mechanical locomotive. January 1961.   *Author*

Miltown Malbay with Down railcar *en route* for Kilrush passing Up goods. May 1958.   *Author*

steamy windows, the women studied their wet muddied legs with indifference. At one point we must have passed a church, for they all crossed themselves. We felt like Unbelievers. Suddenly the silence was broken. We were offered cigarettes and asked about their cost in England ... soon the compartment was full of chatter.

After a burst of speed we reached Miltown Malbay (27 m.), where the railway notionally passes from the West Clare to the South Clare Railway. We made a long stop for water and suddenly the train was almost empty and the platform was thronged with homebound chattering children. We gladly stretched our arms and legs, and lowered the windows. The sea air was a tonic.

For the next hour we passed through treeless upland, a depressing vista unhelped by the foggy weather. At Quilty - a place where a few cottages huddled together by the shore - the remains of the well-known anemometer for measuring wind velocity still stood. The spoons at the top of the mast were now missing. I assume that because all the carriages have been weighted the apparatus was defunct. At an earlier time, if wind-speed reached a certain point unweighted vehicles were not allowed to run. On a siding nearby stood wagons piled high with seaweed which is used as a manure; loading here was very convenient for the beach.

Between here and Moyasta Junction there were spectacular views of the nearby cliffs with Atlantic rollers crashing into the foot of them. As they did so the sea was driven through caves at sea level to escape through fissures and chasms at clifftop height to make a fine display of natural forces accompanied by a tremendous roaring sound.

It was growing dusk when we pulled up at the triangular Moyasta Junction (43 m.) and changed trains into a single coach bound for Kilkee headed by engine No. 6. So sister engines stood side by side in the gathering gloom while we, with a night's sleep at sea already long behind us, and without accommodation booked for the forthcoming night, wondered if we would end up trying to sleep in a primitive compartment coach on an exposed siding ... The two trains moved off simultaneously and silently and we watched the Kilrush rake as it skirted the water's edge wreathed in steam. We were the only passengers for Kilkee.

We passed Blackweir, a short single platform, and then ran over a long straight stretch of bare land to the terminus at Kilkee, a small well-appointed station some distance from the sea. The season was over. The day trippers had all returned to Limerick weeks ago but the station master was kindness itself and showed us the way to a recommended address. It had no electric lighting upstairs but candles and oil lamps in plenty. It was warm and the feather bed was cosy. We could hear the sea beating on the strand and fell asleep well content with the day's adventures and a bookful of notes.

The train for Ennis left at 8 am - the only train. Therefore a vital item of luggage was the alarm clock. I left Dorothy to settle the bill and set off for the station alone. It was deserted but I could see No. 6 poking out of its shed so I wandered up to see what was happening. A young man shortly appeared and said he had been knocking up the driver who was still in bed. The pressure gauge showed 15 lb. and the place was thick with smoke. The fireman - for it

Miltown Malbay with Ennis-bound daily passenger train and No. 5. September 1950.   *Author*

Miltown Malbay looking towards Moyasta. The West and South Clare railways made end-on junction here. January 1961.   *Author*

Moyasta Junction with train from Kilrush *left*, and from Kilkee *right*. Locomotives Nos. 5 and 6.
September 1950. *Author*

Moyasta Junction. May 1958. *Author*

Kilkee. There is only one passenger waiting to see No. 5 back down on the Ennis train.
September 1950.   *Author*

Kilkee 7.45 am. No. 5 limps from the engine shed (*right*) to join the train in the platform!
September 1950.   *Author*

was he - pulled the whistle cord and the whistle produced a gurgle. At 7.55 am the driver turned up and opened the blower a little. Also the drain cocks. When the gauge showed 20 lb. the handbrake was taken off, the regulator opened wide and No. 5 slid out of the shed in a cloud of steam. It was as well that it was all downhill until we reached the carriages again. The guard helped me down from the engine and I joined Dorothy who was alone in the carriage; we set off at a snail's pace as there was hardly any steam. I guessed that staying late in bed and using the gradient to help the engine onto the train was a daily pantomime. We reached Moyasta Junction after one of the slowest short journeys I could recall. The train from Kilrush was waiting for us and we lost no time in changing over and taking a few photographs. It was the same formation which had carried us the night before. Later that day it occurred to me, what did No. 5 and crew do all day until they met again in the evening to make connection with the train from Ennis? I never found out.

The gale and storms of yesterday had blown away and it turned into a lovely day. The sea was magnificent and the coast line clear for miles. The views we had been denied by the mists of yesterday were revealed, and there seemed to be more castles than ever; the flooks of rooks which perched on their crumbling battlements rose in force as the train passed. We re-entered Ennis with a better heart and ready to begin the next stage of our Saga.

Until 1938 when some Tralee & Dingle coaches were drafted in, the WCR pinned its faith in six-wheeled coaches, 30 ft long with Cleminson flexible wheelbases, of compartment or 'Tourist Saloon' arrangement. The latter had tall clerestory roofs. Six-wheeled guard's vans of similar style were used. They had high glass-windowed roof lookouts. One survived.

Our train for Limerick was already at the platform, consisting of No. 8, one of the small ex-GSWR 4-4-0 tender class 'D19' now in its 73rd year and three ex-MGWR 6-wheel carriages (very comfortably re-upholstered) drawn up on the wrong side of the loop to facilitate transfer of luggage. It was a pleasant run to Limerick, through pastoral country very different from that recently tranversed, though fortified ruins persisted. They must have been very warlike hereabouts!

The line was single laid in flat-bottomed rails and a lineside board read 'Prize Length 1950'. Outside Limerick the first junction encountered was that brought into use to serve the Shannon Power Scheme's generating station at Ardnacrusha and was retained for that purpose. There followed a long sweeping curve extending clockwise for almost two miles, firstly over the tidal Shannon River by a steel viaduct and finally onto the double track of the former GSWR main line from Limerick Junction into the terminus. The main line was laid with bull-head rails in chairs. But first a stop was made outside the coaling plant at a narrow wooden Ticket Platform; a few of these still survive in Ireland. Our special tickets were shown here.

Limerick was quite a pretentious station, as befits as the headquarters of the former Waterford & Limerick Railway (W&LR). It had an all-over roof and solidly-built edifice and offices. But accommodation for passengers was very jaded (remember that the date of my notes is 1950) and we had until 5.30 pm before the departure of the daily train to Tralee - 5½ hours later. Despite the extensive Shannon docks there was no rail connection to the quays: what prevented this?

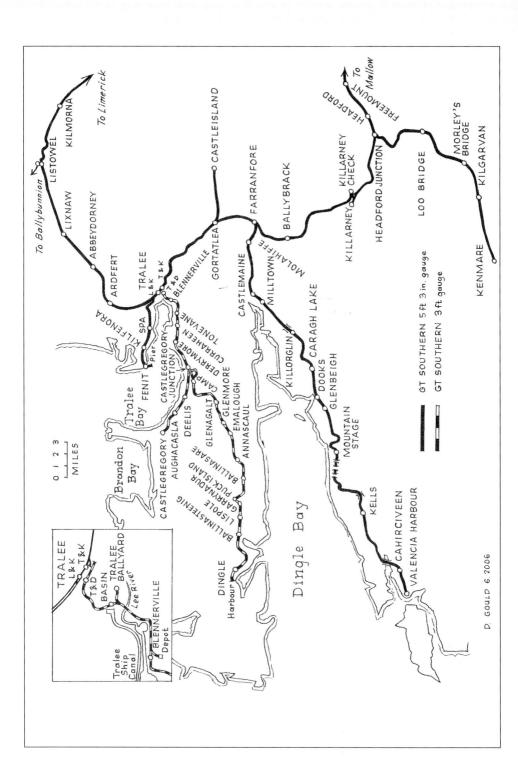

We had anticipated our extended sojourn here by arranging to see the W&LR workshops and engine shed. The former remains in active use as the main wagon repair works. All this was once the domain of J.G. Robinson before he was appointed to the Great Central Railway in England. These are the only CIE workshops outside Inchicore and the young foreman was rightly proud of the fact. The engine shed housed No. 1, 4-4-0 of class 'D17', still with its 'tabernacle' smokebox doors, and No. 295 one of the two 0-4-4T built by Robinson for the WL&WR class 'E2'. This engine had been working the Foynes branch but had sheared two driving wheel spokes; in its place was another Robinson engine, one of the two remaining 2-4-0 class 'G3', No. 291. An interesting trio.

The Tralee line curved very sharply away southward from Limerick's platform ends. There must be few stations without a nameboard in evidence, but perhaps everyone knows they have arrived and should know whence they left! I could see no name on the platforms or signal box. Our engine was an ex-GSWR class 'J15' 0-6-0 No. 130, one of the most numerous class in Ireland which, so we were told, is due to work all CIE branch lines from 2nd October, 1950.

At Ballingrane Junction the Foynes branch runs off to the north-west to reach the south shore of the Shannon estuary; the branch train uses one of the main line platforms, drawing in from a siding after the main line train departs. The Tralee line now curves in almost a complete semi-circle to strike south towards Newcastle. Newcastle is one of those 'unexpected' stations. For apparently no reason at all, the engine is detached and runs forward onto a turntable, turns, and runs round the train to leave eventually in the direction of arrival. The reason for this is historic and is due to the railway terminating at Newcastle originally and then being extended at later date and branching off on a new course. This pantomime cost 20 minutes but we enjoyed every minute! In Ireland such things are taken with leisurely grace. In our case, we simply left the compartment and watched the proceedings from a convenient platform seat.

There now follows a steep climb of 1 in 50 which, for a country not abounding in heavily graded lines with earthworks or tunnels, is worth noting. This is the Barnagh Bank which commences shortly after Newcastle station and rises steeply through a series of fine curves to cross an arm of the Mullaghareirk Mountains in a short single bore tunnel through the limestone. There is a considerable rock-lined cutting at either end of the bore and a small station at the west end of the mouth, Devon Road. Here, by previous arrangement, I joined the men on the footplate and there followed one of the most exciting rides I could wish for. There was a speed restriction down the bank but be that as it may, we fled along with coal on the tender cascading down onto the footplate and ending in a pile below the firehole door. All the same, the elderly six-coupled engine ran smoothly with regulator closed and the reverser screwed well back. Exhilarating! The tender was one of the early type with low side sheets and a yawning gap between cab and tender. I braced myself between the tool locker and hand brake pillar so as not to be pitched off. Now and again the driver applied the train brake and gave me a grin; he was giving his visitor something to remember. We stopped at Abbeyfeale. In a state of enjoyable disarray I rejoined Dorothy in the train. 'There's no need for you to tell me you have enjoyed yourself … how fast were we travelling when we came down the hill?'

No. 1 returns through the streets of Tralee after coaling up at the main station. September 1950.
Author

Tralee engine shed. Nos. 2 and 6. September 1950.
Author

At Abbeyfeale we passed a Special conveying happy throngs of race-goers returning from the last day of Listowel Races. As the two trains stood in the station side by side, the revellers burst into drunken song and there was the sound of breaking glass … When the Special departed, the last carriage was adorned by an extra red tail lamp tied to the coupling chain with binder twine.

In gathering gloom we proceeded to Listowel where I determined to get out to see if there were any vestiges of the long-gone Listowel & Ballybunion mono railway. But no.

There was a long wait here. We must have looked fiercesome as several intending passengers had second thoughts about entering the compartment. The platforms were thronged; everyone was happy - many more so. Another Race Special was drawn up in a siding awaiting our departure. There was more music, more laughter and further sounds of breaking glass. I lowered the window and stood blocking it as I did not fancy my fellow-travellers' company in the state of things. The ruse worked but the remainder of the journey was accompanied by elephantine bumps and crashes emanating from portions of the train. We were relieved to reach Tralee, albeit slightly late, and made our way to Benner's Hotel as recommended. After an excellent meal we joined the driver of our train in the bar. He was quite concerned for our wellbeing saying the crowds had been far worse than any he had experienced. 'Lucky for you to leave the engine when you did'.

Our bedroom at Benner's was on the top floor and shortly after we had got into bed we were aware of strange shuffling noises coming from above the ceiling. These would stop suddenly and then accelerate. We made mention of these sounds to the waitress at breakfast. 'Ach', she said, ''tis the rats. They are far louder in my room'. And that was the last of it.

On the following day the Dingle Cattle Special was due to leave the former T&DR station in two portions at 11 and 12 o'clock respectively. It was some distance away from the main line station but a 3 ft gauge connecting line ran down the middle of the street between the two stations. The weather was what the Irish describe as 'A bit soft', in other words a pitiless, relentless drizzle. We followed the connecting line which was heavily flooded with floating horse muck. An engine with a single low-sided wagon in tow passed us on its way to the main line yard. We reported for duty at the station office and were greeted most cordially and gathered the Dingle line was ours for the day - or almost!

Our visit to the main line engine sheds close by was abruptly halted by torrential rain. Instead we returned to the T&D station per a long island transfer platform between the gauges and used for goods traffic. Since the timetable for the T&D section only listed one cattle run to Dingle and return monthly, it was no surprise to find that everything from rolling stock to track was looking down at heel - serviceable yes, but no more than that.

Even in the heyday of passenger train working, $2\frac{1}{2}$ hours were allowed for the Dingle run with its mountainous terrain and lengths of 1 in 24 (or worse, it was whispered). Today's outing was expected to require at least $3\frac{1}{2}$ hours running time so we had filled the rucksacks with chocolates and fruit as well as the essential cameras, films, notebooks …

Ready for the off. No. 1 at Tralee station. May 1952.   *Author*

Returning to Tralee, Nos. 8 and 1. May 1952.   *Author*

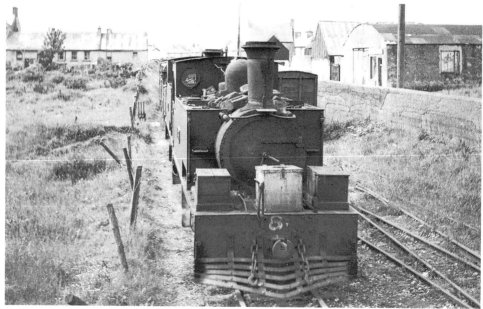

There were five of the original locomotives still on the Dingle section, being Hunslet-built 2-6-0T Nos. 1, 2, 6 and 8 and a fifth Hunslet No. 5, a 2-6-2T which was away at Inchicore for heavy overhaul. For the monthly traffic, four engines have to be steamed, meaning that each had to be taken out of store for the purpose. Nowadays the engines were coaled up at the transfer platform in the main goods yard, and they took it in turn to run down the street for this purpose. Half an hour was allowed for each and it was not surprising that prompt departures were rare! Writing of coal, this was scarce as in every other part of Eire and was bolstered with large briquettes imported from South Wales. As there is no coal available at Dingle, sufficient had to be taken on the outward journey to cover the return; in consequence the cab, bunker and tank tops of the engine were heaped with fuel. For the same purpose the low-sided open wagon coupled to the engine was buried likewise. Each loco had a bell suspended from a trunnion above the boiler, actuated by a cord attached to the motion. This rung continuously as it rumbled along the street. When the engines were new they carried protective side skirts, but these had now been discarded.

Our train consisted of pilot engine No. 8, train engine No. 1, one open wagon full of Cardiff briquettes, 16 empty cattle vans and a passenger guard's bogie van which had had all the glazing removed and replaced with rough timber shuttering. Like all the old T&D passenger stock, the van doors opened inwards. The train was vacuum brake fitted and I noted that the intermediary hoses were properly connected; this seemed to be a priority on a railway with such a reputation for run-away trains!

We left Tralee with the distant Slieve Mish mountain range (which we were destined to cross) covered by heavy clouds. There was another heavy cloudburst and water fell steadily from the roof of the van where the planks had shrunk and the roof canvas had ripped away. There was a strong stench of ammonia here as this end of the vehicle was railed off for carrying calves. Despite this dispiriting start, we anticipated the day with excitement. In the centre of this well-watered space stood the handbrake screw. The guard expostulated, 'How the divil could I be expected to apply the b***** brake while the van is filled with b***** cows and I have to move them before I can reach to turn the b***** handle?' We politely agreed; it was becoming difficult to keep our feet on the greasy floor.

The men on this Dingle job are all former T&DR employees. Broad gauge men could not be bribed into taking on this duty, and after our experiences we appreciate their viewpoint.

We made a confident start from Tralee, for the track was good along the side of the ship canal with rails from the abandoned Cork & Muskerry narrow gauge section of 74 lb. per yard. (The original T&D rails had been upgraded from 45 lb. to 50, 68 and 73 lb. - a mixed bag!) The two engines were anything but steam tight, belching clouds of steam into the damp atmosphere. But the rain had eased into a drizzle and the clouds had lifted and we saw the summits of some of the highest ranges in Ireland. It was like the curtain rising on a stage.

At Blennerville (2¼ m.) the sea encroaches on the land and if the tide was high the train might have to run with its axles at water level. The route up to this

No. 1 has used much of its coal but the sanders are working again. Castlegregory Junction.
September 1950.   *Author*

Trouble with water supply. Castlegregory Junction. September 1950.   *Author*

stage was at sea level and shortly the road to Dingle was joined; the railway followed the verge close beside it, usually along the north edge but occasionally swopping sides with minimal warning. There were danger signs for road users, but no gates or flagmen save at major intersections where a curious double-armed semaphore on a single post was provided. The enginemen kept a good lookout, sounding their whistles continuously until our ears ached, but speed was never slackened. We found it exhilarating - a common reaction to Irish narrow gauge travel! Whenever we ran through a cloudburst, from the back of the train we could watch the rain striking the smokeboxes and chimneys like bullets on a rockface in a 'Western' film. Some of the vans in the rake were beginning to run hot axle boxes which smoked vigorously - not surprising if they had had occasion to run through the sea water near Blennerville …

Further along the railway quitted the road and had its own right of way. Here it became risky to lean out of the van doors as the hedges had not been trimmed, (there was only one platelayer for the current eight miles), so whole boughs flipped inside the van with a frightening crash. We stood back out of harm's way. The railway kept a sinuous course and there were some steep pitches; the leading engine was constantly slipping on the wet vegetation. This had the effect of drying the rails for the second engine which kept its feet.

We continued in this manner for about an hour, occasionally losing balance when the couplings snatched; it was as well there was not much cow muck hereabouts. Shortly we came to Castlegregory Junction, or Lower Camp as the men call it.

The guard informed us that there would be a 10 minute stop here while the engines took water (10 miles). They would have to draw up twice at the water column for this. 'The engines and men are able to get a drink. Would you care for a drink,Boss?' (I should explain that I was 'Boss' throughout this trip.)

'Paddy' is the factotum at the Junction, or in effect the station master without any passenger trains. He handles the parcels etc. for the CIE road lorries and was there to meet us as if we were dignatories from the Far East. Being a conscientious man, he had pulled off all the appropriate signals in this remote spot where there was no possibility of any other movements that month except our two cattle trains travelling in close proximity in the same direction. We were impressed and said so. He was duly chuffed.

I was introduced by the guard as 'Mr Courtney's son' which explained why we were being given the Red Carpet treatment! I gathered that Paddy would meet us all in 'Fitzgerald's Bar' adjacent, and never was a bar so well placed in such an isolated setting I would think.

However, over at the water column all was not so convivial. The stop cock was fully open but not a solitary drop would fall from the hose. A conference was held around the spot and much advice was exchanged. Nothing was done. It was then suggested that water be taken direct from the station tank, though this had not been used for 10 years. This was a dismal failure too. To add to the misery, No. 1 was found to have a hot driving axle box so with half our train was run into a siding in order to work it back to Tralee for repair.

At 2 pm, the stop cock still proving stubborn, various Nabobs arrived from Tralee by van bringing a fitter, his mate and a large plumber's bag with them. It was now obvious to us that we should not reach Dingle to catch the the 4.20

Engines Nos. 1 and 8 take water in turn. Castlegregory Junction. September 1950.   *Author*

Nos. 8 and 1 enter Castlegregory Junction. September 1950.   *Author*

pm CIE Bus before the bus had left Dingle and was well on its way back to Tralee again. The Tralee shed foreman, on his knees in the mud, eventually had water gushing up like a fountain and was able to fill the tanks of No. 8 in the nick of time. They were completely dry. It was a close shave!

After a further conference with the foreman, it was decided to risk No. 1 with its hot box as there would be no time to run it back to Tralee. The second portion of the train meanwhile, had been unable to leave Tralee until the Tralee-Castlegregory Junction single line Tablet (still in our possession) had been put into the Castlegregory Junction instrument, thus releasing a Tablet for the second train.

At 2.55 pm we resumed our belated journey, leaving the Junction at full blast to breast the long climb up to Glenagalt. Below us the course of the abandoned Castlegregory branch swept down in a graceful curve to its roadside location and the Atlantic shore. To the north over the sea was Fenit Harbour and the Co. Limerick coast. To our west the mountains fell sharply down to sea level, their summits shrouded in mist and their flanks dotted by thatched white cottages. Here we were about to descend at 1 in 29, one of the steepest railways in Britain with rails sodden with rain and greasy with vegetation. The guard was pessimistic and told us grim tales of run-away trains and stalling engines. He pointed out the derelict two-arch viaduct at Camp, now bypassed, with its treacherous approach curve where in 1907, a pig train had careered out of control down the bank and pitched over the side of the bridge, killing the crew, the Locomotive Superintendent and most of the pigs as well.

I thought we were travelling well, but obviously the guard did not. The two little engines snaked their way round the long curve ahead, nosing along the mountain as do two small dogs in a gutter, crossing the later-built steel girder bridge which replaced the site of the accident in 1907, and cutting through the hillside to join the original course.

There followed a long exciting grind along the verge of the road, collar work all the way, a sinuous gradient of two miles with a long bleak valley below us which ran to the seashore at length. With the wild hills above and all around, they made a perfect amphitheatre. Even with our enthusiasm for North Wales, we had to admit the scenery and this spectacular railway in concert had us spell-bound! As each locomotive lost its grip on the rails, the speed dropped suddenly and alarmingly. I wondered how the overheated axle box was faring, and could it be felt through the cab floor? I tried to secure a footing to take photographs of the huge smokepall we were making.

We breasted the lonely little passenger platform at Glenagalt (13¾ miles) and the summit. Steam was eased off and the injectors allowed to do their work. The safety valves ceased their incessant clamour and the long descent to Annascaul began. The guard was jubilant and insisted we had knocked 10 minutes off the running time from the Junction. True or not, we were adding a remarkable ride to our Irish experiences.

The railway is about 680 ft above sea level here and the long downhill run extends, with lesser undulations, to the next passing loop at Annascaul. The guard was very insistent that we should have adequate brake availability. The vacuum brake gauge showed only 10 inches. 'Tap the glass, Boss' he said. Eleven inches. The guard came cross and smote the glass in a way no barometer

Anxious moments on Glengalt. Pilot No. 8 is doing all the work while train engine No. 1 is slipping all the way. September 1950.   *Author*

Nos. 8 and 1 slog up Glengalt bank. May 1952.   *Author*

would tolerate, but it held. The needle flicked to 15 and satisfied, the guard leaned from the van and with a wave of his arm, gave the signal to start. In no time at all the train was pushing the engines down a long bleak glacial combe. There were glimpses of turf bogs and occasional snatches of Dingle Bay and the ocean beyond; we were now in the heart of the Slieve Mish range and it would be difficult to describe the wildness of the countryside. On a clear day it was possible to see the steam of the Valencia Harbour branch train as it ran along the south shore of Dingle Bay.

The guard was getting upset again for the vacuum gauge had dropped to nothing (the Rule Book states that 18 inches has to be maintained throughout the T&D section), but with the aid of a herdsman - one of several persons now crowded into the van - managed to screw down the handbrake still further. It seemed to make no difference. We careened over ungated road crossings, screeching whistles blowing, with a bravado which would make me a very nervous motorist in this part of Co. Kerry.

Eventually reaching the road side but continuing to pass through wild scenery we dropped down steeply at 1 in 29 into Annascaul (21¼ miles) barefooted children running in the wet street alongside to meet us. For them the sight of a train once a month must be worth waiting to see! Several stray animals stampeded to avoid an untimely end for the train seemed to be only under partial control as yet. Finally, we abandoned the road and, crossing the Owenascaul River, entered the passing loop and disused island platform. Both engines took water and, as at Corofin two days before, effectively blocked two level crossings. In next to no time, and seemingly from nowhere, the inevitable donkey carts piled with turf, were queing up to cross the railway. The stop was an extended one for the local public house, The South Pole Inn, was even more convenient than the bar at Castlegregory Junction.

From here the railway leaves the company of the road to take a more inland course and climb to a considerable height again, this time along the flanks of Ireland's second mountain, Brandon Hill (3,127 ft). The scenery continues to be of the finest there being no habitation and virtually no trees, in fact there seemed to be a complete absence of trees throughout the route from Tralee. There is another descent after this, abounding in short dips and sharp curves which are best appreciated from the footplate. And so on to Lispole.

It was proposed to swop the engines over here so that No. 1 could pilot No. 8 to give the hot box some respite, but in the event it was decided we should continue as we were. It had been impossible to accommodate three men on an engine until this point on the journey, for over half the cab floor was occupied by coal - it being essential that we had sufficient for the return run as well. By Annascaul much of this fuel had been used so I joined the engine behind the driver of No. 8 to share with a most cheery crew what was to be a monumental trip. The driver intended me to see everything of note. He kept up a running commentary as we proceeded but I could not make out much of it between the frightful clatter and his rich Kerry brogue. Also, there must have been some serious trouble under the footplate for at each revolution of the wheels, a heartstopping crash took place. However, it did not concern the crew at all!

The first of the monthly trains at Annascaul.   *Author*

Engines draw up singly for Annascaul's water. September 1950.   *Author*

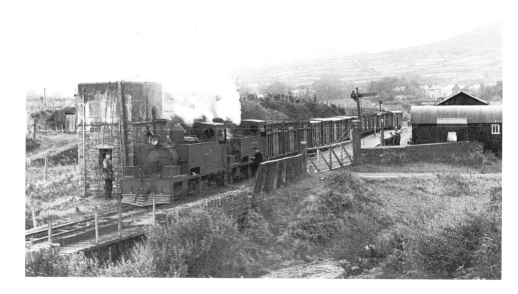

Single line tokens. *Oakwood Press*

A notable hostelry at Annascaul. June 1967. *Author*

For the initial climb from Annascaul the driver started in full forward gear and with half regulator, thereafter controlling the speed by use of the reversing screw. We slipped repeatedly on the grass-covered rails but as previously, cleared them for the train engine behind which 'kept its feet' throughout. I assumed this technique of keeping the train on the move had been learned the hard way. The brickettes had a peculiar smell when burning - more like the native turf - and this billowed about us as No. 8 bellowed upgrade, the smokepall hanging back as far as eye could see.

There is no rear bunker on these engines and leaning out through the square sliding window in the back sheet I could lean out and almost touch the chimney of No. 1. At the summit the regulator was closed and I looked back at the long string of vehicles coming through a trough of bracken. There was no sign of the rails. It would be difficult to describe the sensation as we rolled down the gradient, the train engine still working and we being propelled. The under-floor bang seemed to have become worse and the cab floor jolted vertically with each violent sound, and lurched sideways. I put this down to the considerable rear overhang in the design of the engine. The cab door, against which I was resting, clanged against the side tank due to a broken latch, despite my efforts. All in all, it was a cachophonic ride!

To ease the steamrate and save fuel, the driver kept the valve gear well notched up with the result that the engine ran with that familiar see-saw motion well-known to all enginemen so that the effect of constant babel and lively motion was such that I almost envied Dorothy's situation amongst the livestock! But I would not have exchanged the experience for all the 'Goats in Kerry'.

In time I became used to the motion and racket, but the speed was more than I cared for. Obviously the day still held much for the trainmen and we were being driven as quickly as the track would allow. Watched from the cab the engine seemed to be determined to take a self-destructive plunge off the rails but then recover again as if with second thoughts. I recalled reading the Oakwood Press booklet on the Tralee & Dingle system which quoted a speed limit of 25 mph and added, 'Not much now observed'. How right Roger Kidner was! Looking behind again at No. 1 it presented a peculiar appearance as the chimney and dome literally grew out of a pile of firewood and brickettes on the boiler barrel. The rain, now as heavy as ever, still flew off the smokebox in spurts of steam. All told, it was a strange experience. Now and again the driver would lean unconcernedly far out from the cab to point out some feature on the hills above or the coast far below. As we neared the next summit the racket increased and the see-sawing reached a new pitch. Behind us, the gap between the two locomotives yawned to and fro and watching the movements of No. 1's cowcatcher, showed how imperfectly did the engine follow the rails.

Garrynadur, the next summit, was topped at a crawl and as steam was cut off, the safety-valves of both locomotives blew off with a great roar, sending a column of steam skywards. The fireman quickly grabbed the injector controls and glancing up to see the boiler pressure was 150 lb. and the water level was almost out of sight, turned them on with a deft twist of hand. The response was instant. The safety-valves shut down and there was no noise save that from the same protesting knocks which we had endured all the way. With most of the collar work done, the fireman jammed his shovel under the coalpile and opened the firehole door slightly. We began to drift down the severe and tortuous hill to the Lispole viaduct at its foot.

Driver and fireman together both pulled on the handbrake screw. The vacuum brake was applied but still we rushed on. The driving wheels were locked solidly by the handbrake and simply slid uselessly along the greasy rails. In desperation the driver put the engine into reverse and with wheels revolving backwards and smoking brake blocks, an element of control and calm was obtained. The train brakes were having little effect and the smoke from hot wagon brake blocks and axle boxes was considerable. The train itself moved like a writhing serpent in the long grass.

I expected the train would be stopped before we crossed Lispole viaduct, whose steel spans had been declared unsafe to take the weight of two engines coupled together these many years, but this rule was ignored and as we passed over it the driver drew my attention to the old course of the line where an uncontrollable train had leapt into the river bed.

There is a dip in the middle of the Lispole viaduct which marks the bottom of the decline and then the line climbs through the small station at the roadside (27½ m.). There is no passing loop. A short distance further on the last summit is reached, and in front there stretches a bleak vista of open country, running down to the sea. In a few yards the railway joins the northern edge of the road and passing along the fringes of several farmyards, begins a mile or more of dead straight, roadside run. The weather, being what it was, made this a dreary length, and after the curves and switchbacks which preceded it, an anti-climax. Along here the grass and overgrown hedges were at their most abundant and I carefully kept well within the cab sheets as malignant blackthorn boughs forced their way inside with noisy intent.

Soon we began to encounter herds of livestock all making their way beside us to Dingle for the next day's Cattle Fair. Their drovers were unable to control them and they charged all over the road and track in front of us. Both beasts and men must have walked many miles. They seemed indifferent to the wretched cold and merciless rain, though on the footplate, we were warm enough. I thought of that little huddle of people in the van behind us, and wondered if Dorothy would ever agree to coming to Ireland again.

At the end of this unusual straight piece of railway and road, the line cut over the road at a sharp, crazy angle which I learned had brought many an unwary road user to grief. On breasting the top of a small rise, we saw the whole sweep of landlocked Dingle Bay and harbour below us. It was a magnificent setting, but hardly in the fine weather conditions pertaining when the framed photographs which we had seen, hanging in the porch of Benner's Hotel, Tralee, were taken. They were headed, 'TRALEE & DINGLE RAILWAY'.

The final mile into Dingle is treacherous, combining blind corners and a steep descent, with the road in close proximity all the way to the terminus. With brakes fully applied, we literally skidded all the way. The nearer we came to the station, the more numerous were the cattle on the road and several would have never reached the Fair at all but for some timely lumps of briquette shied from the footplate.

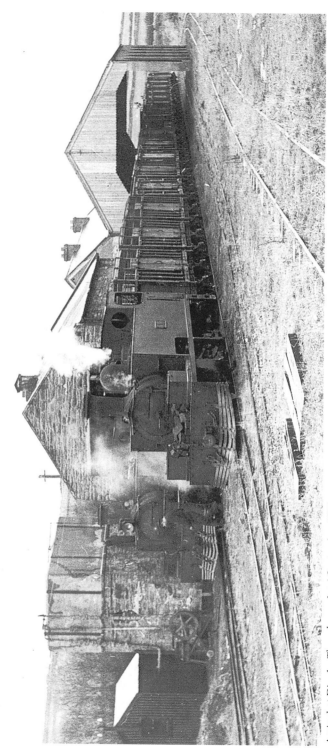

Arrival at Dingle. Three hours late! September 1950.

Dingle at last - six hours and 32 odd miles from the start of our journey, and not much to eat or drink in that time! The men lost no time in shunting the cattle vans into the dock sidings ready for the morning. They turned the engines, made up the fires from the fuel we had brought with us and put them away in the little shed. There were a few farewell photographs and then they were away either to some customary billet or to the unlovely corrugated iron shed adjacent which was fondly termed, 'The Dormitory'. In the latter case, they took their cooking utensils too - pots, pans, onions, potatoes, skillets - a complete portable kitchen. With the complete mastery of a practice long used, all had soon disappeared, leaving Dorothy and I to marvel at the sudden silence which fell upon the station. Silence that is, apart from the noise of rain for which the West of Ireland is renowned. In the far, far distance could be heard the whistles of Nos. 2 and 6 on the second train. We did not wait but followed the steep and rarely used track down to the harbour and pier end, noting the cast steel frog assemblies of the pointwork, a feature I had never seen on the narrow gauge before.

At the pier end we knew we were at the most westerly point of any railway in Europe, exceeding that at Valencia Harbour by a few hundred yards. Then we climbed aboard the forward-control CIE cattle lorry and trailer which the authorities had kept waiting for us as our return bus to Tralee had left several hours earlier. Squashed three together in the cab, we experienced a sick-making ride along the serpentine road through the mountains to the accompaniment of the crashing steel Guinness barrels which leapt about in the empty trailer. Unused to the motion of a forward-control position, we repeatedly feared we would be catapulted over the wall.

A loaded cattle train leaves Dingle with Nos. 8 and 1. May 1952.   *Author*

Cammell cast steel frog, Dingle. May 1952.   *Author*

It was dark and we were mighty wet when the lights of Tralee came into sight. The scrawled hand-written note stuck to the dining room door at Benner's said, 'No meals served after 9 pm' but this was Ireland and we were certainly bona fide travellers. There followed one of those most unforgettable meals and a night's sleep which even the rats in the attic did not disturb.

And did Dorothy refuse to come to Ireland again? Rather the reverse. In a few years we would be in Co. Kerry again to add further experience to this Saga.

Second train engine No. 2 at Dingle, with food basket. May 1952.   *Author*

Chapter Eighteen

Kerry Again!
29th May-2nd June, 1952

The double-event of travelling over two of Co. Kerry's narrow railways during a long weekend break in September 1950 (see Chapter Seventeen) had increased our awareness of the potential of Irish railway travel now that post-war restrictions were being lifted, and coal for steam engines was more available. We had not been been deterred by the disappointing weather which had marked our journeys to Kilkee and Dingle, and were keen to repeat the latter in the hope of better conditions and the continuance of the cattle trains until such date as we could take a weekend's absence. This was to occur during the Whitsuntide Works' Holiday 1952. As before, we would embody two sections of CIE in one long weekend, going first down the Valencia branch and back, and then to Dingle and back the next day.

There was now a through train off the overnight Mail Boat at Dun Laoghaire, departing thence at 7.40 am. In charge was a 'J15' class 0-6-0 at its head and we rounded Dublin Bay with the bright early-morning sun glinting off the sea. There was a short stop in Westland Row before continuing to Amiens Street and a further stop. Thence round the left-hand curve and the Phoenix Park tunnel onto Inchicore bank which heads south out of Kingsbridge station. This was unfamiliar ground to me and for a moment I thought we had taken a wrong train and were bound for some unannounced destination along the ex-GSWR main line - breakfast-less! I was relieved to hear the brakes being applied and we came to rest. Through the open window I spied the Kingsbridge station pilot engine coming up behind us. It made contact in no uncertain manner and I wondered if its driver was allowing a trainee fireman the opportunity for some practice … The guilty party proved to be 4-4-0 No. 538 class 'D' ex-DSER rebuilt with side window cab, somewhat unsuitable for the task, I thought. With engines fore and aft, we drew back into the station at 8.10 am.

There was time for a wander round the station before our train left for Mallow at 10.30 am. The small carriage turntables at the buffer stops which had caught my attention in November 1939 were still in place though clearly, seldom used. The connection to the Guinness brewery yard over Usher's Quay was made through one of the sharpest curves I had seen. A novelty was the new diesel set which was to work the 9 am to Kildare; from the number of spectators it was attracting, it was a rare event.

We left Kingsbridge behind No. 501, a 4-6-0 class 'B1' a mixed traffic engine of which there were only three of its type, a very handsome machine. As we passed Inchicore running sheds I spied the detached portion of the 0-6-4 Steam Cab which was once used to distribute wages to isolated depots on the former GSWR; it looked rather forlorn dumped there and I was glad I had seen it in service - intact! - again in November 1939. The resident Inchicore shunting engine was No. 61 an ex-GSWR 4-4-0 class 'D14'. I managed to scribble a hurried note of all the foregoing which passed quickly from sight as our train gathered speed. At Lisduff quarry there was the railway's stone ballast quarry to be seen and at Maryborough we passed over a single rusted track beneath the main line which was part of a scheme for a railway to Mountmellick, Tullamore and beyond which was never fulfilled. Further on Dorothy drew my attention to the very low platforms at Thurles which were only

Mallow station, view looking north *circa* 1930. Kerry train stock stands in the back platform (*left*).
L&GRP

'D19' class 4-4-0 No. 15 at Killarney. 10th July, 1934.   *H.C. Casserley*

about 18 inches above rail level. Here, the distant signal semaphore arms are painted red but the lens frames are yellow as if in mitigation! I learned that yellow-armed distant signals had only recently been adopted in Eire.

The next place of interest was Limerick Junction and having been there on our previous journey I was ready to get out of the train while it went through its manoeuvres. Luckily I resisted the impulse or I should have lost my seat.

At Mallow the main line for Cork continues southward but the Tralee train veers westward and passes two interesting junction stations which, years later, we explored in full, Banteer for Kanturk and Headford for Kenmare. At Banteer we spotted a small modern diesel locomotive shunting the Kanturk goods train which had a very elderly GSWR timber-framed brake van in tow - a rare treat! At Headford the mixed train for Kenmare was in charge of a 'J15' 0-6--0, a class which had the monopoly of the branch working. The junction platform was a hive of activity and put me in mind of remote stations in the Scottish Highlands.

Onwards the mountain backcloth was delightful, the combination of Kerry scenery threaded by the winding railway kept our eyes busy. Quite soon we ran into another of those Irish railway curiousities, Killarney. Owing to the pattern of railway building, Killarney was at first the end of the line from Mallow but a further extension to Tralee could not be accomplished by a simple furthering of the rails beyond the station. Instead, and involving a considerable gradient, a westward extension was taken from a point eastwards of the station. In practice this means that Tralee-bound trains run into Killarney station and have to reverse out again, past the junction to gain the main line once more. Whereas Limerick Junction, with its reputation for reversing passenger trains (not only into the main line platform), is a curious location, we had in recent months been involved in shunting movements at Newcastle West, and now at Killarney, which we felt were equally rare by English standards and might be better known. I made a note to acquire a copy of the Rule Book for each of these stations as I was sure that propelling passenger trains over facing points was frowned upon back in England!

Musing on these matters our arrival at Farranfore, the junction for the Valencia branch, caught us napping. We hurriedly left the train as we saw our connection was on the opposite side of the platform. It consisted of a mixed bag of elderly ex-GSWR six-wheeled carriage stock with 'J15' No. 146 in front. I had thought it prudent to bring a set of overalls with me and commenced to don these out on the platform; the Tralee train was still awaiting departure and my activities gave its passengers some amusement. The driver, Con O'Connor, of Cahirciveen, had been warned he should expect a visitor on his engine and greeted me most cordially with the bonus of a new engineman's cloth which he insisted I must keep as a souvenir. I still have it!

If there is one thing I cannot do it is to make notes while on the footplate, so I had to choose between soaking up the event as we ran along a most delectable part of Ireland's west coast, or make note of engine performance on this exciting length of railway. In the end I tried to do both. We curved away from Farranfore. Dorothy had chosen a vantage seat in a comfortable compartment and round a bend she leant through the open window and indicated that that she had been well chaperoned by the guard. Whilst ahead could be seen some exciting mountain outlines, for the moment our path lay through low lying land as far as Killorglin which we entered after crossing a three-span steel viaduct over the wide River Laune. The footplate was

'J15' class 0-6-0 No. 127 stands at Farranfore with the 7.30 am from Valencia Harbour to Tralee.
15th April, 1955.   *R.M. Casserley*

'J15' class 0-6-0 No. 194 at Killorglin with the 4.45 pm from Farranfore to Valencia Harbour. 20th
June, 1939.   *W.A. Camwell/Stephenson Locomotive Society*

a fine viewing point and the scene was typical of those late Victorian photographs of idyllic Kerry waterscapes which drew so many to this part of Ireland.

At Killorglin the station was agog with trains as we crossed the daily up goods on its way to Tralee (our own train's starting point). It had waited some time for our arrival and had done some shunting first. Here the train crews were swopped and I had the company of the men who had brought in the goods train from Cahirciveen. I was able to photograph the winding sylvan course as we called at Caragh Lake, Dooks and Glenbeigh. Here we took water for the climbs to Mountain Stage and a second summit of 404 ft at Kells, before a long fall down to sea level at Cahirciveen. Beyond Glenbeigh the climb takes the railway onto a ledge of Drung Hill, passing through three shortish tunnels *en route*. They follow one another in quick succession and are similar to the avalanche tunnels on the Cambrian Railways coast line above Barmouth Bay. They are quite like old friends to us as they appear in Kerry photographs in the first class compartments of electric trains in which we travel daily to Manchester: I little thought I would pass through them for the first time on the footplate of a venerable eighty-year-old Irish goods locomotive! Far below the railway line lap the waves of Dingle Bay with the Slieve Mish mountains beyond and further still, Tralee Bay and the mouth of the Shannon River.

Then came a turn inland and we were over the inspiring Gleesk viaduct, all curved and at great height, with 11 steel spans and a 10 mph speed restriction to boot. I looked back over the carriage roofs and could see Dorothy waving to me. We made another stop at Kells and the driver handed over some fresh mackerel along with the single line staff.

There is a long descent at 1 in 40 of about four miles to sea level and the impressive ten-span steel viaduct over the Fertha River at Cahirciveen. There is a large ruined building of the Constabulary Barracks nearby and a jetty for sea-going ships is adjacent to the station yard. In earlier times there was a weekly steamer calling at ports around the Cork and Kerry coasts.

Our stay in Cahirciveen was quite brief. It was followed by a short run alongside the Fertha to an uninspiring terminus with a fine title, Valencia Harbour. I expected far more! There was a simple platform with run-round and siding, all it would seem, in the middle of a field and with the minimum of facilities. Like many of the GSWR stations in Kerry, the buildings were of corrugated iron. Alongside were the intriguing diamond-shaped marker-boards for the undersea cable to America. Clearly visible across the Sound was Valencia Island; there was a ferry to Knights Town which we vowed to use one day, to explore the adjacent slate quarry.

Meanwhile, No. 146 had run round its train and was ready to return, tender first, to Cahirciveen for the night. Its driver motioned me onto the footplate again and indicated that I could handle the regulator if I liked. I did, even though it was short and very sweet - after all, this was on Europe's most westerly railway!

After a splendid day, we set off along the main street to look for a meal and bed for the night. We soon reached its far end without being tempted. We became acutely concious that Cahirciveen was not a place that tourists visited, the only accommodation being noisy, smoke-filled bars. We chose the least basic we could find and determined to stay in Killorglin if ever we came this way again!

The night was not as bad as we feared and we had to be on our way early to catch the early - and only - morning train. It came in from Valencia having left for there

A general view of Cahirciveen station. 'J15' class 0-6-0 No. 135 is on shed (*right*). The stock of the 10.35 am from Farranfore stands in the platform. 2nd September, 1938. *H.B. Priestley*

A general view of a deserted Valencia Harbour station. 28th April, 1938.
W.A. Camwell/Stephenson Locomotive Society

from Cahirciveen at 7.30 am. The day was fine and the sea air exhilarating. We trundled over the splendid viaduct again with the incoming tide swirling about the feet of its stone piers. The smells of the nearby Atlantic Ocean came up with the tide. No. 146 prepared to do battle with the long steep climb to the summit ahead and her fireman was piling on the coal as if it grew on trees. Her chimney punched the air with blasts of filthy black smoke which blotted out the unsullied vista ahead. As we reached the foot of the gradient the engine slowed to a steady pace which it maintained with dogged determination to the top. I withdrew my head inside the open window as I felt the cinders raining down about me. They pattered on the roof.

It seemed ages before the engine was eased and the safety valves exploded into life. It was safe to look through the open window again and yes, the injectors were both hard at work and the fireman was looking back at me with an enormous grin on his face. I wondered how low the boiler water level had been before there was sufficient pressure for the injectors to pick up!

The return journey took us back through Farranfore where the train continued onwards to its 'home base', Tralee. I was still curious as to why this vintage rake of six-wheeled coaches was still doing duty on the Valencia branch so we called in at the station master's office at Tralee and were shown a copy of the Working Timetable. It contained the footnote that bogie carriages had to fitted with elliptical buffer heads and were disallowed if they still retained the small round heads then commonplace on the ex-GSWR bogie coaches then to be found. Another small feature - easily missed - was that all the vintage coaches still retained the row of brass rings fitted to the cantrail on one side (only) of the roof through which a cord had passed along the train to a bell in the cab, a literal 'Emergency Cord' from the days before the vacuum brake was fitted.

We made our way to Benner's Hotel and after a hearty lunch, took a walk round this most interesting town. We called in at the narrow gauge engine shed where several men were at work preparing Nos. 1, 2, and 4 for duty next day and learned that cattle traffic was passing to road vehicles because only 22 vans were usable. The section was likely to be closed soon.

In the morning there was but one topic of conversation among the T&D railwaymen, the running of The Oaks that day at Epsom. Bets were being placed all round. We made a quick note of what I had omitted last time; the trackwork here embodied the same unusual cast frog pieces by Cammell as I had discovered at Dingle. They were more akin to those used on street tramways, and I have not seen them elsewhere since. The signalling was all by McKenzie & Holland of Worcester or of GSWR fittings. At Lispole later in the day, the ground frame was by 'TWEEDY & CO. (Tyers Patent) CARLISLE'.

The journey to Lispole was uneventful, there were no alarms or extra passengers in the van. The occasional rain was light and short-lived and the train made its way to the eastern side of Lispole viaduct where it made a predetermined stop on the embankment leading to the structure. Adjacent was a ganger's cottage. As portrayed in Western movie films, the train crew lost no time in abandoning their charge and entering the building. Not a word was spoken, no explanation was given. Dorothy and I were left with the locomotives and train to ourselves. However, voices raised in excitement from within the cottage made it plain that racing was in progress and that our arrival had been punctual.

Lispole viaduct c.1950s.   *David Lawrence*

We sat on the grassy slope beside the train and took a picnic lunch from our rucksacks; this included a generous portion of delicious pork sausages which we had arranged with the waitress at our breakfast table. We suppressed any comic notions like sounding an engine whistle - it was all too bizarre! The men seemed very subdued on return and we guessed that the geegees had not lived up to expectations.

The pilot engine was detached as mandatory and ran clear ahead. The handbrakes were taken off the train engine and van, and the gradient did the rest. The whole rake rolled down onto the pilot engine and was coupled together. It was all done with hardly a word or puff of steam to be heard. The guard leant from the van, gave a wave and we set off for Dingle. It was as though we had never been and we wondered if those in posh CIE offices in Dublin had any notion that one of their trains had been to the races that day.

We decided to return to Tralee on the first loaded special. We knew it would take time to load cattle in the morning and strolled round Dingle in bright sunshine. Dorothy spied a narrow entrance with a wonderful garden beyond. At this date most Irish gardens grew vegetables and to see such a colourful picture was irrestible. We peered in and were spotted. A voice invited us to come in. There were Arum Lilies, gigantic Hosters, Palm Trees and multicoloured Fuschia. We were conducted round until we could remain no longer. We had a chat about manure (no shortage!) and accepted a mug of tea. I think the lady was sorry we had to leave for the train and Dorothy would have been there until nightfall! Some seeds in an envelope were pressed into her hand …

They had not finished loading the first train but the driver said he would wait anyway. Of course, we refreshed ourselves at Annascaul and Castlegregory Junction on the way back and there was time at Tralee to see the second portion arrive, and have a meal at the main line station. We caught the 6 pm mixed train to Mallow which enjoyed a slow timing with half an hour to shunt at Farranfore. The train was in charge of No. 370, an ex-GSW 2-6-0 inside cylinder class 'K4' with a very heavy load behind the tender. This was the first time I had seen an engine of this type - nicknamed 'Scotties' - built by The North British Locomotive Co. Ltd. A combination of that wheel arrangement with inside cylinders was due in the first intance to a desire to reduce the weight on the leading axle which would have occurred had it been a purely six-wheeled type. A look inside the cab showed that the Belpaire firebox had caused the firehole door to be very high above the floor so that the fireman would have to lift each shovelful of coal through the hole. No joke. I was not certain if the 'K4' continued beyond Mallow but the train continued overnight to Dublin and we took the morning sailing to Holyhead.

Chapter Nineteen

Footplate in County Cork, August-September 1962

Maps of Ireland at the height of the Railway Age, show an intriguing series of lines which fan out with a backbone based on Cork city, to serve Co. Cork in the south-west of the country. The most important of these, with a main line stretching from Cork to Bantry was, until the formation of the Great Southern Railways in 1925, the Cork, Bandon & South Coast Railway. In former times, the county boasted other smaller concerns as well, some being of narrow gauge but all had succumbed by the date of these reminiscences.

It took me years before a long-planned journey to Skibbereen, at almost the farthest reach of this western leg of the former CBSCR, could be attempted in order to savour the Schull & Skibbereen Railway, and thus I became first acquainted with what Cork railwaymen referred to as the 'Westcorkrailway' (one word), in April 1953 [Chapter Ten].

Way back in 1953 the railways south-west of Cork city were geographically isolated from Ireland's main railway system except by means of the Cork City Railway (CCR), an umbilical which ran through the back streets of Cork and bridged the River Lee in such a way that made it only suitable for freight traffic. Once south of the river, the railways reflected a historic charm to a degree not apparent to the north of it. A case in point was that as the CBSCR had no major engine running shed in Cork, its locomotives were mostly stabled under a conveniently large overbridge. For all but light repairs engines had to traverse the CCR to visit the main line repair shops at Glanmire.

The vintage charm which surrounded the ex-CBSCR system had been partially eclipsed by its dieselation in the late 1950s and the disappearance of elderly bogie and older six-wheeled carriages, all of pre-1925 birth, had a devastating effect on the pleasures of a journey from Skibbereen up to Cork. There had usually been a well-maintained six-wheeled carriage attached to each train and it was the custom to keep it locked to assist platform staff to monitor platform movements. The Baltimore branch had one bogie and a six-wheeler allocated to it and we usually made our way towards the latter when changing to the branch train at Drimoleague Junction. If locked a porter would appear with a carriage key, 'So you want the old-timer?' he would ask. We knew we should have it all to ourselves.

There was less fun in travelling in the replacement train of three near-modern coaches hauled by a Metro-Vick 'C' class diesel locomotive, albeit that the class 'B4' steam engine and its successor had both originated in Manchester factories not many miles apart! Realising that the railway we had almost taken for granted would have vanished before we had our next August holiday near Skibbereen, I took steps to acquire suitable authority for us to travel on the demolition train. This arrived in the form of a letter which in the broadest terms would allow us *carte blanche* and we were to report ourselves to the guard of the train at Drimoleague.

In the first instance we considered it best to 'recce' just what the lifting train was doing and where the track demolition had reached. We found one of the 'B4'

Class 'B4' 4-6-0T No. 464 in Glanmire engine shed. August 1962. *Author*

No. 463 *en route* to Cork with track materials. September 1962. *Author*

engines running light between Skibbereen and Drimoleague where it stopped and assembled a train of carriage frames carrying rails. We soon made friends with the guard who inferred we did not need to bother with a formal letter but could have ridden with them anyway! We made arrangements to come again on the following day and Dorothy suggested we bring Gerard with us.

I must explain the situation a little more. By 1962 our daughters Elizabeth and Diana were in the Sea Rangers at school and our west Cork holidays were entirely given over to sailing our 14 ft boat SHUNA which we kept on a mooring at Castletownshend. In earlier days we had trailed the boat from home but having acquired a convenient barn for it we now left it in Ireland each winter. Gerard lived at Rinneen close by and was not only an Old Boy of Malvern College but possessed a Gauge 1 model railway which gave me many happy hours when not sailing! Furthermore, in the years during which we had brought SHUNA from England on a trailer under a canvas tarpaulin, and when buying models from England which would attract Duty, we would bury them inside the boat to avoid attention from the Customs ...

When we mentioned our intention to ride the brake van to Clonakilty Jn and back and that he should come with us, he was like an excited puppy and met us at Drimoleague saying that he had hardly slept a wink. I felt for his attire too, for he was far too smart for a well-used railway van. However ... Gerard was surprised we had not brought the girls with us so we explained that they preferred to have the day sailing alone and would not embark on any risky japes.

No. 464 was the engine and it was agreed I would ride on the engine, with Dorothy and Gerard on the van balcony. The journey to Clonakilty Junction was, under the circumstances, without remark and we had few stops. The engine was in reasonable condition and the men had become adept at coping with point clips, padlocks and some coal which must have been put aside as only for emergency use. This burnt with a smoke resembling Vesuvius in full eruption, and seen from the engine we made an awesome sight on the gradients.

Once outside Clonakilty Junction we stopped to check the points from the branch which was still intact and to allow me to photograph the unusual signals there. Then we ran into the station yard where we would leave the loaded carriage frames. We were then invaded by a host of small boys who had been waiting to ambush us and for whom this train, on a railway so obviously abandoned, was a gift from heaven in the long summer holiday. They swarmed up into the cab like insects and were treated with great tolerance by the crew who had become used to being waylaid! Meanwhile I left the engine to the mercies of the boys and took photographs of this unusual scenario.

Our shunting duties being done and with a number of empty wagons attached, there were still one or two boys clinging like limpets to the engine; they were allowed to ride the last few yards along the yard. For our return to Drimoleague, Dorothy rode on the footplate and I gather had a difficult but highly amusing time in conversation with the crew who found the occasion a ground-breaking experience. She was allowed to blow the whistle too. Gerard had oviously enjoyed the experience. His dapper Old Malvernian blazer was a little dishevelled and his cravat awry, but both were evidence of pleasure.

Above: Lifting track at Clonakilty
Junction. September 1962.   *Author*

Right: Unusual signalling, Clonakilty
Junction. September 1962.   *Author*

On our return to Castletownsend we were met by the girls in high glee; they had sailed round Horse Island and navigated back through its tricky Sound on their own and hoped we would be going away for another day soon to sample the lifting train. As a matter of fact we were, and a week later Dorothy and I were back at Drimoleague to accept the guard's recommendation that we come again before any more of the line was removed.

The weather was still brilliant. The engine crew had been changed and driver William Lombard from Kinsale had John Hennessy from Creagh, Baltimore, as his fireman. The engine was No. 463, not in quite as good condition as 464 which had gone up to Cork for boiler washout. We had three carriage frames of rails and would return from Clonakilty with a variety of open wagons. The crew opened the firehole door for me to inspect the woeful state of the tubeplate; water was pouring down it from the leaking firetubes to such effect that the fire in the front of the box was cold and black. With the loss of any heat there the remainder of the fire would have to be husbanded carefully to maintain steam pressure as the weight of the load was considerable.

Bill Lombard invited me to share the footplate with them and suggested that on the easier return journey I should try my hand at driving, his mate could then ride in the brake van. I was wearing my Talyllyn Railway 'steaming hat' and the initials on it, 'TR' caught his eye and I explained how I came to own the cap and be familiar with steam engines. Before we left Drimoleague we were visited by another railwayman who was curious to know my situation. 'This gentleman has come from Africa. He is on the Tanganika Railways', Bill said, giving me a broad wink. The visitor seemed impressed, gave a grunt and left us alone. Lombard explained he was the foreman of the track gang and had no authority on the trains. He always interfering in the affairs of others.

We got the right-away from the guard with a wave from a red duster and set off eastwards under a similar cloud of filthy smoke as the last time we were there. The engine laboured somewhat with the weight behind; at the summit of the climb beyond Lombard partially closed the regulator and Hennessy showed me the injector controls - henceforward I was to watch and keep the water level! The Cork road kept us company and we maintained a steady speed of about 35 mph until we reached the outskirts of Dunmanway. Here we were obliged to stop as the gang dismantling the pointwork etc. had removed the locks on the crossing gates which were now closed against the railway and held there with a chain and padlock. Having no padlock key we were obliged to leave the engine in charge of John Hennessy and walk up through the street searching each bar for the foreman. Once found, we marked the occasion in a temperate manner before leaving. We brought the foreman back with us to unlock the signal box and operate the points at the east end of the loop. These had not been disconnected.

Our progress to Clonakilty Junction was now unimpaired and we made good progress before stopping at the junction points and then running right-handed along the platform loop and into the yard beyond. The schools had now gone back and so we were spared the ambush of small boys. It was an an opportunity for me to show Bill my efforts at shunting and we coupled onto a train of empty open wagons. Bill said we would stop at Enniskeen for water and have a bite to

Drimoleague. Baltimore line *left*, Bantry line *right*. September 1962.   *Author*

Lifting track at Drimoleague with No. 464. September 1962.   *Author*

Our motive power at Drimoleague. September 1962. *Author*

Inside Drimoleague engine shed. *Author*

eat. The station nameboards which were large and voluminous, had not been removed but set up for posterity and all to see. I wonder if they have survived?

We came to Enniskeen where the main Cork-Bantry road lies just behind the station and where, in 1953, Walter McGrath had left me to continue on the train to Skibbereen while he waited on the road for the evening Cork bus which never came! It was here that the CBSCR had a ballast pit and over a snack in the van Bill told us what an extensive set of sidings had been located here along with a shed to house three engines, with a boiler and steam pump to supply water. One of the engines was working six days a week. I could not identify the site at all.

On the long fall downgrade into Drimoleague the train was almost pushing the engine and I decided that it would be prudent to pull the reversing lever well back in the quadrant. Regrettably I had not bargained for the well-worn slack in the motion and as soon as I had released the catch-handle the reversing lever shot backwards and took me with it. I managed to retain my foothold and gain my breath. Bill laughed. 'She won't let you notch up like that in her condition. You have to close the regulator first.' He was right and I had no further bother. The guard assisted us with the van brake to stop nicely at Drimoleague and I used the steam brake on the engine to prevent the empty wagons stretching the train. It was all very subdued and I felt quite pleased with myself. 'Well done Sir, I could not have done better myself', said Bill.

It had been a splendid day and one we would never forget. I hope I have recaptured a little of it herein. It seems to be suitable juncture on which to close this Irish Saga.

Cork, Bandon & South Coast Railway and Cork & Bandon Railway chairs at Kinsale Junction. August 1964.   *Author*

Index